INTERNATIONAL TERRORISM: LEGAL CHALLENGES AND RESPONSES

A Report by the
International Bar Association's
Task Force on
International Terrorism

the global voice of
the legal profession

Transnational Publishers

Published and distributed by Transnational Publishers, Inc.
Ardsley Park
Science and Technology Center
410 Saw Mill River Road
Ardsley, NY 10502

Phone: 914-693-5100
Fax: 914-693-4430
E-mail: info@transnationalpubs.com
Web: www.transnationalpubs.com

The views expressed in this report are solely the views of Task Force members and do not necessarily reflect the views of the International Bar Association.

Library of Congress Cataloging-in-Publication Data

International Bar Association. Task Force on International Terrorism.
    International terrorism: challenges and responses: a report from
the International Bar Association's Task Force on International
Terrorism.
        p. cm.
    ISBN 1-57105-301-8
    1. Terrorism.   2. Terrorism—Prevention—International
cooperation.   I. Title.

K5256.I583 2003
341.7'73—dc21

2003056512

Manufactured in the United States of America

CONTENTS

Appendices

ACKNOWLEDGEMENTS

THE TASK FORCE SHOULD LIKE TO THANK THE FOLLOWING FOR THEIR ASSISTANCE:

Dr. Mohamed Al-Roken, Chairman of Board of Directors, Jurists Association, United Arab Emirates, Essam Al-Tamimi, Al Tamimi & Company, Nina Bang-Jensen, Director of the Coalition for National Justice, Nick Cowdery QC, Office Director of Public Prosecutions, New South Wales, Australia, Steven Becker, Assistant Defender, Office of the State Appellate Defender, Ingegard Bredin, Office of the Police Commissioner, Sweden, Nicole Fritz, Cathy Hagel, Emma Jordan, Anton Katz, Advocate, South Africa, Dianna Kempe QC, Former President of the IBA, Jennifer Kent, Luz E. Nagle, Associate Professor of Law, Stetson University College of Law, Francis Neate, Schroders, Chris Newell, Director of Casework, Crown Prosecution Service, England and Wales, Michael Reynolds, Allen and Overy, Dr Andrew Shacknove, Director, International Human Rights Programmes, University of Oxford, Janine Simpson, Constitutional Court of South Africa, Bethany Tarpley, Jim Taylor, Jim Towey, Jennifer Turner, Bruce Zagaris, Berliner Corcoran and Rowe, Phil Zeidman, Piper Rudnick.

THE TASK FORCE SHOULD ALSO LIKE TO THANK THE PEOPLE LISTED BELOW WITH WHOM IT CONSULTED ON THIS PROJECT:

Counter-Terrorism Committee

Anna Clunes, United Kingdom Mission to the UN, New York.
Ambassador Sir Jeremy Greenstock, Former Chairman of the Counter-Terrorism Committee,
Iain MacLeod, United Kingdom Mission to the UN, New York.

Sweden

Christian Ålund, Executive Director of the International Legal Assistance Consortium (ILAC), Sweden.
Catherina Bergqvist Levin, Prosecutor General's Office,
Helsinki Committee for Human Rights,
Holly McMahon, ABA Section on National Security,
Åsa Persson, Deputy Director Division for EU Affairs, Ministry of

Justice,
Fredrik Reinfeldt, Member of Swedish Parliament,
Mr Peter Strömberg, Director General for International Affairs,
Fredrick Wersäll, Ministry of Justice, Sweden.

United Nations

Václav Mikulka, Director, Codification Division, Office of Legal Affairs, UN,
Renan Villacis, Associate Legal Officer, Codification Division, Office of Legal Affairs, UN.

United States

Elliott Abrams, Head of Democracy and Human Rights and International Affairs, National Security Council,
Ronnie Adelman,
John Bellinger, Head of the Legal Office, National Security Council,
Michael Chertoff, Assistant Attorney General,
Mike Fayad, Greeberis Traurig,
John Fox, OSI,
Alice Fisher, Deputy Attorney General in the Criminal Division,
Khalil Jahshan, Director, Arab-American Anti-Discrimination Committee,
Jurists Association,
Cathy Lewis, Vinson and Elkins,
Ambassador John Negroponte, Permanent Representative to the UN,
Kate Martin, Director, Centre for National Security Studies,
Andrew Ness, Thelen Reid and Priest,
Joe Onek, Constitutional Project,
Collete Rausch Programme Officer, Rule of Law, USIP,
Nicholas Rostow Legal Council to Ambassador Negroponte,
Richard N. Seaman, Regional Advisor in the US Department of Treasury for Financial Crimes and Law Enforcement,
William Taft, Legal Advisor the Secretary of State,
Donald Wallace, Georgetown University Law Center and International Law Institute,
Rick Williams,
Carl Zwister, Jenkins and Gilchrist.

United Arab Emirates

Member of the Jurists Association.

FINANCIAL SUPPORT WAS RECEIVED WITH GRATEFUL THANKS FROM:

IBA Educational Trust, IBA Foundation Inc., IBA Section on Business

Law, IBA Section on Legal Practice, IBA Section on Energy and National Resources Law, Human Rights Institute, the General Professional Programme, Swedish International Development Cooperation Agency, His Highness, Dr Sultan Bin Muhammad Al Qasimi, Emir of Sharjah, Arab Lawyers Union.

THE TASK FORCE WOULD ALSO LIKE TO THANK THOSE WHO MADE A FINANCIAL DONATION TO THE WORK OF THE TASK FORCE:

Mr. Kevin Arquit, Clifford Chance Rogers & Wells, Ms Carol Elder Bruce, Tighe Patton Armstrong Teasdale, Deborah A. DeMasi, Esquire, Thelen Reid & Priest, Dennis M. Flannery, Wilmer, Cutler & Pickering, Mark R. Joelson, Law Office of Mark R. Joelson, Andrew P. Loewinger, Buchanan Ingersoll, Keith McGlamery, Jenkens & Gilchrist, John H. O'Neill, Jr., ShawPittman, Steven B. Pfeiffer, Fulbright & Jaworski, Piper Rudnick, Mark H. Tuohey, Vinson & Elkins, Theodore Voorhees, Jr., Covington & Burling, Robert L. Wald, Philip Zeidman, Piper Rudnick.

SPECIAL CONTRIBUTIONS:

Special thanks go to Monty Raphael and David McCluskey from Peters and Peters in London for their expertise and assistance in drafting Chapter 6, to Tom Blass, who acted as consultant editor, Tim Hughes, IBA Deputy Executive Director and Director of Marketing and Public Relations, for his invaluable support and advice, and to Claire de Boursac for her skill and professionalism in the handling of the organisation and administration for the Task Force.

Finally, special acknowledgement is given to Joanna Salsbury and Daniel Moeckli for their extraordinary work in researching and preparing various drafts of the report for consideration by members of the Task Force.

THE IBA'S TASK FORCE ON INTERNATIONAL TERRORISM

Justice Richard Goldstone (Co-Chair), Justice of the Constitutional Court of South Africa. From 1991 to 1994, Justice Goldstone served as Chair of South Africa's Commission of Inquiry regarding Public Violence and Intimidation. From 1994 to 1996, he was Chief Prosecutor of the International Criminal Tribunals for the former Yugoslavia and Rwanda. In 1999, Justice Goldstone was appointed Co-Chair of the Independent Commission on Kosovo which examined key developments before, during and after the crises in Kosovo, including systematic violations of human rights in the region.

Ambassador Emilio Cárdenas (Co-Chair), President of the IBA and Argentina's former Permanent Representative to the United Nations. From 1994 to 1995, he served as a non-permanent member of the UN Security Council. He was also Chair of the Sanctions Committee for the former Yugoslavia and Vice-President of the UN Economic and Social Council. In 1998, he was appointed a member of the International Advisory Group of the High Commissioner for Refugees of the UNHCR.

Professor Badria Al-Awadhi Professor of International Law at Kuwait University. In 1979, Professor Al-Awadhi was appointed as Dean of the Faculty of Law and Sharia, a position she held until 1983. From 1983 to 1993, Dr Al-Awadhi was Deputy Director to the Regional Organisation for the protection of Marine Environment in the Arabian Gulf Region. Dr Al-Awadhi has been a member of human rights organisations in the Arab region and on an international level. She is also the author of many books and articles on a variety of legal subjects including women's issues, international law, and international humanitarian law.

Professor M Cherif Bassiouni President of the International Human Rights Law Institute at DePaul University, Chicago. In 1992, Professor Bassiouni was appointed a member, and later Chair, of the UN Commission to Investigate International Humanitarian Law Violations in the former Yugoslavia. From 1995 to 1998, he served as Vice-Chair of the UN General Assembly's Committee for the Establishment of an International Criminal Court and in 1998, he was elected Chair of the Drafting Committee of the UN Diplomatic Conference on the Establishment of an International Criminal Court. Professor Bassiouni is the author and editor of 54 books and 200 law review articles. 2001 saw the publication of his book entitled **International Terrorism: Multilateral Conventions (1937–2001)**.

Sten Heckscher National Police Commissioner for Sweden. Mr Heckscher has a background as a judge and has also served as Legal Adviser and then Assistant Under-Secretary to the Minister of Justice. From 1987 to 1991, he was the Under-Secretary to the Minister of Justice. In 1991, Mr Heckscher was appointed Director General of the Patent and Registration Office. From 1994 to 1996, he was the Cabinet Minister for Industry and Commerce before accepting his current posting. Mr Heckscher is the author of various publications on penal law, criminal policy and EC law.

Baroness Helena Kennedy QC practises predominantly in criminal law and has acted in many prominent cases including the Brighton bombing trial and the Guildford Four appeal. She is the Chair of the British Council and the Chair of the Human Genetics Commission and is on the Advisory Council of the World Bank Institute. She was created a Life Peer in 1997 and is a Bencher of Gray's Inn.

Fali Nariman President of the Bar Association of India. Mr Nariman is a distinguished lawyer who has played a leading role in the promotion of human rights and the independence of the profession. He is a member of the Advisory Council of Jurists of the Asia-Pacific Forum of National Human Rights Institutions, a former President of LAWASIA and has been made an Honorary Member of the International Commission of Jurists. Mr Nariman is a long-standing member of the IBA and is Co-Chair of its Human Rights Institute.

Professor W Michael Reisman Professor of International Law at Yale University. From 1990 to 1995, he was a member of the Inter-American Commission on Human Rights (President from 1994 to 1995) and from 1998 to 2003 was co-Editor-in-Chief and then Editor-in-Chief of the American Journal of International Law. Since 2000, he has served as President of the Arbitration Tribunal for the Bank of International Settlements, President of the Ireland-United Kingdom *OSPAR* Tribunal, and member of the UN Boundary Commission for Eritrea and Ethiopia. He is author of numerous publications on international law, including the law of war and legal responses to terrorism. His most recent books are **Law in Brief Encounters (1999)** and **Jurisdiction in International Law (1999)**.

PREFACE

"No person is an island, entire of itself; every person is a piece of the continent, a part of the man. . . . Any person's death diminishes me because I am involved with mankind. . . ."

(John Donne, 1624)

On 11 September, 2001, I had just finished a luncheon meeting with Richard Goldstone, Justice of the Constitutional Court of South Africa and former Chief Prosecutor of the International Criminal Tribunals for the former Yugoslavia and Rwanda. As we walked back to the IBA office, I was struck by the anxiety registered in the faces of the people we passed. Something was clearly amiss. As we entered the IBA office, there was not a sound from members of the staff. They were huddled around a television where the silence was pierced only by the endless replay of an airline jet crashing into a tower of the World Trade Center. Minutes later, silence turned into open grief, fear and dismay as another plane hit the second tower.

The next 24 hours are a distant memory for me with countless phone calls, meetings and prayers. I do remember turning to Justice Goldstone. Without speaking a word, we both knew the world had changed that day in ways we could not fully comprehend.

The events of 11 September set governments, international law-making bodies, and non-governmental organisations on a long journey to tackle a number of complex legal challenges in terms of responding to global terrorism. The core of this journey is the task of countering the very threat of terrorism without diminishing the protection of civil liberties and internationally accepted norms of human rights.

As the global voice of the legal profession, it was important for the IBA to become engaged with these challenges. As an Association comprising over 193 Law Societies and Bar Associations from over 183 countries, and with over 16,000 individual members, I felt we could contribute to a better understanding of the complex and testing problems of modern terrorism against the backdrop of domestic and international law and practice. Representing an exceptional gathering of international experts and lawyers, the IBA could approach the threat of international terrorism from a balanced and global perspective.

At the 2001 Annual IBA Conference in Cancun, Mexico, the IBA leadership supported the request to create an IBA Task Force on

International Terrorism. The five major entities of the IBA (Section on Legal Practice, Section on Business Law, Section on Energy & Natural Resources Law, Human Rights Institute and the General Professional Programme) each agreed to contribute funding necessary to launch the Task Force.

Recognising the multidisciplinary nature of the legal issues involved, it was imperative that we attract a range of high-profile international experts, including judges, academics and legal practitioners, to serve on the newly created Task Force.

There was no doubt in my mind who should Co-Chair the Task Force. Justice Goldstone is one of the most pre-eminent legal scholars in the world. I worked with him in 2000 when he co-chaired the International Independent Commission on Kosovo. When asked, he did not hesitate to accept. For the other Co-Chair, the IBA was fortunate to have already Ambassador Emilio J. Cárdenas as the President-Elect of the Association. As Argentina's former Permanent Representative to the United Nations and a world renowned diplomat, he was the perfect candidate.

We then looked for diversity among other members of the Task Force to reflect both the IBA's own membership and the need to have a broad spectrum of opinion when dealing with the complex issues of international terrorism. The pool of potential candidates was immense and in the end we selected six additional members of the Task Force, all of whom are prominent legal scholars and practitioners.

M Cherif Bassiouni is one of the world's leading experts in the area of international criminal law. He is currently the President of the International Human Rights Law Institute at DePaul University, Chicago. Sten Heckscher is the National Police Commissioner for Sweden and is recognised as one of the most progressive leaders in the European Union in the areas of penal law and criminal policy. Baroness Helena Kennedy QC is a title Peer in the House of Lords. She is Chair of the British Council and is one of England's leading barristers. Fali Nariman is President of the Bar Association of India. A distinguished lawyer who has played a leading role in the promotion of human rights and the independence of the profession, Mr Nariman is Co-Chair of the IBA Human Rights Institute. Dr Badria Al-Awadhi is former Dean of the Faculty of Law and Sharia at Kuwait University. She is one of the leading human rights experts in the Arab region. Michael Reisman is Professor of International Law at Yale University. He is a past member of the Inter-American Commission on Human Rights and is one of the leading scholars in the field of international law (see page xiii).

With appointments to the Task Force made, it quickly started its work. Beginning with its first meeting in London in January 2002, the Task Force held subsequent meetings in Washington DC and New York

(April 2002), Stockholm, Sweden (July 2002), Durban, South Africa (October 2002), and Dubai, United Arab Emirates (January 2003).

During these meetings, the Task Force undertook an extensive process of consultation with governments, intergovernmental organisations, NGOs, policy advisers and lawyers to consider how the international community could approach the difficulty of balancing protection of individual rights while protecting the wider community from terrorist violence. It critically examined legal issues crucial to the problem of international terrorism against the backdrop of existing national and international law.

Throughout its work, the Task Force enjoyed tremendous support, expertise and technical assistance from many IBA members worldwide. In particular, Chistian Åhlund, Essam Al-Tamimi, Francis Neate and Phil Zeidman who provided tremendous support to the Task Force. The Task Force also benefited from the generous funding of a number of groups and individuals, including the Swedish Government, the IBA US Foundation, the IBA Educational Trust, the Arab Lawyers Union and the Office of the Emirate of Sharjah of the United Arab Emirates.

The work of the Task Force would not have been possible without the IBA staff. Joanna Salsbury deserves the most praise as the programme lawyer assigned to the Task Force. She delicately, and with great purpose and wisdom, led the Task Force through a multitude of complex legal issues and positions to help formulate and structure the overall report. She was ably assisted by Daniel Moeckli, a lawyer whose own background in researching and writing in the area of terrorism added significantly to the production of this report. The skills of Claire de Boursac who, on her own, was the administrative arm of the Task Force were indispensable.

Finally, this report remembers the victims of 11 September, 2001, their families, and others whose lives have been ravaged and destroyed by senseless acts of terror and violence. International terrorism is not a new phenomenon; its victims have been counted for as long as history has recorded these types of acts. The methods and means may have changed, but the results are equally as devastating on the victims, their families, friends and communities. September 11, however, completed the global dimension of this heinous crime and forever shattered the myth of invulnerability for countries which were previously spared these hardships. Terrorism is a global phenomenon that demands a global response.

This report, therefore, reflects the global challenge that we now face. Finding answers to the complex issues surrounding international terrorism requires a multilateral approach, similar to the diverse membership of the Task Force. Multilateral cooperation through new international legal instruments, with effective enforcement mechanisms, are required now more than ever. Combating international terrorism also requires insight from a number of different perspectives, often contradictory, with the goal of reaching consensus on as many issues as possible. This is the approach taken by the IBA Task Force. We hope the end result will generate further debate and cooperation while all of us continue to struggle to find the answers.

Mark S Ellis
Executive Director
International Bar Association

INTRODUCTION

The objective of this project has been to explore a number of the legal issues relevant to the prevention of terrorism and the lawfulness of responses to it domestically and within the international community. We have been extremely fortunate at having been joined in this task by a group of exceptional international lawyers with whom it has been an absolute pleasure to work. This report draws upon the experience of each member of the Task Force and aims to provide an informative exploration of this most complex and challenging of legal topics.

From the outset the Task Force unanimously condemned acts of terrorism, believing its use against civilians particularly insidious. Even where it is argued that violence is justified by legitimate political goals, the Task Force agreed that all violence against civilians is abhorrent and inexcusable. From this starting position we resolved that the aim of the Task Force was to contribute to international standards and practice in the field of terrorism. Our mission statement, appended to this report, expresses our desire to reaffirm the rule of law and civil liberties while taking necessary measures to protect both individuals and societies in a manner consistent with the maintenance of international peace and stability. This is a theme which has increasingly come to the attention of the United Nations Security Council which, in Resolution 1456 (adopted on 20 January 2003), stipulated that States must ensure that any measure taken to combat terrorism complies with their obligations under international law, and in particular international human rights law.

As international lawyers we have focused our efforts on considering the challenge of international terrorism from a legal perspective. Whilst individually we may have views on the causes of terrorism, we concluded that our deliberations should focus exclusively on the law. As noted elsewhere in this report, agreement upon a definition of terrorism has eluded the international community for many years. After grappling with this issue for some time, the Task Force felt that it was not necessary to come to a conclusive definition. Instead, it noted that acts of terrorism are defined as crimes in virtually all countries around the world and that, within a domestic context, it may not be necessary to agree upon a specific crime of terrorism. Notwithstanding this, we also appreciated that to achieve greater co-operation between states in areas such as criminal justice and the prevention of terrorism finance, it would be beneficial if agreement on a comprehensive international convention on terrorism could be reached.

This report is not merely a recitation of the Task Forces' deliberations; it contains interpretations, analyses and assessments on current legal developments pertinent to international terrorism. Our findings have been agreed by general consensus and it should not, therefore, be assumed that every member of the Task Force subscribes to all observations and comments.

To conclude, we should like to pay tribute to members of the Task Force for their diligence, commitment and dedication. This has been an extraordinary and rewarding process from which we have all learnt and been inspired. We should also like to thank the IBA Executive Director, Mark Ellis, for his vision and support throughout this project. Finally we should like to thank Joanna Salsbury and Daniel Moeckli from the IBA's Human Rights Institute who have played a significant role in helping shape this report.

Justice Richard Goldstone   Ambassador Emilio Cárdenas
Co-chairs of the IBA's Task Force on International Terrorism

EXECUTIVE SUMMARY

1. INTRODUCTION

While terrorism is a phenomenon that has blighted communities for centuries, it is now perceived to be an increasing threat to international peace and security. The events of September 11 and elsewhere have widely been regarded as a renewal of the challenge to combat terrorism. The Task Force unanimously condemns terrorism, even where it is argued that the use of violence is justified by legitimate political goals such as self-determination and believes its application against civilians is particularly insidious.

It is vital to acknowledge that the use of violence to instil terror among civilians is not exclusively the preserve of the non-state actor. Although some state violence is popularly referred to as 'state terrorism', this term is not recognised in international law. However, a framework within the UN and regional bodies governs the behaviour of state forces and their agents. Whilst this report does not intend to discuss the various causes of terrorism, the Task Force recognises that violence by state forces may be one factor encouraging terrorism. By the same token, it emphasises that respect for human dignity, the rule of law and democracy weakens ground support for terrorist causes.

Although attempts to agree upon an international definition of terrorism have thus far failed, acts of terrorism nonetheless constitute crimes under almost all domestic laws and in many cases under international law. For this reason the Task Force believes it unnecessary to come to a conclusive definition, although a definition would constitute an important component in improving international cooperation in criminal justice, and combating terrorism finance

There appears to be a growing trend for states to deal with international terrorism by unilateral action. The deliberative processes of collective action should, wherever possible, be preferred over unilateral action. The Task Force believes that the role of multilateral organisations must be enhanced wherever possible to make the multilateral effort more effective in the field of cooperation to prevent and suppress terrorism.

The Task Force has concluded that judges and lawyers play a crucial role in protecting the rule of law when threats are posed to national security. They should be at the forefront of monitoring anti-terrorist laws which confer powers on the executive and have the potential to violate fundamental human rights. The judiciary should be alert to, and resist, being collusive in the erosion of the rule of law and its own independence by, for instance, presiding over tribunals which fail to provide due process guarantees. Equally, lawyers should not be exposed to undue pressures when they take on roles as prosecutors and defenders in terrorist cases.

A role too exists for the media in helping ensure protection for the rule of law, civil liberties and human rights standards. When national security is under threat it is crucial that the media offer independent and balanced information. This task may be made more difficult when governments attempt to control information and restrict freedom of expression.

RECOMMENDATIONS

1) The threat of terrorism should not be used by states as a reason to disregard fundamental norms of international law.

2) Adherence to the rule of law and established international standards will help to facilitate international cooperation in areas such as information sharing and law enforcement.

3) Even in a political climate generated by fear of terrorism, judges must be free to act independently and impartially.

4) Lawyers defending suspected terrorists should not be deterred from carrying out their professional duty even in the face of adverse public opinion.

5) It is crucial that the media offer independent and balanced information, including in times of threats to national security. Censorship, either self-imposed or through government restrictions, should be approached with extreme caution.

2. THE USE OF FORCE AS A RESPONSE TO TERRORISM

In the past, some forcible responses to terrorism have been criticised for failing to abide by the standards set down in international law. It is premature to suggest that the response of the international community to the attacks on September 11 marks the emergence of a new, incontrovertible legal regime governing the use of military force against terrorist groups. Nonetheless, there appears to be an acceptance that international law is accommodating the threat posed to international peace and security by non-state actors. However, any extension of the *jus ad bellum* (law regulating the use of force) must be consistent with the settled principles of international law.

The Task Force has grave doubts as to whether claims of self-defence justify, *per se*, unilateral action to engage in armed intervention in any country that has not attempted an attack or threatened international peace and security. In all cases multilateral action through the auspices of the United Nations is a preferable option. Failing success, new criteria for determining the lawfulness of military responses to terrorism must be agreed upon.

Recommendations

6) Any act of self-defence must conform to the legal requirements of the United Nations Charter.

7) A searching debate about the lawful contingencies for self-defence in an environment of international terrorism is urgent and the Task Force recommends that it be undertaken in the United Nations as well as in the college of international lawyers.

3. RESPONSES TO SEPTEMBER 11 WITHIN THE INTERNATIONAL COMMUNITY

Security Council Resolution 1373 has clearly led member states to reconsider the effectiveness of their anti-terrorist strategies and how to facilitate international cooperation. However, not all legislative measures being adopted and action taken in the name of combating terrorism are consistent with fundamental human rights principles—something which the Task Force believes the Security Council and the Counter Terrorism Committee (CTC) should be mindful of. New laws which may restrict human rights and civil liberties should be considered carefully by legislative bodies, with emphasis placed on the likely effectiveness of such measures.

Recommendations

8) The CTC should undertake to include in its consideration of state reports an assessment of whether measures taken to comply with Security Council Resolution 1373 are consistent with international human rights obligations.

9) States should not use the fight against terrorism as a pretext to adopt measures which unlawfully restrict the rights to freedom of expression, religion, opinion and belief, nor the rights of minorities.

4. UPHOLDING HUMAN RIGHTS AND CIVIL LIBERTIES IN THE FIGHT AGAINST TERRORISM

Despite a public perception to the contrary, the Task Force believes that the protection of human rights and civil liberties is not incompatible with the safety and security of the wider community. It is at times of stress to the nation that human rights and civil liberties take on even greater importance and yet are under the greatest threat. Governments must strike a balance between national security and the protection of civil liberties and human rights. Yet some states with a tradition of human rights protection appear to be shifting the balance away from commonly accepted standards, undermining their credibility as good examples to the international community, and eroding the applicability of universal human rights.

During extreme threats to the nation many treaties permit the suspension of certain human rights to the extent strictly required. However, governments might be tempted to use threats to national security to justify human rights restrictions that go further than required and may fail to respect fundamental guarantees that can not be derogated from under any circumstances. Moreover, there is a danger that restrictions of human rights applied to suspected terrorists will be in place for longer than strictly necessary, allowing such procedures to be embedded in the general fabric of the law.

Procedural rights such as those protecting from arbitrary arrest and unfair trial are particularly at risk when a state faces terrorist threats. Whilst human rights treaties allow for the restriction of these rights, certain fundamental guarantees must be respected at all times and failure to apply them may result in miscarriages of justice.

Restrictions of substantive rights, such as the freedom of association and assembly, might be used by states to suppress legitimate political dissent. Such action constitutes a blunt instrument which may have little effect in combating threats to national security. Similarly, overbroad measures which target asylum-seekers or citizens of certain states may be both discriminatory and ineffective.

Yet these concerns do not necessarily conflict with the ability of states to take preventative and effective measures to protect themselves from threats to national security, including terrorism. The Task Force believes that in order to both respect human rights and be effective, any anti-terrorist activity should be based on sound investigative and intelligence gathering methods, thus promoting a targeted approach over sweeping measures.

Recommendations

10) When states intend not to comply with certain obligations contained within human rights treaties to which they are parties, they can only do so for reasons of state of emergency and provided the criteria for derogating are observed. Further, the suspension of human rights should be regularly reviewed and must be limited in time.

11) All restrictions of substantive human rights must be expressly provided by law, must be necessary and proportionate, and must not exclude the possibility of judicial review.

12) At all times arrested or detained individuals must be accorded the right to promptly challenge the actions of the state before a court. Nobody should be held in administrative detention indefinitely.

13) Even during states of emergency the fundamental principles of the right to a fair trial must be respected. This necessitates at the least protecting the presumption of innocence, the right to be tried by an independent and impartial court, access to counsel and the right to appeal. Upholding these fair trial guarantees is even more crucial in cases attracting the death penalty.

5. TERRORISM AND INTERNATIONAL HUMANITARIAN LAW

Whilst the Task Force recognises the threat posed by international terrorism to the security of nations, it is troubled by certain failures to take into account and apply fundamental principles of international humanitarian law. The consequences of such action are grave and may undermine the binding force of the humanitarian law regime. It is vital that the treatment of those captured during armed conflict conforms to both international humanitarian law and fundamental human rights standards, regardless of the scenario in which they were captured and suspicions as to their criminal activities. Similarly, those prosecuted for acts committed before or during an armed conflict must be afforded fundamental fair trial guarantees.

It must be acknowledged that states might find it difficult to apply international humanitarian law to combatants who themselves do not comply with the same provisions. In addition, the humanitarian law regime is not without ambiguity, gaps or flaws. Yet in dealing with new situations states should act in accordance with the spirit and fundamental objectives of international humanitarian law and, in this regard, take due note of the views of the ICRC, which is assigned a special role in this process.

Recommendations

14) Without exception the determination of POW status must continue to be made strictly in accordance with Article 4 of the Third Geneva Convention.

15) States can not hold detainees, for which they are responsible, outside of the jurisdiction of all independent courts or tribunals competent to determine the legality of their detention. All detainees must have the right to challenge their detention before an independent court or tribunal.

16) Treatment in detention must comply with the fundamental standards. Detainees must never be held in prolonged incommunicado detention or solitary confinement.

6. PREVENTING THE FINANCING OF TERRORISM

The effectiveness of legislation against terrorist financing can only be determined by evaluating its success in frustrating, deterring or preventing an act of terrorism. The problem lies in assessing such effectiveness—a thwarted terrorist act will probably only be known as such if it is prevented very shortly before it is carried out, in which case the probability is that the terrorists were able to access funds to get as far as they did. Effective restriction of funding to terrorists should mean that any planned activity is stifled early, and it is therefore difficult to truly measure the efficacy of anti-terrorist finance legislation.

Further, it should not be assumed that all terrorist acts can be prevented by blocking funds belonging to or intended for terrorists. Not all such funds flow through the regulated financial systems and those that do are often extremely difficult to identify. In any event, a terrorist act does not necessarily require significant quantities of funding to be perpetrated.

The efforts of international organisations combating terrorist finance have been most effective in identifying areas or countries of concern and bringing pressure to bear on jurisdictions to tighten money laundering controls. However, international cooperation could be impeded by the CTC's lack of any regulatory teeth.

International efforts to eradicate terrorism finance have unfortunately led some states to implement measures which can significantly erode the rights of individuals. The lack of a legal framework regulating the seizure and freezing of assets commonly leaves those affected without means of obtaining the evidence against them or legally challenging the actions of the state. As a matter of urgency the international community should agree upon certain minimum evidential and due process requirements.

Recommendations

17) In order to tackle terrorism finance globally, all states must put in place measures to detect and suppress funds used to support terrorist activities. Such measures must be consistently and universally enforced, taking account of guidelines developed by international expert bodies.

18) The system of asset seizure must be placed within a more regulated framework, in particular to ensure transparency and protect due process guarantees.

7. INTERNATIONAL COOPERATION IN COMBATING TERRORISM

As the world perceives the terrorist threat to be increasing in severity and breadth, there is a corresponding imperative to look at and evaluate existing mechanisms of international cooperation. The present weaknesses of cooperation include: i) failing to provide an overall framework that integrates all the applicable modalities of international cooperation (*eg* extradition, legal assistance, transfer of criminal proceedings etc.); ii) depending almost entirely on the effectiveness of national legal systems; iii) lacking a policy that provides continuity and progressive development; iv) placing the sole duty on states to act in conformity with treaty obligations without international constraints; v) over-reliance on bilateralism; vi) failing to provide a mechanism for the resolution of conflicts that arise between states; and vii) lacking adequate safeguards to insure 'due process.'

A priority is to clarify and reinforce the obligations of states under the maxim *aut dedere aut judicare* (duty to extradite or prosecute) and to develop an integrated approach for all the modalities of international cooperation. The cumbersome, costly, and lengthy bilateral approach must give way to a more effective multilateral process or at least to an integrated bilateral approach which can strive for greater national similarities.

Where international, transnational, and national criminal phenomena are not effectively controlled, governments may either reduce the procedural safeguards of due process or engage in questionable and even illegal practices under their domestic laws and under international law.

This state of affairs may be due to a lack of vision on the part of responsible officials and the fact that there are insufficiently knowledgeable experts on international criminal law advising governments, particularly in developing countries. Yet developed countries and intergovernmental organisations offer little technical legal assistance and support to developing countries. Moreover, administrative and bureaucratic divisions among the national organs of law enforcement and prosecution impair the effectiveness of international cooperation in penal matters.

Recommendations

19) Recognition of the maxim *aut dedere aut judicare* as a *civitas maxima* and the development of international standards, including standards for effective and good faith prosecution and extradition.
20) Developing a model international criminal code to serve as a model for codifying national legislation.
21) Developing specialised parts in national legislation on international cooperation in penal matters which integrate all the modalities of international cooperation.
22) Adopting a multilateral convention on cooperation between law enforcement and intelligence agencies setting forth the means, methods, and limitations of such cooperation, including the protection of fundamental human rights and the right to privacy.

8. FORA FOR TRYING INTERNATIONAL TERRORISTS: THE ROLE OF THE INTERNATIONAL CRIMINAL COURT

The field of law dealing with terrorism needs to be developed to cater for such forms of criminality with the possibility of exploring new fora for the prosecution of the perpetrators. It is clear that terrorism has well and truly moved into the international arena and that commonly the most appropriate forum to deal with the problem is an international one. As far as the International Criminal Court (ICC) is able to exercise its jurisdiction over acts of this nature, it should be allowed and encouraged to do so. The question of what impact the 'complementarity principle' (meaning that the ICC will only prosecute if a state with jurisdiction is unwilling or unable to do so), absence of jurisdiction over the crime of terrorism *per se*, and the limitations inherent in fitting the acts into the three existing crimes under ICC jurisdiction will have, remains to be seen. The Task Force hopes that these issues will not handicap the ICC to such an extent that this preferred forum will not be able to prosecute acts of international terrorism effectively. It is further hoped that the introduction of bilateral agreements, which provide immunity from surrender to the ICC for nationals of the two states parties, will be a trend that does not perpetuate. The Task Force believes that this thwarts the very object and purpose of the Rome Statute—to end impunity for the worst crimes.

Recommendations

23) Where a state has a choice as to which forum may legitimately try suspected terrorists, ensuring respect for the fundamental due process guarantees must be a major factor in reaching the decision.
24) When choosing a forum, consideration should also be given to the interests of the victims and their families.
25) In many instances international tribunals or, where it has jurisdiction, the ICC are the preferred fora to try suspected international terrorists.

SELECTED ABBREVIATIONS

ACHR	American Convention on Human Rights
ATCSA	Terrorism, Crime and Security Act 2001
AU	African Union
CERD	Convention on the Elimination of all Forms of Racial Discrimination
CIA	Central Intelligence Agency
CTC	Counter Terrorism Committee
DOD	US Department of Defense
ECHR	European Convention for the Protection of Human Rights and Fundamental Freedoms
EU	European Union
FATF	The Financial Action Task Force on Money Laundering
FBI	Federal Bureau of Investigation
FISA	Foreign Intelligence Surveillance Act
GA	General Assembly
IBA	International Bar Association
ICC	International Criminal Court
ICCPR	International Covenant on Civil and Political Rights
ICJ	International Court of Justice
ICRC	International Committee of the Red Cross
ICTY	International Criminal Tribunal for the Former Yugoslavia
IHL	International Humanitarian Law
IMF	International Monetary Fund
INA	Immigration and Nationality Act
INS	Immigration and Naturalization Service
NATO	North Atlantic Treaty Organisation
OAS	Organization of American States
OSCE	Organisation for Security and Cooperation in Europe
POTA	Prevention of Terrorism Act
POW	Prisoner of war
SAARC	South Asian Association for Regional Cooperation
SIAC	Special Immigration Appeals Commission
UDHR	Universal Declaration of Human Rights
UN	United Nations
UNHCR	United Nations High Commissioner for Refugees
UNODC	United Nations Office on Drugs and Crime

CHAPTER 1

THE CHALLENGES OF MODERN TERRORISM

1.1 INTRODUCTION

This Task Force was established as a reaction to the IBA's abhorrence at the perpetration of massive atrocities against civilians on September 11. The Task Force notes that the term 'terrorism' is emotive and has such strong political connotations that it has thus far proved impossible for the international community to agree a definition. Terrorism is not a new phenomenon but has existed for thousands of years. It has been defined as 'a method of combat in which random or symbolic victims serve as an instrumental target of violence. These instrumental victims share group or class characteristics which form a basis for their selection for victimization. Through previous use of violence or the credible threat of violence other members of that group or class are put into a state of chronic fear (terror).'[1]

Terrorist acts are normally designed to attract publicity both to spread fear and to draw attention to the perpetrators' agenda. Terrorism can be an inexpensive means of publicising a particular ideological viewpoint and circumventing normal political processes. Nonetheless, the commission of terrorist acts constitutes a crime under almost all domestic laws and in many cases under international law.[2] Further, terrorism commonly engages the international community with respect to the funding and planning which often occur outside of the target state.

---

1.   Schmid, Alex P. and Jongman, Albert J., *Political terrorism: a new guide to actors, authors, concepts, data bases, theories and literature*, North-Holland Publishing (1988), pp. 1–2.

2.   Some crimes are so serious that they are considered international crimes. These include piracy, war crimes, crimes against humanity, genocide, torture, aggression. See Cassese, *International Law*, Oxford University Press (2001), p. 246. Where an act is considered an international crime, the perpetrator can be tried under the principle of universal jurisdiction. Some acts of terrorism may constitute one of these crimes. In addition, the international community has adopted a number of treaties on terrorism some of which provide for universal jurisdiction.

1

The Task Force unanimously condemns the use of terrorism, believing its use against civilians particularly insidious. Even where it is argued that the use of violence is justified by legitimate political goals, such as self-determination, the Task Force is of the view that all brutality against civilians is abhorrent and inexcusable.

1.2 THE PROBLEM OF DEFINING TERRORISM

Attempts to agree on a definition of terrorism have failed for two main reasons. Firstly, some governments seem to have no interest in defining the term, preferring to keep it vague or to only identify prohibited means. Secondly, a great amount of confusion exists as to the legitimacy of wars of national liberation (which some states believe should be excluded from the definition entirely) and their permissible means.[3]

The prevention of international terrorism has been considered at successive sessions of the General Assembly (GA) of the United Nations (UN), which first set up an *ad hoc* committee on international terrorism in 1972.[4] A new *ad hoc* committee was created in 1996, including as its mandate the elaboration of a comprehensive convention on terrorism.[5] A working group established by the committee has recently considered an extensive draft convention prepared by India.[6] At the 56th Session of the working group, terrorism was defined in Article 2 as follows[7]:

'Any person commits an offence within the meaning of this Convention if that person, by any means, unlawfully and intentionally, causes:
(a) Death or serious bodily injury to any person, or:
(b) Serious damage to public or private property, including a place of public use, a State or government facility, a public transportation system, an infrastructure facility or the environment; or

---

3. See Bassiouni, Cherif, *International Terrorism: Multilateral Conventions (1937–2001)*, Transnational Publishers (2001), pp. 15 and 19. For example, Article 2 of the Convention of the Organisation of the Islamic Conference on Combating International Terrorism excludes from the definition of terrorism armed struggle for liberation and self-determination. Similar provision is found in Article 2 of the Arab Convention for the Suppression of Terrorism.

4. See General Assembly Resolution No. 3034 (XXVII) of 18 December 1972, para. 9, and Oppenheim, Lassa F.L., *Oppenheim's International Law*, Vol. I, Part I, Longman (1992), 9th edition, p. 402.

5. See General Assembly Resolution No. 51/210 of 17 December 1996, UN Doc. A/RES/51/210.

6. See General Assembly, *Draft comprehensive convention on international terrorism; Working document submitted by* India, 28 August 2000, UN Doc. A/C.6/55/1.

7. Measures to Eliminate Terrorism: Report of the Working Group Fifty-sixth session, 29 October 2001, UN Doc. A/C.6/56/L.9.

(c) Damage to property, places, facilities, or systems referred to in para. 1 (b) of this article, resulting or likely to result in major economic loss,

  when the purpose of the conduct, by its nature or context, is to intimidate a population, or to compel a Government or an international organization to do or abstain from doing any act.'

It is, however, unlikely that this proposed convention will progress further than the drafting stage as there remains a lack of consensus on how to define terrorism.

Agreement on a definition would constitute an important component in improving international cooperation in criminal justice and may facilitate procedures such as extradition. Even if a definition remains elusive, the Task Force believes at the least a convention standardising and improving cooperation to combat international terrorism is crucial.

1.3 'STATE TERRORISM'

The Task Force believes it vital to acknowledge that the use of violence to instil terror among civilians is not exclusively the preserve of the non-state actor. A number of states have engaged and continue to engage in violence against populations in a manner designed to create fear among them, particularly in internal conflicts. Insufficient attention is paid to such state violence, despite the vast majority of those affected by political violence in the modern world being victims of state forces.

Although some state violence is popularly referred to as 'state terrorism,' this term is not recognised in international law. There is, nonetheless, a framework within the UN and regional bodies governing the behaviour of state forces and their agents. Violence perpetrated by a state may constitute violations of international humanitarian law and international human rights treaties. In addition, individuals acting on behalf of a state in carrying out crimes against humanity, genocide and war crimes may be prosecuted under international humanitarian law (the laws of war) and now under the Statute of the International Criminal Court (ICC). Where a state has been involved in systematic violence against its civilians, this may constitute a threat to international peace and security, following the declaration of which, the Security Council may invoke its powers under Chapter VII.[8] Further, states have claimed a right to intervene unilaterally on humanitarian grounds where another state

---

8. According to Article 39 of the UN Charter, the Security Council can determine the existence of a threat to international peace and security and invoke its powers under Chapter VII of the Charter, which include ordering economic sanctions against a state under Article 41 and taking military action under Article 42.

is engaged in systematic abuse of human rights.[9] Thus, states are subject to international legal requirements which prohibit 'state terrorism' on many grounds. A comparable comprehensive legal regime does not apply to non-state actors. It is for this reason that the activities of international terrorists are of special concern to the international community and are the focus of this report.

Alternatively, if a state has engaged in, or sponsored terrorism, the Security Council may again utilise its powers pursuant to Chapter VII, which include ordering economic sanctions, or taking military action. In addition, it is possible that action, such as the suspension of membership, may be taken by regional organisations. Finally, states sponsoring terrorism may incur liability under the law of state responsibility.

Whilst this report does not intend to discuss the various causes of terrorism, the Task Force recognises that violence by state forces may be one factor encouraging terrorism. By the same token, the Task Force emphasises that respect for human dignity, the rule of law and democracy weakens ground support for terrorist causes.

1.4 RESPONDING TO MODERN TERRORISM

Over the years, terrorists have kept abreast of the developments in weaponry and other technologies. The dissemination of propaganda and the creation of global terror networks has been made easier by communications technology and access to international travel. Further, the prospect of terrorists gaining access to weapons of mass destruction now appears more a possibility. While terrorism is a phenomenon that has blighted communities for centuries, it is now perceived to be an increasing threat to international peace and security.

These developments require responses in international law enforcement and, under certain circumstances, military force. States, regional organisations and the UN have adopted a range of new measures designed to prevent and deter terrorism.[10] There is a trend that these measures

---

9. International law is presently unclear as to the extent to which another state, or states, can intervene to prevent human rights abuses, including state-sponsored terrorism. There is much debate amongst scholars and governments as to the existence of such a right as an exception to the general prohibition on the use of force set out in Article 2(4) of the UN Charter. For a discussion of differing legal perspectives see, for example, Simma, NATO, the UN and the Use of Force: Legal Aspects, 10 *European Journal of International Law* 1 (1999); Cassese, *Ex iniuria ius oritur*. Are We Moving towards International Legitimation of Forcible Humanitarian Countermeasures in the World Community?, 10 *European Journal of International Law* 23 (1999); Kritsiotis, Reappraising Policy Objections to Humanitarian Intervention, 19 *Michigan Journal of International Law* 1005; The Independent International Commission on Kosovo, *The Kosovo Report: Conflict, International Response, Lessons Learned*, Oxford University Press (2000); Holzgrefe, and Keohane, (eds.), *Humanitarian Intervention*, Cambridge University Press (2003).

10. See Chapter 3 for details.

either take no account of, or violate, fundamental principles of international law. Whether terrorism is dealt with as a law enforcement matter or through military coercion, the Task Force believes that fundamental norms of international law remain applicable and must be observed universally. Further, while it is crucial for states to have sufficient tools to combat terrorism, they must be consistent with the rule of law[11] and established international standards. Adherence to common standards will help facilitate international cooperation in areas such as information sharing, extradition and law enforcement.[12] In turn, enhanced cooperation may be an additional tool in the prevention and deterrence of terrorism.

Finally, the Task Force believes it to be vital that judicial review is maintained over any measures restricting or interfering with individual rights and liberties.

1.5 INTERNATIONAL COOPERATION IN THE PREVENTION AND DETERRENCE OF TERRORISM

A number of international treaties deal with specific manifestations of terrorism and, *inter alia,* aim to enhance international cooperation in criminal justice.[13] Most embody the principle requiring states to try or

---

11. The preamble to the Universal Declaration of Human Rights (UDHR) refers to the rule of law. The rule of law is a fundamental principle of human rights law, requiring that within a state, rights must themselves be protected by law; and any disputes about them must not be resolved by the exercise of some arbitrary discretion, but must be consistently capable of being submitted for adjudication to a competent, impartial, and independent tribunal, applying procedures which will ensure full equality and fairness to all the parties, and determining the question in accordance with clear, specific, and pre-existing laws, known and openly proclaimed. See Sieghart, *International Law of Human Rights*, Clarendon Press (1983), pp. 18–19.

12. For example, international cooperation in matters such as extradition can be impeded by a lack of fair trial guarantees in another state.

13. Convention on the Prevention and Punishment of Crimes against Internationally Protected Persons, including Diplomatic Agents, adopted by the General Assembly of the United Nations on 14 December 1973; International Convention against the Taking of Hostages, adopted by the General Assembly of the United Nations on 17 December 1979; International Convention for the Suppression of Terrorist Bombings, adopted by the General Assembly of the United Nations on 15 December 1997; International Convention for the Suppression of the Financing of Terrorism, adopted by the General Assembly of the United Nations on 9 December 1999; Convention on Offences and Certain Other Acts Committed on Board Aircraft, signed at Tokyo on September 1963; Convention for the Suppression of Unlawful Seizure of aircraft, signed at the Hague on 16 December 1970; Convention for the Suppression of Unlawful Acts against the Safety of Civil Aviation, signed at Montreal on 23 September 1971; Convention on the Physical Protection of Nuclear Material, signed at Vienna on 3 March 1980; Protocol on the Suppression of Unlawful Acts of Violence at Airports Serving International Civil Aviation, supplementary to the Convention for the Suppression of Unlawful Acts against the Safety of Civil aviation, signed at Montreal on 24 February 1988; Convention for the Suppression of Unlawful Acts against the Safety of Maritime Navigation, signed at Rome on 10 March 1988; Convention on the Marking of

hand-over (*aut judicare aut dedere*) those suspected of having committed a terrorist act. An additional common feature of most of these conventions is that all states parties can try suspected terrorists regardless of the location of the offence or the nationality of the defendant. Other shared elements include the six modalities of international cooperation in criminal justice: extradition, legal assistance, execution of foreign penal sentences, recognition of foreign penal judgments, transfer of criminal proceedings, and freezing and seizing of assets deriving from criminal conduct. However, the treaties vary as to whether or not all six modalities are included. No treaty so far deals with law enforcement and intelligence sharing.

None of the anti-terrorist conventions contains effective enforcement provisions to ensure that state parties effectively and fairly fulfil their treaty obligations, and in particular, take appropriate steps to investigate, arrest, and alternatively extradite, suspected terrorists. International cooperation between states is indispensable in order to prevent and suppress terrorism, and all other forms of transnational and international criminality. As noted above, the Task Force believes the adoption of a comprehensive multilateral convention to integrate means of inter-state cooperation in criminal justice will enhance cooperation and engender uniformity of practice among states. A similar treaty could be developed to enhance cooperation between law enforcement agencies with appropriate guarantees for the right of privacy and protections against erroneous information. National bureaucratic difficulties must be resolved to ensure the efficacy of national law enforcement and that of international cooperation.

Although there are some notable efforts being made to improve international cooperation with regard to counter-terrorism,[14] there is a trend towards unilateral action which is bolstered by failures in multilateral cooperation efforts. International organisations have not been suf-

---

Plastic Explosives for the Purposes of Detection, signed at Montreal on 1 March 1991; Arab Convention on the Suppression of Terrorism, signed at a meeting held at the General Secretariat of the League of Arab States in Cairo on 22 April 1998; Convention of the Organization of the Islamic Conference on Combating International Terrorism adopted at Ouagadougou on 1 July 1999; European Convention on the Suppression of Terrorism, concluded at Strasbourg on 27 January 1977; OAS Convention to Prevent and Punish Acts of Terrorism Taking the Form of Crimes against Persons and Related Extortion that are of International Significance, concluded at Washington D.C. on 2 February 1971; Inter-American Convention Against Terrorism, adopted by the General Assembly of the Organization of American States on 3 June 2002; OAU Convention on the Prevention and Combating of Terrorism, adopted at Algiers on 14 July 1999; SAARC Regional Convention on Suppression of Terrorism, signed at Kathmandu on 4 November 1987; Treaty on Cooperation among States Members of the Commonwealth of Independent States in Combating Terrorism, done at Minsk on 4 June 1999.

14. See Chapter 3 for details.

ficiently active in many areas, particularly in regard to technical legal assistance for developing countries. The Task Force is concerned that these failings may lead to unlawful unilateral action which detracts from the legitimacy of the efforts to combat terrorism. Moreover, it believes that even where unilateral action is, in the circumstances, lawful, international cooperation is always to be preferred.

1.6 STRIKING THE BALANCE

The Task Force is of the view that governments should strike a balance between national security, including the protection of persons and property on the one hand, and the protection of civil liberties and human rights on the other. Since September 11, factors, including public expectation and media pressure, have led governments to tighten their security measures to the extent that certain principles are compromised. Despite a public perception to the contrary, the Task Force believes that the protection of human rights and civil liberties is not incompatible with the safety and security of the wider community. It is at times of stress to the nation that human rights and civil liberties take on even greater importance and yet are under the greatest threat. Most human rights treaties already allow for states to suspend certain rights during states of national emergency.[15] (Although any suspension must be to the extent strictly required by the exigencies of the situation.) Even some states with a tradition of human rights protection appear to be moving away from commonly accepted standards, undermining their credibility as good examples to the international community, and eroding the applicability of universal human rights.

1.7 THE ROLE OF JUDGES AND LAWYERS

It is the duty of judges and lawyers to respect the rule of law, protect human rights, apply standards of international law, and preserve the integrity of the judiciary. When national security is under threat, the role of an independent judiciary becomes even more important. Judges and lawyers should be at the forefront of monitoring anti-terrorist laws which confer powers on the executive and have the potential to violate fundamental human rights.

In a political climate generated by fear of terrorism, members of the judiciary may be subject to a host of pressures: to interpret the law so as to prejudice the interests of alleged 'terrorists', or to let legislation of dubious constitutionality go unchallenged. Judges have conceded that

---

15. See Article 4 of the International Covenant on Civil and Political Rights (ICCPR), Article 15 of the European Convention for the Protection of Human Rights and Fundamental Freedoms (ECHR), and Article 27 of the American Convention on Human Rights (ACHR).

they are subject to 'hydraulic pressure [. . .] which makes what was previously clear seem doubtful, and before which even well settled principles of law will bend.'[16] But for members of the judiciary to do anything other than to remain independent, including from the executive, and to administer justice fairly and in accordance with the constitution, is unacceptable in any circumstances. Judges should be cautious to ensure that they remain impartial even in the face of extraordinary events.

Principle 2 of the UN Basic Principles on the Independence of the Judiciary[17] requires judges to:

'. . . decide matters before them impartially, on the basis of facts and in accordance with the law, without any restrictions, improper influences, inducements, pressures, threats of interferences, direct or indirect, from any quarter or for any reason.'

The judiciary should be alert to, and resist being collusive in the erosion of the rule of law and its own independence by, for instance, presiding over tribunals which fail to provide due process guarantees and the highest standards of independence and impartiality.[18]

Lawyers defending suspected terrorists should not be deterred from carrying out their professional duty even in the face of adverse public opinion. Instead, they should be encouraged and supported in the fulfilment of what is undoubtedly a crucial role in the administration of justice. According to the UN Basic Principles on the Role of Lawyers, defence lawyers should not be identified with their clients or their clients' causes and must be allowed to perform all of their professional functions without intimidation, hindrance, harassment or improper interference.[19]

Prosecution lawyers involved in terrorist cases may be subject to pressure to obtain a successful conviction. However, the UN Guidelines on the Role of Prosecutors state that prosecutors must be able to per-

---

16. See the decision by the US Supreme Court in *Northern Securities Co. v. United States,* Holmes Dissenting, 24 S.Ct. 436 (14 March 1904), at 468. Likewise, in a British case concerning a non-citizen detained for reasons of national security, Lord Hoffman acknowledged 'the need for the judicial arm of government to respect the decision of ministers of the crown on the question of whether support for terrorist activities in a foreign country constitutes a threat to national security.' In so stating, he indicated the additional weight that the House of Lords gave the executive in the particular circumstances. See the decision of the House of Lords in *Secretary of State for the Home Department v. Rehman,* 11 October 2001, [2001] UKHL 47, [2003] 1 AC 153, para. 62.

17. UN Basic Principles on the Independence of the Judiciary, adopted by the Seventh UN Congress on the Prevention of Crime and the Treatment of Offenders in 1985, UN Doc. A/CONF.121/22/Rev.1 at 59 (1985).

18. See Chapter 4, Section 4.6.

19. See Principles 18 and 16(a) of the UN Basic Principles on the Role of Lawyers, adopted by the Eighth UN Congress on the Prevention of Crime and the Treatment of Offenders in 1990, UN Doc. A/CONF.144/28/Rev.1 at 118 (1990).

form their functions without intimidation or hindrance and must act with objectivity.[20]

Both judges and lawyers face the hazard of security threats. It is therefore crucial that states take the necessary protective measures to ensure their personal integrity, independence and impartiality.[21] However, any such measures should not interfere with due process guarantees.[22]

1.8 THE ROLE OF THE MEDIA

Like judges and lawyers the media have a special role in helping ensure protection for the rule of law, civil liberties and human rights standards. When national security is under threat it is even more important that journalists and broadcasters offer independent and balanced information. This task may be made more difficult when governments attempt to control information and restrict freedom of expression, as may be more prevalent at times of stress to the nation.

1.8.1 Freedom of Expression and the Media

Freedom of expression, of which a free media is an essential component, is recognised as a fundamental right in international law, to which all citizens are entitled. It includes the freedom to seek, receive and impart information and ideas without interference and regardless of frontiers.[23] Restrictions of this right are only allowed as far as they are provided by law, and are necessary for respect of the rights or reputations of others, or for the protection of national security, public order, public health or morals.[24] The press is a crucial watchdog over the power of government and must be permitted to report freely. The role of the press is recognised in Article 79 of Additional Protocol I to the Geneva Conventions which provides safeguards for the protection of journalists.

---

20. See Principles 3 and 13(b) of the UN Guidelines on the Role of Prosecutors, adopted at the Eighth UN Congress on the Prevention of Crime and the Treatment of Offenders in 1990, UN Doc. A/CONF.144/28/Rev.1 at 189 (1990).

21. See Principle 2 of the UN Basic Principles on the Independence of the Judiciary, Principle 5 of the UN Guidelines on the Role of Prosecutors, and Principle 17 of the UN Basic Principles on the Role of Lawyers.

22. In Peru, the practice of holding secret trials for terrorism and drug-related offences was criticised by the Human Rights Committee which urged the reinstatement of public trials. See Human Rights Committee, Preliminary Observations, UN Doc. CCPR/C/79/Add. 67, 25 July 1996, para. 25.

23. See Article 19 of the UDHR, Article 19(2) of the ICCPR, Article 10 of the ECHR, Article 13 of the ACHR, and Article 9 of the African Charter on Human and People's Rights (African Charter).

24. See Article 19(3) of the ICCPR, Article 10(2) of the ECHR, and Article 13(2) of the ACHR.

1.8.2 Terrorism and the Media

Publicity is the life-blood of terrorism, the medium by which it gains attention, spreads fear, delivers messages, demonstrates the vulnerability of the state and attracts support. Terrorists are adept at using media and select their targets accordingly. The September 11 attacks, for example, were almost certainly orchestrated to demonstrate the vulnerability of the United States, but were also of sufficient scale, prominence and audacity to ensure that they were seen live on television broadcasts across the globe. Terrorists' preoccupation with publicity has also led to a growing number of threats and acts of terrorism directed against journalists and media organisations.[25]

By the same token, media organisations should be aware of their own symbiotic relationship with terrorism. Dramatic, violent events can have a positive effect on television ratings and newspaper circulation.[26] With technological advances in global communication, media organisaions have the ability to play a greater role in the spreading of fear and the psychological effects of terrorism. Thus, they can be exploited by terrorists. Therefore it becomes even more important for them to report in a responsible and balanced manner when covering terrorism news, avoiding overstating terrorist threats. However, this notion should in principle not be used to unduly restrict the freedom of press. Clearly, there is a need to tread a fine line to ensure both freedom of expression and responsible journalism, which should be determined by self-regulation rather than government restriction.

However, there are instances where self-regulation may be insufficient and governments may legitimately restrict the freedom of expression. For example, the media may be restricted in order to protect the presumption of innocence and refrain from publishing material that could prejudice any trial.[27] Restrictions may also be applied to protect the reputation and privacy of individuals alleged to be involved in terrorist activities.

In addition, in countries in which the Convention on the Elimination of Racial Discrimination applies, media organisations are prohibited from

---

25. For example, terrorists have assassinated investigative reporters in Spain and Northern Ireland. In January 2002, the Wall Street Journal journalist Daniel Pearl was kidnapped and killed by Islamic militants in Pakistan. See International Federation of Journalists, Journalism and the War on Terrorism, 3 September 2002.

26. For example, over 16 million viewers in the UK tuned onto their televisions as the events of September 11 unfolded. See Jason Deans, 16m Glued to News as Tragedy Unfolds, *The Guardian*, 12 September 2001.

27. For example, the British Attorney General issued a warning to newspaper editors against publishing material that could prejudice the case of three men charged under the Terrorism Act 2000. See Ciar Byrne, Warning Over Terror Charge Suspects, *The Guardian*, 22 November 2002.

reporting in a manner that would violate the prohibition on the dissemination of racist material.[28] With media interest focused on international terrorism, news coverage in connection with foreign nationals, immigration and asylum may be more likely to violate this prohibition.

1.8.3   Restrictions on Media

The crucial and challenging role played by media organisations in shaping public opinion on terrorist issues may tempt governments to curtail press freedom, for example by banning the dissemination of statements by terrorists,[29] criminalising meetings with suspected terrorists,[30] or introducing a duty to disclose to the authorities information on terrorist activities.[31] In addition, the pressure exerted on journalists from within the media industry itself may be even greater. At times of national crisis, many media outlets will be particularly wary not to appear unduly unpatriotic, which could create an atmosphere of self-censorship.[32] Further, with the popularity of 'embedding' journalists within military units, it may be even more difficult to obtain an independent perspective on news events. The Task Force believes that even at times of threats

---

28. Article 4 of the Convention on the Elimination of All Forms of Racial Discrimination (CERD) requires states parties to restrict all dissemination of ideas based on racial superiority or hatred and incitement to racial discrimination.

29. For instance, in the 1980's the British Government banned the broadcasting of statements by members of the Irish Republican Army (IRA), much to the chagrin of the British media. Following September 11, the United States administration asked TV stations and newspapers to restrict coverage of statements from Osama bin Laden. See Ron Hutcheson, Newspapers are asked to limit use of bin Laden quotes, *The Seattle Times*, 12 October 2001.

30. The Indian Prevention of Terrorism Act (POTA) criminalises anyone arranging or managing a meeting which he or she knows is 'to be addressed by a person who belongs or professes to belong to a terrorist organisation.' See POTA, Section 21(2)(c). 'Meeting' is defined as 'a meeting of three or more persons whether or not the public are admitted', thus including private meetings and discussions. See POTA, Section 21. This means that anybody meeting with any member, even if inactive, of a 'terrorist organisation' would be guilty under POTA—even if the purpose of the meeting is different from supporting the organisation and completely peaceful. For instance, a journalist arranging an interview with a member of a 'terrorist organisation' would commit an offence under POTA, as long as a third person (e.g. a photographer) attends the meeting. The penalty for this offence would be imprisonment for up to 10 years. See POTA, Section 21(4).

31. For example, Section 14 of POTA allows an investigating officer to require any person to furnish information in relation to an offence under the Act. Failure to furnish the required information is punishable with imprisonment for up to three years. Similarly, the British Terrorism Act 2000 and the Anti-Terrorism, Crime and Security Act 2001 (ATCSA) contain a duty to disclose certain information on terrorist activities. See Section 19 and Schedule 5, para. 13 of the Terrorism Act 2000, and Section 117 of the ATCSA.

32. For example, following September 11 several journalists were dismissed in the United States for writing articles that were critical of the President. See Howard Kurtz, Journalists Caught in Backlash against Dissent, *The Washington Post*, 4 October 2001.

to national security, media organisations must ensure that their role as public watchdogs is not diminished, and that they retain their perspective and critique. After all, it is in times when national security is under threat and governments may take measures to limit human rights and civil liberties that the media's role in scrutinising government actions is particularly important.

CONCLUSION

Several themes emerge from the Task Force's consideration of the fundamental issues discussed above.

First, the contemporary phenomenon of international terrorism is nothing new, rather a renewed challenge that was faced by many societies in the past. Any responses to terrorism must be in accordance with the rule of law and established international norms and standards of due process. The law should facilitate counter-terrorism within the parameters of the values and principles reflected in national constitutions and international and regional human rights treaties.

Second, there appears to be a growing trend for states to deal with international terrorism by unilateral action. The deliberative processes of collective action should, wherever possible, be preferred over unilateral action. The Task Force believes that the role of multilateral organisations, such as the United Nations, must be enhanced wherever possible to make the multilateral effort more effective in the field of cooperation to prevent and suppress terrorism.

Third, international cooperation in criminal matters must be made more effective to deter, prevent and suppress terrorist acts without sacrificing international norms and standards of due process.

Fourthly, where national security is under threat, judges and lawyers play a crucial role in ensuring respect for the rule of law and human rights. To achieve that goal it is necessary to uphold the independence and integrity of the judiciary. Further, it is crucial that judges retain judicial supervision over any anti-terrorist laws.

Fifthly, the media have a crucial role in helping protect the rule of law, human rights and civil liberties. For this reason, they must be protected from undue restriction by the state, whilst upholding the highest standards of independent and balanced reporting.

Many of these themes are explored throughout the chapters of this report and where appropriate the Task Force makes a number of recommendations.[33] Starting with the most extreme response to terrorism, the exercise of force, the Task Force considers the circumstances in which such action is lawful. Chapter 3 reviews the legal changes adopted both

---

33. These recommendations are not listed on the basis of any priority or ranking.

within the international community and individual states since September 11. A number of states have adopted stringent anti-terrorism laws, raising concerns with respect to the rule of law, individual civil liberties and human rights, which are dealt with in Chapter 4. Chapter 5 considers the application of international humanitarian law to terrorists, whilst Chapter 6 focuses on the legal developments in the area of terrorism finance. Chapter 7 reviews the means of inter-state cooperation and explores whether, and by what means, these can be improved to more effectively deter and combat terrorism. To conclude, Chapter 8 considers the role of the newly-created International Criminal Court in the prosecution of acts of terrorism.

Recommendations

1) Even if a definition of terrorism remains elusive, the Task Force believes at the least a convention standardising and improving cooperation to combat international terrorism is crucial.
2) The threat of terrorism should not be used by states as a reason to disregard fundamental norms of international law.
3) Adherence to the rule of law and established international standards will help to facilitate international cooperation in areas such as information sharing and law enforcement.
4) International cooperation is to be preferred over a range of unilateral actions in combating terrorism.
5) States must strive to balance national security and the protection of human rights and civil liberties. Failure to do so serves to undermine the universality of human rights.
6) Especially in a political climate generated by fear of terrorism, judges must be free to act independently and impartially.
7) Lawyers defending suspected terrorists should not be deterred from carrying out their professional duty even in the face of adverse public opinion.
8) States must protect judges and lawyers dealing with terrorist cases from threats to their personal integrity.
9) When national security is under threat, it is even more important that the media offer independent and balanced information, a task that may be made more difficult when governments attempt to restrict freedom of expression or the media employ self-censorship.

Failure to define terrorism —

— state based terrorism

— recognition of SD/NL.

— limits states in a way — they
   can use it to justify repressive
   means

CHAPTER 2

THE USE OF FORCE AS A RESPONSE TO TERRORISM

2.1 INTRODUCTION

Acts of terrorism are commonly defined as criminal and are dealt with through mechanisms of law enforcement. In limited situations, a state may seek to exercise military force in the face of terrorism. This chapter explores the circumstances in which such a response is permissible under international law.

When the United Nations (UN) Charter was framed in the wake of the Second World War, the drafters had in mind a legal regime that promoted the peaceful settlement of disputes and prohibited the use or threat of force. But the provisions of the Charter are predicated on the regulation of relations between nation states. The exercise of force in self-defence against non-state terrorist groups, which have no legal personality within international law, sits uneasily within this framework. Given that the conditions under which states can act in self-defence against another state are not directly transposable to a situation involving non-state actors, there is no settled law governing the use of force against terrorist groups. Without clear legal standards governing the use of force, the risk of its overuse is increased, potentially eroding the potency of its fundamental prohibition.

Section 2.2 of this chapter sets out the basic principles on the use of force governing conduct between states. It considers the circumstances in which states, that are the victim of aggression by another state, may take military action in self-defence. From these rules it might be possible to extrapolate a framework regulating the use of force against non-state actors.

Section 2.3 explores whether states subject to terrorist attacks can respond with military force and the consequences of the complicity of 'host states'.

This chapter discusses the most pressing challenges facing the *jus ad bellum* (law regulating the use of force). The Task Force hopes that it will add to debate within the international community on the use of armed force against non-state actors.

2.2 MILITARY RESPONSES TO ARMED ATTACKS BY OTHER STATES

The United Nations Charter was drafted, *inter alia,* to establish legal principles promoting the peaceful settlement of disputes between states, based upon the overarching principle of territorial integrity. The Charter specifically prohibits member states from 'the threat or use of force against the territorial integrity or political independence of any State or in any other manner inconsistent with the purposes of the United Nations.'[1] This is coupled with the requirement that 'all Members shall settle their international disputes by peaceful means in such a manner that international peace and security, and justice, are not endangered.'[2]

There are a number of exceptions to the Charter's prohibition on the use of force. The two most relevant are: i) Article 51, which provides for the right of individual or collective self-defence in the face of an 'armed attack' until such time as the Security Council takes measures necessary to ensure international peace, or in the absence of any such action;[3] ii) Article 39, under which the Security Council may determine the existence of a threat to international peace and security and invoke its powers pursuant to Chapter VII. These powers include, *inter alia,* the right to authorise military action. In addition to these exceptions to the Charter, the right to exercise self-defence exists in customary international law.[4] This customary international law right to self-defence is said to be recognised in Article 51, as the text of this article incorporates the '*inherent*' right to self-defence.[5]

According to Article 51 of the Charter, an act of self-defence is only permissible after an 'armed attack occurs'. The international community has not, however, settled upon a definition of the term 'armed attack'. In the *Nicaragua* case, the International Court of Justice (ICJ) concluded that the sending of armed rebels could amount to an armed attack if it were of sufficient 'scale and effects'.[6] In this case the court found that the supplying of arms to rebels did not amount to an armed attack justifying military action. Thus, the threshold set by the ICJ is considerable, and,

---

1. Article 2(4).

2. Article 2(3).

3. Article 51 states: 'Nothing in the present Charter shall impair the inherent right of individual or collective self defence if an armed attack occurs against a Member of the United Nations, until the Security Council has taken measures necessary to maintain international peace and security.'

4. Confirmed in the *Case Concerning the Military and Paramilitary Activities in and Against Nicaragua (Nicaragua v. United States of America) (Merits)* (Nicaragua case), ICJ Reports, June 1986, para. 176.

5. In the *Nicaragua* case, the ICJ found that the term 'inherent' ('droit naturel' in the original text) in Article 51 could only be a reference to the inclusion of a customary law right to self-defence. See *id.*

6. *Id.*, para. 195.

seemingly excludes low-level persistent aggression. Undoubtedly this is derived from a policy intended to minimise the use of force in self-defence and reduce the number of potential conflicts.[7] But in a minority opinion Judge Jennings found the armed attack threshold to be 'neither realistic nor just in the world where power struggles are in every continent. . . . [I]n this situation it seems dangerous to define unnecessarily strictly the conditions for lawful self-defence. . .'[8] It has been suggested that the interpretation of a legal principle based upon the size of an attack, the amount of destruction to property and the numbers of victims does not constitute a 'satisfactory criterion for legal decision-making'.[9]

Military action in self-defence cannot, in international law, be taken unless it meets the requirements of necessity and proportionality, now recognised as principles of customary international law.[10] These are drawn from the *Caroline* incident, which took place during the 1837 Canadian rebellion, in which British forces attacked and destroyed an American rebel ship, 'the Caroline', that had joined forces with the Canadians. In the ensuing correspondence between the British and the United States governments, it was agreed that the defending state must show:

> 'a necessity of self-defence [that is], instant, overwhelming, leaving no choice of means, and no moment for deliberation. It will be for it to show, also, . . . [it] did nothing unreasonable or excessive; since the act, justified by the necessity of self-defence, must be limited by that necessity, and kept clearly within it.'[11]

Thus, the exercise of force in self-defence must, under the principle of necessity, be i) the only means available of repelling the attack, and ii) within the confines of what is necessary to deter the attack. The principle of proportionality requires that in the conduct of hostilities, military action taken should not cause excessive loss of life or damage in relation to the military advantage to be gained. Thus, in order to sufficiently satisfy the proportionality test, the choice of weapons used should be discriminate and should be aimed at the structures and groups responsible for the attack or the imminent attack. It would not, therefore, be proportionate to retaliate to the initial aggression with the sole aim of creating destruction equivalent to the initial attack.

---

7. Reisman, International Legal Responses to Terrorism, 22 *Houston Journal of International Law* 3 (1999), p. 37.

8. *Supra* note 4, p. 543.

9. *Supra* note 7, p. 37.

10. The ICJ in the Nicaragua (Merits) case, *supra* note 4, para. 176, confirmed that necessity and proportionality are 'well established in customary international law'.

11. See Jennings, R.Y., The Caroline and McLeod Cases, 32 *American Journal of International Law* 82 (1938), at. p. 89.

Any response to an act of aggression must also be within reasonable time of the attack. The longer the delay between the initial aggression and the act of self-defence, the more likely it is that the response could constitute a reprisal and thus be unlawful.[12] It is possible, however, that some delay might reasonably be incurred, for example, to enable preparations to be made, while still fulfilling the requirements of proportionality and necessity.

2.2.1 Anticipatory Self-Defence and Pre-emptive Strikes

While 'anticipatory' and 'pre-emptive' self-defence are often used interchangeably, in the view of the Task Force they have different meanings. The doctrine of anticipatory self-defence is considered to authorise an armed response to an imminent attack, or pending attacks which are part of an ongoing series of armed attacks. Pre-emptive self-defence, by contrast, is claimed as justification for force used to prevent aggression, even where there is no reason to believe that an attack is planned and where no prior attack has occurred.[13]

The extent to which an attack can justifiably be anticipated or pre-empted is intensely debated by legal academics. According to Article 51 of the Charter, armed action by way of self-defence is only legitimate 'after an armed attack occurs'. Literal interpretation of this principle suggests that a state must wait for an armed attack before it can respond in self-defence. Yet as noted earlier, Article 51 incorporates the right to self-defence that existed in customary international law prior to the adoption of the Charter. The *Caroline* incident is widely accepted as the authority for the existence of a right to anticipatory self-defence in customary international law. In this case, the British fired at the US rebel ship *before* it had launched an attack. It was later agreed between the US and British governments that the British had 'no choice of means, and no moment for deliberation'.[14] Some argue that this right to self-defence was left entirely unaffected by the Charter and was not superseded by Article 51.

---

12. Legitimate self-defence is distinguishable from military action that seeks to punish another state by way of reprisals. Reprisals are recognised as being 'punitive in character; they seek to impose reparation for the harm done, or to compel a satisfactory settlement of the dispute created by the initial illegal acts, or to compel the delinquent state to abide by the law in future.' See Bowett, Reprisals Involving Recourse to Armed Force, 66 *American Journal of International Law* 1 (1972), at p.3. The difficulty of determining the motive of the states and the complexity of discerning the exact facts surrounding the aggression makes anticipatory self-defence sometimes difficult to distinguish from reprisals. Further, the longer the delay between the initial aggression and the act of self-defence, the more likely becomes the argument that the response is a reprisal.

13. O'Connell, The Myth of Preemptive Self-Defense, American Society of International Law, Task Force on Terrorism Paper, August 2002, p. 2, note 10, available at http://www.asil.org/taskforce/oconnell.pdf.

14. See, *supra* note 11.

However, the extent to which customary law and in particular the right to anticipate an armed attack is applicable has not been finally settled in international law. The ICJ in the *Nicaragua* case confirmed that Article 51 refers to a pre-existing right to self-defence and that the two rights continue to exist alongside each other.[15] The ICJ did not, however, elaborate upon the extent of the customary right to be read into Article 51.

There has been a long standing reluctance on the part of the international community to accept the unilateral use of force by a state on the basis of anticipatory or pre-emptive self-defence. Frequently such actions have been condemned as punitive or retaliatory.[16] Israel was condemned for its attack of Palestinian bases in Lebanon in December 1975[17] and for its destruction of a nuclear reactor in Iraq.[18] Similarly, after complaining of acts of aggression emanating from Yemeni territory, British forces bombed Harib Fort in the Yemen, claiming to be acting in self-defence. The Security Council adopted a resolution in which it condemned the British action.[19]

There are clear policy reasons for limiting anticipatory and pre-emptive self-defence due to the obvious dangers of expanding the right of states to take unilateral military action. Expansion of the right to self-defence may undermine the principle that links the necessity for self-defence with the imminence of the attack. Additionally, universal acceptance of the right to act pre-emptively could be perceived as eroding the accepted prohibition on the use of force.

There is, however, apparent acceptance that states can use force to repel attacks that are underway but have yet to reach their shores.[20] States may also be permitted to respond in anticipatory self-defence to pending attacks if they are part of an ongoing series of armed attacks.[21] Evidence of this is found in the responses to the attacks of September 11. In his letter of 7 October 2001 to the President of the Security Council, the United States Permanent Representative asserted that there is an ongoing threat to the United States and its nationals posed by al-Qaeda.[22]

---

15. See *supra* note 4, para. 176.

16. See O'Brien, Reprisals, Deterrence and Self-Defense in Counterterror Operations, 30 *Virginia Journal of International Law* 421 (1990), and Bowett, *supra* note 12.

17. Although the Security Council unanimously condemned Israel's action, it did not pass a resolution as the United States used its power of veto. See O'Brien, *id.*, pp. 432–433.

18. UN Security Council Resolution 487, adopted on 19 June 1981.

19. UN Security Council Resolution 188, adopted on 9 April 1964.

20. *Supra* note 13.

21. Henkin, L., *International Law: Politics, Values and Functions 1990*, pp. 142–62, cited in O'Connell, *supra* note 13, pp. 9–10.

22. See Letter dated 7 October 2001 from the Permanent Representative of the United States of America to the United Nations addressed to the President of the Security Council, UN Doc. S/2001/946.

Through Resolutions 1373 and 1368, the Security Council recognised the right to respond in self-defence to the attacks in the United States.[23] NATO, relying on a briefing from the United States Department of State, found the evidence sufficiently compelling to be regarded as justifying collective self-defence.[24] Thus there is evidence of wide acceptance within the international community that self-defence can anticipate a future imminent attack, once an initial armed attack has occurred.

In favour of a wider doctrine of anticipatory self-defence is the notion that in an age where weapons can be dispatched to rapid and deadly effect, and with the sophistication of intelligence gathering, for states to wait to be attacked before responding, challenges logic. Further, it has been argued that the UN Charter incorporates existing customary law on the right to self-defence that includes anticipatory action.

Responses to the United States' use of missile attacks in Sudan and Afghanistan in 1998 may indicate a softening of the international community's position on anticipatory action. Following attacks on the US embassies in Kenya and Tanzania, the United States attacked alleged terrorist training camps in Afghanistan and a Sudanese pharmaceutical plant, suspected of producing chemical weapons. The United States explained that it was acting to prevent terrorist attacks in accordance with its right to self-defence according to Article 51.[25] In response to this justification, the international community was divided. There were varying degrees of acceptance by Japan, the United Kingdom, France, Germany, Spain and Australia. Other states, including, Iran, Iraq, Libya, Russia, Pakistan and the League of Arab States condemned the strike on Sudan.[26] No resolution condemning the action was passed by the United Nations.

Following September 11 some states have reasserted the right to pre-emptive strikes. The United States has been increasingly prepared to incorporate a right to pre-emptive action as part of its defensive strategy. The White House National Security Strategy, issued in September 2002, states: 'To forestall or prevent such hostile acts by our adversaries, the United States will, if necessary, act pre-emptively.'[27] Similarly, the National Strategy to Combat Weapons of Mass Destruction confirms that the United

---

23. See UN Security Council Resolution 1373, adopted 28 September 2001, UN Doc. S/RES/1373 (2001), see Appendix IV, and UN Security Council Resolution 1368, adopted 12 September 2001, UN Doc. S/RES/1368 (2001).

24. According to Article 5 of the Washington Treaty, an armed attack on one or more of the Allies in Europe or North America shall be considered an attack against them all.

25. See Letter dated 20 August 1998 from the Permanent Representative of the United States of America to the United Nations addressed to the President of the UN Security Council, UN Doc. S/1998/780 (1998).

26. See Reisman, *supra* note 7, p.49.

27. See The National Security Strategy of the United States of America, Chapter V, para. 13, The White House, United States Department of State, September 2002, available at http://usinfo.state.gov/topical/pol/terror/secstrat.htm.

States proposes to respond to adversaries with weapons of mass destruction through pre-emptive measures where appropriate.[28] The United States is not alone in adopting such an approach. Support for pre-emptive action comes from the Australian[29] and British Prime Ministers.[30]

However, there is not yet evidence of a sufficiently widespread acceptance of the right to act pre-emptively to create a new principle of customary international law. Until recently, the fact that states engaging in coercive responses to terrorism have tended to do so on the basis of self-defence instead of the doctrine of pre-emption, has indicated a lack of willingness on the part of the international community to fully accept a departure from the existing legal norms. Yet, the spectre of non-state groups threatening states with force akin to that of regular armed forces represents a challenge to the parameters of the law of self-defence. The international community must determine the extent to which it is prepared to see self-defence not only as reactive, but also as a proactive policy.

To conclude this section, it can be seen that the legality of self-defence still raises a number of as yet unanswered questions. In practice, states taking *anticipatory* military action that satisfies the principles of necessity and proportionality are unlikely to receive condemnation from the international community. This, however, may also depend upon the political allegiances of the state concerned. Even more questionable is the legality of *pre-emptive* military action.

2.2.2 Acts Imputable to a State

Charter law is predicated on a legal regime regulating relations between states, hence it refers to the concept of 'armed attack' only in the context of nation states. Where an act of aggression amounts to an armed attack and is imputable to a state, the legal regime discussed above

---

28. See National Strategy to Combat Weapons of Mass Destruction, December 2002, p. 3, available at http://www.whitehouse.gov/news/releases/2002/12/WMDStrategy.pdf.

29. The Australian Prime Minister said: 'It stands to reason that if you believed that if somebody was going to launch an attack against your country, either of a conventional kind or of a terrorist kind, and you had a capacity to stop it and there was no alternative other than to use that capacity, then of course you would have to use it.' See Channel 9, Australian broadcasting Corporation, 2 December 2002, Transcript available at www.abc.net.au/7.30/s739334.htm.

30. The British Prime Minister stated on 16 July 2002: 'The one thing we have learned post-11 September is that to take action in respect of a threat that is coming may be more sensible than to wait for the threat to materialise and then to take action.' See House of Commons Liaison Committee, Session 2001–02, evidence presented by the Rt Hon Tony Blair MP, Prime Minister, HC 1095, Question 93. This was reinforced by the Foreign Secretary who stated: 'If any nation feels that it is threatened in a direct way then under Article 51 it has an inherent right to take action pre-emptively.' See Select Committee on Foreign Affairs, Session 2001–02, uncorrected evidence presented by the Rt Hon Jack Straw, Foreign Secretary, on 25 September 2002, Question 32.

is invoked. Thus it is necessary to determine the circumstances in which acts are imputable to a particular state.

It is a principle of international law that the conduct of any organ of a state must be regarded as an act of that state.[31] Where state officials perform outside of their official capacity, those acts may be imputed to the state where they used the means attached to their public function.[32] The UN General Assembly Resolution on the Definition of Aggression, seen as a guide to the UN in its interpretation of the Charter, encapsulates this concept when it includes the following as an aggressive act by a state:

'The sending by or on behalf of a state of armed bands, groups, irregular or mercenaries, which carry out acts of armed force against another state of such gravity as to amount to the acts listed above, or its substantial involvement therein.'[33]

Where the relationship between the state and the individual is less clear, international law does not offer a precise set of rules. Acts may occur which, in certain circumstances, turn their authors into *de facto* organs of the state.[34] Generally, individuals will be regarded as organs of the state if they receive orders from a state, are under overall control of a state or behave as state officials.[35]

---

31. See the decision by the ICJ in *Immunity from Legal Process of a Special Rapporteur of the Commission on Human Rights*, Advisory Opinion of 29 April 1999, as cited in Cassese, *International Law*, Oxford University Press (2001), p. 187.

32. Article 9 of the International Law Commission's Draft Articles on State Responsibility, 2000.

33. Article 3(g), UN General Assembly Resolution, 3314 UN GAOR, 29th Sess. Supp. No. 31, adopted 14 September 1974. Article 3 is recognised as reflecting customary international law. See Nicaragua case, *supra* note 4, para. 195.

34. See Article 8 of the International Law Commission's Draft Articles on State Responsibility, 2001, which provides: 'The conduct of a person or group of persons shall be considered an act of a State under international law if the person or group of persons is in fact acting on the instructions of, or under the direction or control of, that State in carrying out the conduct.' This test is similar to that cited in the *Nicaragua* case by the ICJ, *supra* note 4. Here, the ICJ concluded that for the conduct of individuals not part of the apparatus of the state, it must be demonstrated that they are under the 'effective control' of that state. Effective control amounts to whether they were financed by the state, their actions had been supervised by the state and the state had issued specific instructions concerning each of their unlawful actions. See para. 195. In the case of *Tadic (Prosecutor v Dusko Tadic)*, Case No. IT-94-1, Appeals Decision of 15 July 1999, paras. 137–144, the Appeals Chamber of the International Criminal Tribunal for the Former Yugoslavia (ICTY) concluded that there are different tests to establish whether an individual acts as a *de facto* organ of the state. i) A single private individual or a group not militarily organised must receive specific instructions or subsequent approval from a state; ii) for militarily organised groups it is sufficient that they are under the 'overall control' of the state; and iii) private individuals may be assimilated to state organs on account of their actual behaviour within the structure of a state and regardless of any possible requirement of state instructions (*de facto* organs).

35. See Cassese, *supra* note 31, p.189.

2.3 NON-STATE ACTORS

As we have seen, if the nexus between the state and the non-state group is sufficiently close, liability may be imputed to the state for the group's acts. If a state is prohibited from responding in self-defence to an attack merely because it is not the legal responsibility of a particular state, then many governments will feel vulnerable, particularly given the prospect of terrorist groups having access to weapons of mass destruction. Yet for the reasons enunciated above, it is not clear whether in such circumstances states can lawfully exercise force against an attack from non-state actors. A strict interpretation of the UN Charter suggests that whilst it might be permissible for a state to take defensive action against groups mounting ongoing attacks, taking military action against another state which is not directly participating in attacks perpetrated by terrorists based within its borders, would be impermissible.[36]

However, international law has also long tolerated the use of force against pirates which is analogous to the exercise of military action against terrorist groups. Although it must be acknowledged that pirates operate on the high seas and do not carry the flag of a nation state, there is authority in the *Caroline* incident suggesting that in the gravest of cases the territorial integrity of a nation state can be breached in the face of an imminent attack by non-state actors.[37] In the diplomatic exchange following this incident the British representative, having acknowledged that 'respect for the inviolable character of the territory of independent nations is the most essential foundation of civilization', said:

> 'but however strong this duty may be it is admitted by all writers, jurists, by the occasional practice of all nations, not excepting your own, that a strong overpowering necessity may arise, when this great principle may and must be suspended.'[38]

The right of states to protect their citizens abroad also supports this principle. This is explored in more detail below.

If it is accepted that states may use military force in self-defence against non-state actors based in another state, further consideration must be given to the circumstances in which such action is permissible. The requirements that apply to self-defensive action against states must be transposed to situations that involve the use of military force against non-state actors. An assessment of the lawfulness of such action must take into account the extent to which it is necessary and proportionate. The answer

---

36. See Paust, Symposium: The Legal Implications of the Response to September 11th 2001, Use of Armed Force against Terrorists in Afghanistan, Iraq and beyond, 35 *Cornell International Law Journal* 533 (2002), at pp. 539–540.

37. *Supra* note 11.

38. *Id.*

to this question largely depends, in the view of the Task Force, on the complicity of the state in which a terrorist group is based.

Complicity, but not state responsibility, was invoked against Afghanistan to justify military action following September 11. Through its representative to the UN, the United States indicated its intention to take self-defensive military action against Afghanistan because of the 'decision of the Taliban regime to allow the parts of Afghanistan that it controls to be used by [al-Qaeda] as a base of operation.'[39] The Security Council specifically acknowledged the inherent right of individual and collective self-defence.[40] Likewise, the Secretary-General of NATO invoked the right to collective self-defence without invoking the liability of the Taliban government.[41] These responses are notable because at no time did the United States impute al-Qaeda's acts to the Taliban regime under the law of state responsibility. Instead, reliance was placed on collusion between the Taliban and al-Qaeda. Thus military action was taken on grounds that the Taliban harboured a terrorist group, not because they exerted 'overall control'. The subsequent response from the international community was at the most supportive and at the least unchallenging.[42]

It is possibly too early to say that a clear international rule on the right to respond with military force to an armed attack from a non-state actor operating from a base in the territory of another state has emerged. In any event there are few legal parameters currently in existence from which states can assess the legality of any similar responses. The Task Force sets out below what it believes to be sensible criteria to facilitate consideration of the lawfulness of military responses to non-state actors.

2.3.1   Determining the Lawfulness of a Military Response to an Attack by Non-State Actors

State practice on the use of force to rescue citizens abroad may provide important guidance in determining the lawfulness of a military response to an attack by a terrorist group based in another state.[43] There are a number of examples of states claiming a right to use force to protect their nationals who are threatened abroad. In the *Entebbe Incident* Israel rescued hostages held on a hijacked plane which was flown to Uganda.[44]

---

39. *Supra* note 22.

40. UN Security Council Resolution 1373, adopted on 28 September 2001. See Appendix IV.

41. Statement by Lord Robertson, Secretary-General of NATO, 2 October 2002. Available http://www.nato.int/docu/speech/2001/s011002a.htm

42. Ratner, Jus ad Bellum and Jus in Bello after September 11, 96 *American Journal of International Law* 905 (2002), pp. 909–910.

43. According to Paust, *supra* note 36, p. 538, legitimate self-defence can include action taken to protect nationals abroad.

44. See Harris, D.J., *Cases and Materials on International Law*, Sweet & Maxwell (1998), 5th edition, pp. 909–912.

There was evidence that the Ugandan authorities had not taken sufficient steps to end the hijack situation. In response, Israel flew soldiers to Entebbe, rescuing the hostages by force, in the course of which a number of Ugandan soldiers were killed. While the matter was debated in the Security Council, this did not result in a condemnation of the Israeli action.[45] It is therefore not clear whether such action constitutes self-defence under Article 51. However, the international community tends to accept it under certain strict conditions. These include i) the absence of any alternative peaceful means; ii) the response must be proportionate; and iii) force should be discontinued once the mission has been accomplished.[46]

The second authority from which a right to respond to attacks by non-state actors may be derived is the abovementioned *Caroline* incident. This case concerned self-defence in anticipation of an attack from non-state actors. From the facts, it is clear that the US rebels fighting for the Canadians were not linked to the US government. This case provides some authority to suggest that when a state is the victim of an attack or threat of attack by non-state actors, it may respond with military force, subject to the following considerations, derived from the principle of necessity: (i) The attack is so imminent that there is no alternative but the use of force; or (ii) the host state has been asked to deal with the terrorist threat but is unwilling or unable to do so.[47]

If the scenarios in (i) or (ii) apply, any military response by the victim state must also comply with the principle of proportionality. By extension of this argument, the victim state may be required to consider the degree of complicity of the host state with the terrorist group. Thus, a proportionate self-defensive action against a terrorist group based in a complicit host state will not necessarily be proportionate in relation to a non-complicit state. If a state has been an unwitting host to a terrorist group, use of force will only be proportionate if this lack of complicity is taken into account.

Thus, consideration must be given as to how the requirements for a defensive response differ between state A, an unwitting refuge for a terrorist group, and state B, which is complicit with terrorist groups in its territory. If an attack by a terrorist group based in state A is imminent or underway against state C, and there is no time for state A to be asked for assistance, any response by state C must be limited to repelling the immediate attack regardless of the ongoing threat posed by the terrorist group. Support for this proposition can be found in the *Caroline* incident in which the British Government agreed that territorial integrity can only be breached for the:

---

45. *Id.*
46. See Cassese, *supra* note 31, p.315.
47. *Supra* note 7, pp. 46–47.

'shortest possible period, during the continuance of an admitted overruling necessity, and strictly confined within the narrowest limits imposed by that necessity.'[48]

Following the limited defensive action, state C would be expected to ask state A for assistance to deal with any further aggression by the terrorist group. Crucially, only the most limited loss of civilian life or property could be considered proportionate and therefore lawful.

This may differ from a response against a terrorist group based in state B where greater force may be permissible given the improbability of the state preventing future attacks. It follows from the principle of proportionality that the extent of the lawful collateral damage may be higher in state B than state A.

It must be conceded that there are risks attached to expanding the right to self-defence to non-state actors. There are, as yet, no standards from which to determine the complicity of states in which terrorist groups exist. Firstly, any such standards would have to take account of a lack of infrastructure impeding the ability of a host state to take action against terrorist groups. Secondly, a lack of standards upon which to base an assessment of the legitimacy of military action increases the possibility of unjustified unilateral action. Thirdly, permitting military action against non-state groups could be seen as a further erosion of the prohibition on the use of force as a general rule.

CONCLUSION

In the past, some forcible responses to terrorism have been criticised for failing to abide by the standards set down in international law, (although often they have met with little more than verbal condemnation). It is premature to suggest that the response of the international community to the attacks on September 11 marks the emergence of a new, incontrovertible legal regime governing the use of military force against terrorist groups. Nonetheless, there appears to be an acceptance that international law is developing to accommodate the threat posed to international peace and security by non-state actors, which may contribute to the deterrence of terrorist activities. However, any extension of the *jus ad bellum* must be consistent with the settled principles of international law as agreed between nation states.

The Task Force has grave doubts as to whether claims of self-defence justify, *per se*, unilateral action to engage in armed intervention in any country that has not attempted an attack or threatened international

---

48. The Avalon Project at Yale Law School: *The Caroline Case*, p. 13. Lord Ashburton to Mr Webster, 28 July 1842. Available http://www.yale.edu/lawweb/avalon/diplomacy/britain/br-1842d.htm

peace and security. In all cases multilateral action through the auspices of the United Nations is a preferable option. Failing success, new criteria for determining the lawfulness of military responses to terrorism must be agreed upon.

Recommendations

1) Any act of self-defence must conform to the legal requirements of the United Nations Charter.

2) In accordance with Article 51 of the UN Charter, states must report to the Security Council on measures taken in self-defence against an armed attack. The Task Force recommends that states submitting such reports must demonstrate the conformity of their actions with international law.

3) The Task Force believes that a searching debate about the lawful contingencies for self-defence in an environment of international terrorism is urgent and recommends that it be undertaken in the United Nations as well as in the college of international lawyers.

4) Recognising that there are few legal parameters in existence against which a state can assess the legality of a military response to armed attack from non-state actors, the Task Force proposes that a group of internationally renowned experts should be assembled to make recommendations on a legal framework. The IBA would consider convening such a forum.

Restrictions on the Use of Force to respond to terrorist threat

must be post attacks + future ones
must be imminent - extent of the
post 9/11 response recognises the
int community

No acceptance of pre-emptive
right

CHAPTER 3

TRENDS IN ANTI-TERRORIST MEASURES AFTER SEPTEMBER 11

3.1 INTRODUCTION

This chapter gives an overview of the most significant legislative developments and other trends within the international community since September 11, some of which are discussed in more detail in later chapters.

At the United Nations (UN) level the most important development has been the adoption of Security Council Resolution 1373, which sets out a range of far-reaching measures designed to deter terrorism. Regional organisations have similarly been active in this field, with the Organization of American States (OAS) having adopted a new convention on combating terrorism. Within the international community, there has been a diversity of response. While some states have adopted new anti-terrorism laws, others have deemed their existing legislative framework sufficient. The chapter first considers the response of the UN to the events of September 11.

3.2 UNITED NATIONS

On 12 September 2001 the UN General Assembly adopted Resolution 56/1 in which it condemned the 'heinous acts' committed on September 11 in the United States and urgently called 'for international cooperation to prevent and eradicate acts of terrorism.'[1] Similarly, the Security Council, in Resolution 1368, condemned the acts as 'a threat to international peace and security' and called on the international community to redouble its efforts to prevent and suppress terrorist acts.[2] On 28 September 2001, the Security Council, acting pursuant to its powers under

---

1. UN General Assembly Resolution 56/1, 12 September 2001, UN Doc. A/RES/56/1 (2002), paras. 1 and 4.
2. UN Security Council Resolution 1368, 12 September 2001, UN Doc. S/RES/1368 (2001), paras. 1 and 4.

Chapter VII of the UN Charter, adopted Resolution 1373.[3] This legally binding resolution requires states to take measures to prevent and suppress the financing, preparation and commission of acts of terrorism. States are obliged to prevent their territory from being used as a safe haven, to share information with other governments on terrorist activities, and to refrain from either actively or passively engaging in terrorist acts.[4] Finally, the resolution calls upon states to become parties to and fully implement the relevant international conventions relating to terrorism.[5] The United Nations Office on Drugs and Crime (UNODC) has prepared an overview of the 12 international conventions,[6] intended to inform legislative drafters of the development and requirements of these instruments.[7]

Paragraph 3(6) of the resolution establishes the Counter-Terrorism Committee (CTC). Member states were initially required to submit reports to the CTC on measures taken to comply with the requirements of Resolution 1373 within 90 days of the passing of the resolution. The CTC is tasked with assessing state reports and advising on compliance with Resolution 1373. To facilitate this process it has issued specific guidelines to member states advising on the information they should include in their national reports[8] and has established internal mechanisms for the orderly process of the incoming responses.[9] Further, it has created a directory of resources from which states can obtain expert advice from other states or organisations.[10]

The Task Force has some concerns with regard to the text of Resolution 1373 and the CTC's procedures. It is concerned that Resolution 1373 requires states to introduce a range of far-reaching measures, but does so without defining the key terms 'terrorism' and 'terrorist acts'. Paragraph 2(e), for example, requires states to establish terrorist acts as serious crim-

---

3. UN Security Council Resolution 1373, 28 September 2001, UN Doc. S/RES/1373 (2001), see Appendix IV.

4. *Id.*, paras. 2(c), 2(b), 3(a), 3(b), and 2(a).

5. *Id.*, paras. 3(d) and (e).

6. See Chapter 1, note 13.

7. See *UN Legislative Guide to the Universal Anti-Terrorism Conventions and Protocols*, Draft as of 18 March 2003, available at http://www.unodc.org/pdf/crime/terrorism/explanatory_english2.pdf

8. See CTC, *Guidance for the Submission of Reports pursuant to Paragraph 6 of Security Council Resolution 1373 (2001) of 28 September 2001*, 26 October 2001, available at http://www.un.org/Docs/sc/committees/1373/.

9. See CTC, *Guidelines of the Committee for the Conduct of its Work*, 16 October 2001, UN Doc. S/AC.40/2001/CRP.1, available at http://www.un.org/Docs/sc/committees/1373/.

10. See CTC, *Directory of Counter-Terrorism Information and Sources of Assistance*, available at http://www.un.org/Docs/sc/committees/1373/ctc_da/index.html.

inal offences in domestic laws, with penalties that reflect the seriousness of the acts. It is conceivable that states could define the term 'terrorist acts' so broadly as to criminalise legitimate political dissent.

Secondly, the mandate of the CTC does not include monitoring compliance of counter-terrorist measures against international human rights standards. The UN High Commissioner for Human Rights has expressed reservations about the impact of new anti-terrorism legislation on human rights and has recommended that the CTC appoint a human rights advisor and strengthen links with the Human Rights Committee and other relevant UN human rights bodies and mechanisms.[11] The CTC is understood to be giving a prominent role to the issue of human rights.[12] However, it might be more transparent if the CTC were to adopt guidelines outlining human rights obligations that states should take into account when implementing Resolution 1373, as proposed by the Office of the High Commissioner for Human Rights.[13] The Task Force believes that the CTC should avail itself of *all* possible means to ensure that implementation of the measures required by Resolution 1373 is consistent with existing international human rights standards.

The biggest difficulty facing the CTC is the issue of compliance. Though Resolution 1373 is detailed as to the measures states should implement, it is silent as to how to deal with non-compliant states. For the moment, the CTC has chosen to engage member states in constructive dialogue and cooperation. However, it is still unclear as to what extent its experts are in fact providing the required technical assistance to countries experiencing difficulties in implementing the resolution. Further, whilst the CTC does not see itself as a policing body, the potency of Resolution 1373 will be diminished if some form of penalty is not contemplated. In the future, more coercive methods may need to be employed, including naming those states that fail to comply and possibly the imposition of sanctions or other penalties.

---

11. See Address by Sergio Vieira de Mello, the High Commissioner for Human Rights, to the Counter-Terrorism Committee of the Security Council, 21 October 2002, available at http://www.un.org/Docs/sc/committees/1373/.

12. The Chairman of the CTC, Ambassador Sir Jeremy Greenstock, expressed such a view at a special meeting of the CTC with international, regional and subregional organisations on 6 March 2003, which was attended by the Executive Director of the IBA, Mark Ellis. See also the Outcome Document of the special meeting, 31 March 2003, UN Doc. S/AC.40/2003/SM.1/4, available at http://ods-dds-ny.un.org/doc/UNDOC/GEN/N03/286/30/PDF/N0328630.pdf?OpenElement

13. See Report of the United Nations High Commissioner for Human Rights and Follow-up to the World Conference on Human Rights, 27 February 2002, UN Doc. E/CN.4/2002/18, para. 30 and Annex: Proposals for 'further guidance' for the submission of reports pursuant to paragraph 6 of Security Council resolution 1373 (2001).

3.2.1   Freezing of Assets

Through the United Nations, action to freeze the assets of terrorists has been increased. Security Council Resolution 1390, adopted on 16 January 2002, reaffirms earlier resolutions[14] and requires member states to implement a range of measures with respect to Osama bin Laden, al-Qaeda, the Taliban and associated individuals, organisations and entities, as named in a list created pursuant to Resolutions 1267 and 1333.[15] Resolution 1267, adopted on 15 October 1999, established a Committee, which is tasked with maintaining this list.[16] Under Resolution 1390 states are required to freeze assets of the listed individuals, groups and entities, and to prevent entry into, and support from, their territories.[17] Resolution 1373 requires states to freeze the assets of any person who commits, attempts to commit, participates in or facilitates terrorist acts and of entities controlled by, or acting on behalf of, such persons. Assets that can legitimately be frozen include those owned and controlled directly or indirectly by such persons or entities, as well as those derived or generated from these sources.[18] Once on the list, all assets, including a basic living allowance, are to be frozen.

Neither resolution requires states to provide for due process standards, judicial review, right of appeal or other legal safeguards. Yet, freezing orders can eventually affect innocent third parties.[19] Further, Resolution 1390 is silent as to the means and/or legal procedures by which individuals or organisations may have their names removed from the list.

3.3 REGIONAL ORGANISATIONS

Many regional organisations promptly condemned the terrorist attacks of September 11,[20] and have since adopted declarations, plans of action, and, in some instances, new treaties, requiring member states to take a number of measures to combat terrorism.

---

14. In particular, UN Security Council Resolution 1267, adopted on 15 October 1999, UN Doc. S/RES/1267 (1999), UN Security Council Resolution 1333, adopted on 19 December 2000, UN Doc. S/RES/1333 (2000), and UN Security Council Resolution 1363, adopted on 30 July 2001, UN Doc. S/RES/1363 (2001).

15. See UN Security Council Resolution 1390, adopted on 16 January 2002, UN Doc. S/RES/1390 (2002), see Appendix III, para. 2.

16. See para. 6.

17. See para. 2.

18. See para. 1(c).

19. For a more detailed discussion see Chapter 6, Section 6.5.

20. See, for example, Communiqué issued by the Arab League Council's extra-ordinary meeting, 13 September 2001, Press communiqué issued by the Ministerial Council of the Gulf Cooperation Council at its twenty-fifth special session, 23 September 2001, and APEC Leaders Statement on Counter-terrorism, 21 October 2001.

The African Union (AU), for example, adopted a Plan of Action on the Prevention and Combating of Terrorism in Africa,[21] intended to implement the commitments under the Convention on the Prevention and Combating of Terrorism (Algiers Convention) and UN Security Council Resolution 1373, and to establish a counter-terrorism cooperation framework in Africa.[22] Accordingly, the AU member states undertook to sign, ratify and fully implement the Algiers Convention and all relevant international instruments concerning terrorism.[23] The Plan of Action further spells out a range of specific measures which the AU member states must adopt, including enhancing border control and surveillance, adopting certain legislative and judicial measures, suppressing the financing of terrorism, and enhancing the exchange of information and intelligence.[24]

Similarly, members of the Organisation for Security and Cooperation in Europe (OSCE) adopted a Decision and Action Plan on Combating Terrorism,[25] pledging to become parties to all 12 UN conventions and protocols relating to terrorism by 31 December 2002 and to implement all the obligations assumed under these conventions and protocols.

The Commonwealth of Nations established the Commonwealth Committee on Terrorism (CCT), which drafted a plan of action to assist member countries in implementing UN Security Council Resolution 1373.[26] In March 2002, the Commonwealth Heads of Government endorsed the plan of action and requested member states to implement the measures identified by the CCT, including the ratification and implementation of all the existing anti-terrorism conventions, enhancing international cooperation in criminal matters, reviewing domestic laws on extradition, enacting mutual legal assistance legislation, and preventing the abuse of financial services sectors.

The Heads of State or Government of the South Asian Association for Regional Cooperation (SAARC) expressed their support for UN Security Council Resolution 1373, reaffirmed their commitment to the SAARC Regional Convention on the Suppression of Terrorism, and reiterated 'their firm resolve to accelerate the enactment of enabling legis-

---

21. See Plan of Action of the African Union High-Level Inter-Governmental Meeting on the Prevention and Combating of Terrorism in Africa, 14 September 2002, Doc. Mtg/HLIG/Conv.Terror/Plan.(I).

22. *Id.*, paras. 8 and 9.

23. *Id.*, paras. 10(a) and (b).

24. *Id.*, paras. 11–14.

25. See OSCE, *Decision on Combating Terrorism and the Bucharest Plan of Action for Combating Terrorism*, 3–4 December 2001, Doc. MC(9).DEC/1.

26. See Report of the Commonwealth Committee on Terrorism (CCT): Commonwealth Plan of Action, 29 January 2002, available at http://www.thecommonwealth.org/dynamic/whatisnew/Pdisplay.asp?id=506.

lation within a definite time-frame for the full implementation of the Convention.'[27]

By far the most significant and far-reaching legal developments following September 11 have, however, taken place within the European Union, the Council of Europe, and the Organisation of American States. These organisations have adopted important new legal instruments which will be considered below.

3.3.1   European Union

Due to its highly integrated political and legal system, the European Union (EU) was able to adopt more far-reaching measures than other regional organisations. At a special meeting on 20 September 2001, the EU Council of Justice and Home Affairs ministers decided on a number of measures to combat terrorism, including enhanced judicial cooperation and cooperation between police and intelligence services, measures to combat the financing of terrorism, controls at external borders, and improved cooperation with the United States.[28] As an instrument for monitoring implementation of these measures, an anti-terrorism 'roadmap' was adopted on 17 October 2001.[29] Most of the measures, including the introduction of a European arrest warrant and the creation of the EU public prosecutions agency 'Eurojust', had been proposed prior to September 11. The only genuinely new response was a commitment to review the immigration and asylum legislation with reference to terrorist threats. All the new measures, save the Framework Decision on Terrorism, discussed below, have applications beyond combating terrorism.

Prior to the adoption of the Framework Decision on Terrorism, a number of member states of the EU had no specific anti-terrorism laws in place.[30] Even amongst those states that had, standards and definitions were inconsistent. The Framework Decision on Terrorism, which came into force on 22 June 2002, includes a common definition of various types

---

27. See SAARC Heads of State or Government, Declaration of the Eleventh SAARC Summit, 4–6 January 2002, paras. 42 and 44, available at http://www.saarc-sec.org/publication/11summitdec.pdf.

28. See Conclusions adopted by the Council (Justice and Home Affairs), 20 September 2001, Doc. SN 3926/6/01 REV 6.

29. See Council of the European Union, Coordination of implementation of the plan of action to combat terrorism, 17 October 2001, Doc. 12800/01 REV 1. This is updated monthly. See http://register.consilium.eu.int/scripts/utfregisterDir/WebDriver.exe?MIval=result&MIlang=EN&key=REGISTER&what=advanced&ff_COTE_DOCUMENT=&ff_COTE_DOSSIER_INST=&ff_TITRE=update+of+the+road+map&ff_FT_TEXT=&ff_SOUS_COTE_MATIERE=&dd_DATE_DOCUMENT=&dd_DATE_REUNION=&dd_FT_DATE=&fc=REGAISEN&srm=5&md=100&ssf=&button1=Search+Now.

30. The United Kingdom, Germany, France, Italy, Portugal, Greece and Spain already had such legislation.

of terrorist offences and serious criminal sanctions, and aims at promoting extradition and information-exchanging procedures across Europe.[31] It lists a number of acts, which, if intentionally committed with the aim of intimidation, compelling a government or international organisation to perform or abstain from performing any act, or seriously destabilising or destroying the fundamental political, constitutional, economic or social structures of a country or an international organisation, must be punished as terrorist offences. This list includes: murder; attacks on the physical integrity of a person; hostage taking; causing extensive destruction to a government or public facility, an infrastructure facility, a public place or private property likely to endanger human life or result in major economic loss; seizure of means of public or goods transport; release of dangerous substances; interfering with a natural resource the effect of which is to endanger human life; and threatening to commit any of the acts listed.[32] Member states are also required to punish the following as terrorist offences: directing a terrorist group or participating in its activities; theft, extortion and drawing up false administrative documents with a view to committing one of the listed acts; and inciting, aiding, abetting or attempting to commit one of these acts.[33] The Framework Decision establishes a number of minimum sentences for these offences.[34]

There are concerns that the definition of 'terrorist offence' contained in the Framework Decision is overly broad. For example, the destruction of private property or the seizure of a bus during a legitimate political demonstration could well be intended to compel 'a government or international organisation to perform or abstain from performing any act' and would thus have to be punished as a terrorist offence. Indeed, an 'explanatory memorandum' to the proposal for the Framework Decision states that the list of terrorist offences could include 'acts of urban violence'.[35] Whilst the Task Force condemns *any* acts of violence, it is concerned that a too far-reaching designation of acts as 'terrorist', attracting severe penalties, might go further than required for combating terrorism and might thus be disproportionate.

Another element of the EU's efforts to combat terrorism is the Framework Decision on the European arrest warrant and the surrender procedures between Member States, adopted by the EU Council of min-

---

31. Council Framework Decision on combating terrorism, 13 June 2002, Doc. 2002/475/JHA

32. *Id.*, Article 1.

33. *Id.*, Articles 2–4.

34. *Id.*, Article 5.

35. See Commission of the European Communities, Proposal for a Council Framework Decision on combating terrorism, Explanatory Memorandum, 19 September 2001, Doc. COM(2001) 521 final, p. 9.

isters on 13 June 2002.[36] The objective of the Framework Decision, which came into force on 7 August 2002, is to replace the extradition system by a European arrest warrant, thus simplifying and speeding up the procedure of transferring people from one member state to another. It requires each national judicial authority to recognise, *ipso facto* and with a minimum of formalities, requests for the surrender of a person made by the judicial authority of another member state. For a number of offences, including terrorism, the surrender of a person does not require the verification of the double criminality of the act (whereby an offence in the requesting state must be recognised as a criminal offence in the requested state).[37]

The Framework Decision on the European arrest warrant and the surrender procedures between Member States constitute an important step towards a single European judicial area. It improves judicial cooperation between states trusting each other's legal systems and sharing the same conception of the rule of law. However, this automatically brings with it reduced safeguards for requested persons, as evidenced by the abolition of the double criminality rule. Further, under the Framework Decision it will no longer be possible for a member state to refuse to surrender one of its citizens who has committed a crime in another EU state on the ground that the individual concerned is a national. The surrender of nationals may require legislative changes in states where the refusal to extradite own citizens is guaranteed by law.[38]

3.3.2 Council of Europe

The Council of Europe was the first international body to produce guidelines on human rights and the fight against terrorism.[39] While reaffirming the obligation on states to protect their citizens from the threat of terrorism,[40] the guidelines also reiterate the need to avoid arbitrariness[41] and the absolute prohibition of torture.[42] They require that all measures taken by states to combat terrorism be lawful and that all human rights restrictions be defined as precisely as possible and be necessary

---

36. Council Framework Decision on the European arrest warrant and the surrender procedures between Member States, 13 June 2002, Doc. 2002/584/JHA.

37. *Id.*, Article 2.

38. For example, according to Article 16(2) of the German constitution ('Grundgesetz') German citizens can only be extradited to another EU member state if a legislative act provides that extradition is permissible.

39. See Council of Europe, *Guidelines on Human Rights and the Fight against Terrorism*, adopted by the Committee of Ministers of the Council of Europe on 11 July 2002.

40. *Id.*, Section I.

41. *Id.*, Section II.

42. *Id.*, Section IV.

and proportionate to the aim pursued.[43] Further, they establish minimum standards for measures interfering with privacy, arrests, police custody and pre-trial detention, legal proceedings, extradition and the compensation of victims.[44] Finally, the guidelines state that a person accused of terrorist activities must under no circumstances be subject to the death penalty and that, where such a sentence is imposed, it may not be carried out.[45]

Following September 11, the Council of Europe also updated the European Convention on the Suppression of Terrorism of 1977. On 13 February 2003 the Committee of Ministers adopted the Protocol amending the European Convention.[46] One of the main features of the Convention is that it does not oblige state parties to criminalise the offences defined therein, but provides that none of the offences in question shall be regarded as a political offence, which would prevent extradition. The amending Protocol does not change the nature of the Convention. Rather, it extends the list of offences to be 'depoliticised' in order to increase its effectiveness.[47]

3.3.3 Organization of American States

The Inter-American Convention against Terrorism, adopted and opened for signature by the General Assembly of the Organization of American States (OAS) on 3 June 2002, is the first international treaty on this subject since the September 11 attacks.[48] In this convention, which came into force on 14 July 2003,[49] OAS member states reaffirm the need to adopt effective steps to prevent, punish and eliminate terrorism through the broadest cooperation.[50] The convention contains a range of measures designed to prevent the financing of terrorism, to enhance closer cooperation in law enforcement and afford greater mutual legal assistance.[51] By virtue of Article 15, these provisions must be carried out by the states parties 'with full respect for the rule of law, human rights

---

43. *Id.*, Section III.

44. *Id.*, Sections VI–XIII and XVII.

45. *Id.*, Section X(2).

46. See Protocol amending the European Convention on the Suppression of Terrorism, approved by the Committee of Ministers at Deputies' level on 13 February 2003, available at http://www.coe.int/T/E/Legal_affairs/Legal_co-operation/Fight_against_terrorism/Texts_&_documents/Draft%20Protocol%20Final%202002cm149rev2.asp. The Protocol was opened for signature on 15 May 2003.

47. *Id.*, Articles 1 and 2.

48. Inter-American Convention against Terrorism, adopted at the thirty-second regular session of the OAS General Assembly, 3 June 2002, Doc. A-66.

49. *Id.*, Article 22.

50. *Id.*, preambular para. 3 and Article 1.

51. *Id.*, Articles 4–10.

and fundamental freedoms.' The states parties will not be obliged to provide mutual legal assistance if they have substantial grounds for believing that the request has been made for the purpose of prosecuting or punishing a person on account of that person's race, religion, nationality, ethnic origin, or political opinion, or that compliance with the request would cause prejudice to that person for any of these reasons.[52]

Rather than attempting to define terrorism, Article 2(1) lists terrorist offences by reference to the offences listed within a number of UN Conventions.[53] Those states that have not ratified these conventions are encouraged to do so, and to implement them,[54] or may make a declaration that the particular instrument is not applicable in the context of determining terrorist offences.[55]

3.4 INDIVIDUAL STATES

In terms of domestic policy, states have responded in various ways to the events of September 11. For the present purpose, three broad categories of responses can be distinguished. First, several states have introduced new anti-terrorism legislation. Some countries have adopted comprehensive new acts, addressing issues ranging from terrorist organisations to the financing of terrorism and immigration law. Others, stopping short of adopting comprehensive acts, have introduced specific new measures, such as the establishment of special tribunals to try suspected terrorists. Second, there are countries which have used the 'war against terrorism' as justification for taking repressive actions whilst not adopting new anti-terrorism legislation. Often, these repressive measures are largely unrelated to combating terrorism, were already in place or would have been pursued anyway. Third, some states have not adopted any new significant measures or made any major changes to their legal systems after September 11. Instead, they are trying to deal with the problem of

---

52. *Id.*, Article 14.

53. The following conventions are referred to: Convention for the Suppression of Unlawful Seizure of Aircraft; Convention for the Suppression of Unlawful Acts against the Safety of Civil Aviation; Convention on the Prevention and Punishment of Crimes against Internationally Protected Persons, including Diplomatic Agents; International Convention against the Taking of Hostages; Convention on the Physical Protection of Nuclear Material; Protocol on the Suppression of Unlawful Acts of Violence at Airports Serving International Civil Aviation; Convention for the Suppression of Unlawful Acts against the Safety of Maritime Navigation; Protocol for the Suppression of Unlawful Acts against the Safety of Fixed Platforms Located on the Continental Shelf; International Convention for the Suppression of Terrorist Bombings; International Convention for the Suppression of the Financing of Terrorism.

54. *Id.*, Article 3.

55. *Id.*, Article 2(2).

international terrorism within the established legal framework of existing criminal laws and procedures.

3.4.1   States with New Anti-Terrorism Legislation

While important legal measures have been introduced in a range of countries, some of them, in the view of the Task Force, deserve special attention. In the United States, the adoption of the USA PATRIOT Act[56] and other legislation in the same spirit constitutes arguably the most important change in the legal landscape anywhere in the world. The United Kingdom is the only European country which has declared a public emergency and has opted out of part of the European Convention on Human Rights (ECHR) following September 11. Germany is an example of the numerous European states having adopted specific new anti-terrorism measures. The Task Force believes that focus on these countries is also justified by the fact that the policy of western states in general, and the United States in particular, often serves as a benchmark for other governments.[57] Important legal developments since September 11 have, however, not been confined to the west. Several countries in the Asian region have implemented new far-reaching anti-terrorism measures. India, for example, has adopted a comprehensive new act, covering a whole range of issues. The Pakistani and the Indonesian governments have introduced several specific anti-terrorist measures, including administrative detention.

3.4.1.1 United States

The main anti-terrorism act passed in the United States after 11 September 2001 is the USA PATRIOT Act 2001. The Act amends, among others, the Federal Criminal Code, the Foreign Intelligence Surveillance Act (FISA), and the Immigration and Nationality Act (INA). It expands the definitions of 'international terrorism' and of 'federal crime of terrorism' under the United States Code,[58] as well as creating the new crimes of 'domestic terrorism'[59] and of 'harboring or concealing terrorists'.[60] It gives the police and the FBI greater powers to keep suspected terrorists

---

56. Uniting and Strengthening America by Providing Appropriate Tools Required to Intercept and Obstruct Terrorism (USA PATRIOT Act) Act of 2001, Public Law No. 107–56, signed into law on 26 October 2001.

57. For example, the Pakistani government replied to criticism of its new anti-terrorism laws by stating that they were similar to anti-terrorism legislation passed in several European countries and less severe than America's indefinite detention of the prisoners in Guantánamo Bay. See Paul Haven, Pakistan Touts New Anti-Terror Law, *Associated Press*, 22 October 2002.

58. See USA PATRIOT Act § 802(a)(1) and (2), amending U.S. Code § 2331, and USA PATRIOT Act § 808(2), amending U.S. Code § 2332b(g)(5)(B).

59. USA PATRIOT Act § 802(a)(4).

60. *Id.*, § 803.

under surveillance and monitor their conversations, to share intelligence with other agencies, and to conduct covert searches.[61] Title III of the USA PATRIOT Act, the 'International Money Laundering Abatement and Anti-Terrorist Financing Act', expands the authority of the Secretary of the Treasury to regulate the activities of US financial institutions, contains a number of new money laundering crimes, and allows confiscation of all of the property of individuals or entities involved in terrorism and of any property derived from or used to facilitate terrorism. The House of Representatives and the Senate approved the bill in less than six weeks, bypassing much of the normal committee process.

Among the most important changes introduced by the USA PATRIOT Act are those made to the INA, tightening immigration laws and restricting the due process rights of immigrants. The class of non-citizens subject to removal from the United States on grounds of terrorism has been expanded.[62] Further, the Attorney General now has authority to indefinitely detain non-citizens if he has 'reasonable grounds to believe' that they are or have engaged in a terrorist activity or otherwise endanger national security.[63]

In addition to the USA PATRIOT Act, numerous other federal and state acts and resolutions have been signed into law, and a multitude of executive orders, directives and interim regulations have been issued.[64]

On 20 September 2001, the Immigration and Naturalization Service (INS) issued a new interim regulation on custody procedures.[65] The regulation allows the INS to detain non-citizens without charge for up to 48 hours instead of the previous 24 hours and permits further detention for an unlimited 'additional reasonable period of time' in the event of 'emergency or other extraordinary circumstance.' These powers of detention go further than the ones contained in the USA PATRIOT Act.[66] Another regulation sets out additional security procedures for certain immigration cases, notably requiring immigration judges to close hearings to the public, whereas previously immigration proceedings were closed on a case-by-case basis.[67]

---

61. *Id.*, §§ 201–225.

62. See *id.*, § 411, and the broad definitions of the terms 'terrorist activity', 'engage in terrorist activity', and 'terrorist organisation'.

63. *Id.*, § 412.

64. An overview is available at http://jurist.law.pitt.edu/terrorism/terrorism3.htm

65. Interim regulation on custody procedures, 20 September 2001, 66 Fed. Reg. 48,334 (amending 8 CFR 287.3(d)).

66. For a detailed analysis of this regulation see Different authors, Administrative Comment: Indefinite Detention without Probable Cause: A Comment on the INS Interim Rule 8 C.F.R. § 287.3, 26 *New York University Review of Law and Social Change* 397 (2001–01).

67. See Internal Memorandum by the Chief Immigration Judge, *Cases Requiring Special Procedures: Internal Memorandum*, 21 September 2001, available at http://news.findlaw.com/hdocs/docs/aclu/creppy092101memo.pdf.

By the 'Executive Order on Terrorist Financing'[68] the President blocked all property and interests in property of foreign individuals and entities listed in the order. The Secretary of State and the Secretary of the Treasury have been authorised to designate additional individuals and entities, which have committed acts of terrorism. Apart from blocking financial assets, the order also prohibits US transactions with the designated individuals and entities.

A new Department of Justice rule authorises the Attorney General to direct the Bureau of Prisons to monitor all communications between persons in federal custody and their lawyers where he certifies 'that reasonable suspicion exists to believe that a particular inmate may use communications with attorneys or their agents to further or facilitate acts of violence or terrorism.'[69]

Most prominently among the executive orders figures the military order entitled 'Detention, Treatment, and Trial of Certain Non-Citizens in the War Against Terrorism' ('Military Order'),[70] issued by the President on 13 November 2001. The Military Order directs the Secretary of Defense to detain and try before military commissions appointed by him certain non-US citizens suspected of being involved in international terrorism.[71]

On 25 November 2002, the President signed the Homeland Security Act into law, setting in motion a vast bureaucratic reorganisation. The Act creates a new Department of Homeland Security which brings together nearly 170,000 employees from 22 agencies with widely varying missions, including, amongst others, the INS, the Coast Guard, the Secret Service, the federal security guards in airports and the Customs Service.

3.4.1.2 United Kingdom

Prior to September 11, the United Kingdom had already enacted a wide range of legislative measures to counteract terrorist activity.[72] Nevertheless, on 15 October 2001 the Government announced proposals to adopt new legislative steps 'necessary to counter the threat from international terrorism.'[73] The new Anti-Terrorism, Crime and Security Act 2001 (ATCSA) became law on 14 December 2001.

---

68. *Executive Order Blocking Property and Prohibiting Transactions with Persons Who Commit, Threaten to Commit, or Support Terrorism,* signed 23 September 2001.

69. See Department of Justice Rule of 31 October 2001, 66 Fed. Reg. 55061 (Attorney General Order No. 2529-2001 amending 28 CFR Parts 500 and 501), at 55066.

70. 66 Fed. Reg. 57833 (16 November 2001)

71. See Chapter 5, Sections 5.4 and 5.5 for a more detailed discussion of the Military Order.

72. The centrepiece of this legislative framework was the Terrorism Act 2000, which had come into force on 19 February 2001.

73. See House of Commons Debates, volume 372 column 923, 15 October 2001, the Secretary of State for the Home Department.

The ATCSA contains a range of new powers. As far as the financing of terrorism is concerned, cash may now be forfeited in civil proceedings where an authorised officer has reasonable grounds for suspecting that it is intended to be used for the purposes of terrorism, comprises the resources of a terrorist organisation, or was obtained through terrorism.[74] The Treasury is permitted to make a freezing order if it reasonably believes that a foreign government or resident is engaged in action detrimental to the economy of the United Kingdom or constituting a threat to the life or property of one or more citizens of the United Kingdom.[75] The ATCSA also introduced new restrictions on the right to seek asylum. The Secretary of State may certify that an individual is excluded from refugee status or not entitled to the protection of the principle of *non-refoulement* on grounds that Article 1(F) or 33(2) of the Refugee Convention applies and that their removal 'would be conducive to the public good'.[76] Where such a certificate is made, only a limited asylum appeal is permissible to the Special Immigration Appeals Commission (SIAC).[77] There may no longer be substantive consideration of such asylum claims[78] and no consideration of the balance between an individual's fear of persecution against the government's perceived threat to national security.[79]

The ATCSA also contains some significant disclosure powers and provisions governing the retention of communications data. Public authorities are now permitted to disclose information to each other for the purposes of any criminal investigation, including investigations outside the United Kingdom.[80] The disclosure powers are far-reaching[81] and not confined to terrorist investigations but relate to criminal investigations generally.[82]

The most controversial feature of the Act is the introduction of the power of internment without trial, which was omitted from the Terrorism Act 2000. Part 4 of the ATCSA authorises the Secretary of State to certify a person as a 'suspected international terrorist' if he 'reasonably (a)

---

74. See ATCSA, Section 1(1) and Schedule 1, para. 2.

75. *Id.*, Section 4.

76. *Id.*, Section 33(1) and (2). Article 1(F) of the Refugee Convention excludes from refugee status persons who have committed a crime against peace, a war crime, a crime against humanity, a serious non-political crime outside the country of refuge, or acts contrary to the principles of the United Nations. Article 33(2) of the Refugee Convention allows for the return of refugees who are a danger to the security of the host country.

77. The SIAC was set up specifically to deal with cases involving security matters by the Special Immigration Appeals Commission Act 1997.

78. See ATCSA, Section 33(3) and (4)

79. *Id.*, Section 34.

80. *Id.*, Part 3.

81. Schedule 4 to the ATCSA lists 66 acts under which disclosure of information is authorised.

82. ATCSA, Section 20.

believes that the person's presence in the United Kingdom is a risk to national security, and (b) suspects that the person is a terrorist.'[83] Upon certification as a 'suspected international terrorist', a non-UK citizen can be detained without charge or trial, for an unspecified period of time, if his or her removal or deportation from the United Kingdom is prevented as a result of the UK's international obligations or for practical reasons.[84] Appeals against the certification as a 'suspected international terrorist' can only be made to the SIAC.[85]

The wide powers of detention without charge or trial have made it necessary to derogate from Article 5(1) of the ECHR.[86] However, Parliament insisted on limits on the duration of these powers. Thus the provisions on detention will expire after a period of 15 months beginning with the day on which the Act was passed.[87]

3.4.1.3 India

On 26 March 2002, the Indian parliament passed a new anti-terrorism law, the Prevention of Terrorism Act (POTA). POTA reinstates a modified version of the Terrorist and Disruptive Activities (Prevention) Act (TADA), which had come into force in 1987.[88] Over 76,000 people had been arrested under TADA, only one percent of who were ultimately convicted of a criminal offence.[89] TADA was finally repealed in May 1995,

---

83. *Id.*, Section 21(1)

84. *Id.*, Section 23. Detainees cannot be removed where, for example, removal or deportation to a country where the individual concerned may face the death penalty is prevented by the United Kingdom's obligation under Protocol No. 6 to the ECHR concerning the Abolition of the Death Penalty. Further, the European Court of Human Rights has ruled that no one can be removed to a state where he or she would face a real risk of being subjected to treatment contrary to the prohibition of torture. See *Chahal v. United Kingdom,* Judgment (Merits and just satisfaction), 15 November 1996, para. 80. See also *Soering v. United Kingdom,* Judgment (Merits and just satisfaction), 7 July 1989, paras. 90–91. Finally, removal or deportation could be impossible for practical reasons, for instance, because the individual concerned is a stateless person or because the British authorities are unable to find a country willing to accept him or her.

85. ATCSA, Sections 21(8) and 25.

86. See Human Rights Act 1998 (Designated Derogation) Order 2001 (SI 2001/3644).

87. See ATCSA, Section 29(1). The Secretary of State may continue in force or revive the sections for a period not exceeding one year. See Section 29(2) and (3). But any renewal is subject to the 'sunset clause' of Section 29(7) which provides that sections 21 to 23 will automatically lapse on 10 November 2006.

88. See R. Shunmugasundaram, Can POTO achieve what TADA could not?, *The Hindu,* 1 January 2002.

89. See Praful Bidwai, The perils of POTO, *Frontline,* Volume 18, Issue 24, 24 November 2001, and Human Rights Watch, India: Human Rights Press Backgrounder, 20 November 2001. In the state of Jammu and Kashmir alone, 16,620 persons were detained since 1990; of these, 1,640 were brought to trial and 10 were convicted. See R. Shunmugasundaram, Can POTO achieve what TADA could not?, *The Hindu,* 1 January 2002.

following widespread allegations of misuse and criticism by human rights organisations, lawyers and even officials themselves.[90] Since then, several attempts have been made to introduce a new anti-terrorism law. As a result of the incidents of September 11, the issue of new anti-terrorism legislation resurfaced and POTA was passed.

POTA sets forth broad definitions of 'terrorist act' and 'membership of terrorist organisations' and provides for strong penalties, including the death penalty.[91] The government can declare an organisation as a 'terrorist organisation' by listing it in a schedule, 'if it believes that [the organisation] is involved in terrorism.'[92] The invitation of support for a terrorist organisation, the arrangement or management of a meeting where a member of a terrorist organisation is speaking, and the raising of funds for a terrorist organisation also constitute criminal offences.[93] The holding of any proceeds derived from terrorism is illegal,[94] and any property of a person convicted under POTA may be forfeited.[95]

POTA also sets up special courts to deal with terrorist offences. Both the central government and state governments are permitted to constitute such courts for certain notified areas or groups of cases.[96] The proceedings before the special courts may be held *in camera* 'if the Special Court so desires.'[97]

Further, POTA extends the powers of the police to hold people without bringing charges. Terrorist suspects can now be detained for 90 days without charge or trial.[98] The Special Court can extend this period to 180 days on application by the Public Prosecutor.[99] Further, no accused may be released on bail unless the Court gives the Public Prosecutor an opportunity of being heard.[100] Where the Public Prosecutor opposes release on bail, the accused may not be released 'until the Court is satisfied that there are grounds for believing that he is not guilty of committing such offence.'[101] Finally, POTA introduces new provisions governing surveillance measures, authorising police officers to intercept communications.[102]

---

90. See Amnesty International, India: Briefing on the Prevention of Terrorism Ordinance, 15 November 2001, p 2.

91. POTA, Section 3.

92. *Id.*, Section 18.

93. *Id.*, Sections 21 and 22.

94. *Id.*, Section 6.

95. *Id.*, Section 16(2).

96. *Id.*, Section 23.

97. *Id.*, Section 30(1).

98. *Id.*, Section 49(2) in connection with section 167 of the Code of Criminal Procedure.

99. POTA, Section 49(2)(b).

100. *Id.*, Section 49(6).

101. *Id.*, Section 49(7).

102. *Id.*, Section 36–48.

3.4.1.4 Pakistan

In Pakistan, the Anti-Terrorism Act of 1997 gives police far-reaching powers to arrest suspects, and special anti-terrorist courts have been established under its authority. The new courts consist of a judge, a magistrate and an army officer not below the rank of Lieutenant Colonel, and can convene in military or jail premises. According to the amendment, which was introduced to expedite terrorist cases, the new courts must pass judgment within 15 days.[103]

On 16 November 2002, the government added a further amendment to the Anti-Terrorism Act.[104] The amendment authorises the government to list, based on information received from any source, any person suspected of being concerned or affiliated with a 'terrorist organisation' or with any group or organisation suspected of being involved in terrorism or sectarianism.[105] Once included in this list, suspects can be arrested and detained without charge for a period which may be extended for up to twelve months.[106] Alternatively, under the new law, listed persons can be required to execute a bond for their good behaviour; to seek prior permission from the police before moving from their permanent place of residence for any period of time; not to visit schools, places of public entertainment, airports, railway stations, bus stands, parks, and scenes of any public meeting without prior permission from the police.[107] In addition, the police are allowed to check and probe the assets of such persons or their immediate family members.[108] The Interior Minister defended the amendment against criticism by human rights organisations[109] by stating that the new measures were in line with tough laws passed by several Western countries since the September 11 attacks; and were similar to anti-terrorism legislation passed in several European coun-

---

103. See Rafaqat Ali, Army officers to be part of new ATCs: Law amended to expedite terrorism cases, *Dawn*, 31 January 2002, and New ATCs termed setback for democracy, *Dawn*, 1 February 2002, and Amnesty International, Press Release, Pakistan: New anti-terrorist courts breach fair trial norms, 4 February 2002.

104. See Anti-terrorism (Amendment) Ordinance 2002, promulgated on 16 November 2002, available at http://www.satp.org/satporgtp/countries/pakistan/document/actsandordinences/anti_terrorism_ordin_2002.htm

105. Anti-Terrorism Act 1997, Section 11EE, heading 'Security for good behaviour', para. 1, as inserted by the Anti-terrorism (Amendment) Ordinance 2002.

106. Anti-Terrorism Act 1997, Section 11EE, heading 'Power to arrest and detain suspected persons', para. 1, as inserted by the Anti-terrorism (Amendment) Ordinance 2002.

107. Anti-Terrorism Act 1997, Section 11EE, heading 'Security for good behaviour', para. 2, as inserted by the Anti-terrorism (Amendment) Ordinance 2002.

108. *Id.*, para. 2(e).

109. See Amnesty International, Press Release, Pakistan: No need for more laws to fight political violence, 19 November 2002.

tries. He further claimed they were less severe than the United States' indefinite detention of the prisoners in Guantánamo Bay.[110]

3.4.1.5 Indonesia

Less than a week after the bomb attack in Bali on 12 October 2002, the Indonesian government enacted two new anti-terrorism decrees.[111] A similar draft anti-terrorism law had been debated in parliament earlier, but met strong opposition. However, after the Bali bombing, the Indonesian government came under intense pressure from the United States, Australia and other foreign countries to move firmly against terrorism.[112] The new 'Government Regulation in lieu of Law' No. 1 defines as a 'terrorist' any person 'who intentionally uses violence or the threat of violence to create a widespread atmosphere of terror or fear in the general population or to create mass casualties, by forcibly taking the freedom, life or property of others or causes damage or destruction to vital strategic installations or the environment or public facilities or international facilities.'[113] The regulation allows for the death penalty.[114] It permits police to detain terrorist suspects for seven days without charge, based on any intelligence reports as 'preliminary evidence', and for a further six months for investigation and prosecution.[115] Based on such preliminary evidence investigators can also intercept and confiscate a suspect's mail and tap telephone conversations or other forms of communication.[116] Government Regulation No. 2 stipulates that the provisions of Regulation No. 1 may be applied retroactively to cover the Bali attack. Human rights organisations pointed out that Indonesia already had appropriate criminal laws to deal with terrorist crimes and expressed apprehension that the regulations could be misused.[117]

---

110. See Paul Haven, Pakistan Touts New Anti-Terror Law, *Associated Press*, 22 October 2002.

111. Government Regulations in lieu of Law No. 1 and No. 2. An English translation of the regulations is available at http://www.law.unimelb.edu.au/alc/indonesia/perpu_1.html and http://www.law.unimelb.edu.au/alc/indonesia/perpu_2.html respectively. For a detailed analysis of the regulations, see Todung Mulya Lubis, The Antiterrorism Regulations—Indonesia's Miracle Drug?, *Tempo Magazine*, 5–11 November 2002, and Leonard C. Sebastian, The conundrum of Jakarta's anti-terrorism moves, *Straits Times*, 3 November 2002.

112. See Ellen Nakashima and Alan Sipress, Indonesia Issues Anti-Terror Order, *Washington Post*, 19 October 2002.

113. See Government Regulation in lieu of Law No. 1, Section 6.

114. *Id.*

115. *Id.*, Sections 25(2), 26(1) and 28. Such intelligence reports have to be approved by a court within three days. See *id.*, Section 26(2) and (3).

116. See Section 31.

117. See Tapol, Indonesia's Anti-Terrorism Decree a threat to basic rights, 27 October 2002, Human Rights Watch, Indonesia: Bali Attack Should Not Undermine Civil Liberties, 18 October 2002.

3.4.1.6 Germany

Shortly after the events of 11 September 2001, the German government introduced its first ever anti-terrorism package into parliament. An amendment to the Act Governing Private Associations, which came into effect on 8 December 2001, now makes it possible to ban religious groups showing extremist tendencies.[118] In addition, the Penal Code has been amended, making the founding, membership and support of terrorist organisations a criminal offence, even if the groups are based abroad.[119]

On 20 December 2001, the German parliament approved a second anti-terrorism package, the Anti-Terrorism Act, which took effect in January 2002 and comprehensively changed a number of existing laws.[120] In particular, the Act introduces important new provisions governing the gathering of information. Different intelligence services can now request user information from postal services, airlines and telecommunication companies, as well as from financial institutions on accounts, account-holders, and monetary transactions.[121] In addition, the Federal Office for the Protection of the Constitution now has the authority to locate mobile phones and to establish the number of the phone as well as of the phonecard.[122] The Anti-Terrorism Act also provides for the enhanced sharing of data between immigration authorities, social insurance authorities and the intelligence services.[123] A further amendment provides that passports, identity cards and residence permits may include biometric data relating to a person's fingers, hands or face in addition to their photograph and signature.[124] Finally, the reasons for which associations of non-citizens and foreign organisations can be banned have been expanded.[125]

3.4.2 States using the 'War on Terrorism' as a Justification for Other Measures

A number of states seem to have taken advantage of the change in the political landscape after September 11 by using the fight against terrorism to justify measures inconsistent with international human rights standards.

---

118. By way of deleting § 2(2)2 of the Act Governing Private Associations (Vereinsgesetz).

119. See the new § 129b of the German Criminal Code, which came into effect on 1 September 2002.

120. The text of the Anti-Terrorism Act (Gesetz zur Bekämpfung des internationalen Terrorismus (Terrorismusbekämpfungsgesetz)) is available (in German) at http://eng.bundesregierung.de/Anlage17379/Terrorismusbekaempfungsgesetz_Wortlaut.pdf

121. See Anti-Terrorism Act, Articles 1–3.

122. *Id.*, Article 1.

123. *Id.*, Articles 1, 11 and 16.

124. *Id.*, Articles 7, 8 and 11.

125. *Id.*, Article 9.

The government of the People's Republic of China, for example, linked its support for the global campaign against terrorism to American support for China's 'fight against terrorism and separatists', in particular, those advocating independence for the Xinjiang Uighur Autonomous Region (XUAR), a far western Muslim region.[126] Following 11 September 2001, the Chinese government has reportedly intensified its crackdown on Uighur opponents of Chinese rule in XUAR. Several thousand people are reported to have been detained for investigation and a number of them charged or sentenced under the Criminal Law. At the same time, the government has further restricted the religious rights of the Muslim population in the XUAR.[127] In December 2001, China amended its Criminal Law, tightening the provisions on 'terrorist crimes'.[128] The law lacks a definition of the terms 'terrorism', 'terrorist crime' or 'terrorist organisation', thus creating uncertainty as to the prohibited conduct and raising concerns that these provisions could be used to criminalise peaceful political dissent.

Similarly, the Russian government has increasingly tried to link its operation in Chechnya with the global fight against terrorism.[129] It has equated its campaign in Chechnya to US counter-terrorist actions, suggesting that criticisms of its human rights record in Chechnya are unfounded.[130]

The Uzbek government has used the events of September 11 to justify its own long running campaign against independent Islamic congregations and followers of independent Islamic leaders. Repressive measures, including systematic arrests and harsh prison sentences, have been presented as necessary to combat the Islamic Movement of Uzbekistan, an armed Islamic opposition group reportedly operating from Afghanistan and allegedly linked to the Taliban and al-Qaeda.[131]

---

126. See China sets terms for backing US war on terror, *Reuters*, 18 September 2001.

127. See Amnesty International, People's Republic of China: China's Anti-Terrorism Legislation and Repression in the Xinjiang Uighur Autonomous Region, 22 March 2002.

128. See Amendments to the Criminal Law, adopted by the Standing Committee of the National People's Congress on 29 December 2001. An English translation of the Amendments can be found in the People's Republic of China's report to the UN Counter-Terrorism Committee, UN Doc. S/2001/1270/Add.1.

129. See, for example, press release of the Russian embassy in Prague, On Russian President Vladimir Putin's Telegram of Condolence to US President Bush, 17 September 2001.

130. See Russia launches aerial assaults in Chechnya, *USA Today*, 12 January 2002. The Kremlin was quoted as stating the following: 'Our experience in Chechnya and America's experience in Afghanistan show how hard it is sometimes to reach terrorists and to prevent any harm on civilians. Nevertheless, that is the goal of Russia and the United States.' See also Human Rights Watch, Human Rights in the New Russia-U.S. Relationship, 13 November 2001.

131. See Amnesty International, Central Asia: No Excuse for Escalating Human Rights Violations, 11 October 2001, and Human Rights Watch, In the Name of Counter-Terrorism: Human Rights Abuses Worldwide, 25 March 2003.

In Egypt, measures which are apparently inconsistent with international human rights standards have been taken against people suspected of having links with Islamist groups. Many of the hundreds of people arrested have been referred to military and state security courts.[132] Although Egypt has a long history of using emergency rule and anti-terrorism decrees, the Egyptian government has frequently cited the attacks of September 11 and the global campaign against terrorism to justify its repressive policies.[133]

Malaysian officials argued that the September 11 attacks demonstrated the importance of the Internal Security Act (ISA), which had been enacted in 1960 to fight a communist rebellion, as a preventive measure and arrested several alleged Islamic militants under the act.[134] The ISA allows for indefinite detention without charge or trial of any person suspected of posing a threat to national security and has been used to arrest political opponents, including the former deputy prime minister Anwar Ibrahim.[135]

As a final example, the Australian government has used the September 11 attacks to justify its policy of tighter border controls and of restricting, and in some cases preventing, asylum-seekers from entering Australia.[136]

3.4.3 States Without New Significant Measures

A number of states have not adopted any new significant anti-terrorist measures following September 11. Some of them, for example Croatia,[137] Tajikistan[138] and Turkey,[139] already had specific anti-terrorist legislation in place and did not consider it necessary to introduce new laws.

---

132. See Human Rights Watch, In the Name of Counter-Terrorism: Human Rights Abuses Worldwide, 25 March 2003.

133. For example, President Hosni Mubarak referred to new anti-terrorist measures in the United Kingdom and the United States as proof that military trials and other emergency measures in place in Egypt for the past 20 years were always the 'right' policy. He added, 'There is no doubt that the events of September 11 imposed a new concept of democracy that differs from the concept that Western states defended before these events, especially in regard to the freedom of the individual.' See Amil Khan, Mubarak says military trials were always 'right' policy, *Middle East Times*, 21 December 2001.

134. See Human Rights Watch, Malaysia's Internal Security Act and Suppression of Political Dissent, 13 May 2002, and Malaysia detains nine 'Afghan-trained militants' for two years, *AFP*, 26 September 2001.

135. See Amnesty International, Malaysia: Human Rights under Threat—the Internal Security Act (ISA) and other restrictive laws, 24 October 2001.

136. See Australia warns of 'terrorist pipeline', *CNN.com*, 14 September 2001.

137. See Croatia's report to the CTC of 27 December 2001, UN Doc. S/2001/1271, and its additional report of 21 June 2002, UN Doc. S/2002/727.

138. See Tajikistan's additional report to the CTC of 21 January 2003, UN Doc. S/2003/147.

139. See Turkey's report to the CTC of 31 December 2001, UN Doc. S/2001/1304, and its additional report of 20 August 2002, UN Doc. S/2002/948.

Other states deemed their established legal frameworks of existing ordinary criminal laws and procedures to be sufficient to combat international terrorism. In Switzerland, the government tried to introduce a new offence of 'terrorism' in the criminal code. But parliament refused to adopt the amendment, arguing that there was no need for a new specific offence, since the existing norms of the criminal code covered all possible acts of terrorism.[140] The Saudi Arabian government stated that in its country crimes of terrorism were already covered by the Islamic Shariah law, attracting severe penalties.[141]

In Paraguay there was a proposal for a new anti-terrorist law that introduced the offence of 'international terrorism'.[142] But parliament indefinitely postponed consideration of the draft act, as it was feared that it might be applied in a manner that infringes civil liberties and safeguards.[143]

Finally, other states without specific anti-terrorism legislation, including Gabon,[144] Ghana,[145] Jamaica,[146] Nigeria,[147] Panama,[148] Tanzania,[149] Uruguay,[150] and Senegal,[151] have announced that they will adopt such legislation in the future. Rwanda is an example of a state lacking a specific anti-terrorism law and has requested technical assistance in drafting such national legislation.[152]

---

140. See Keine übereilten neuen Terrorismus-Strafnormen, *Neue Zürcher Zeitung*, 6 September 2002.

141. See Saudi Arabia's report to the CTC of 27 December 2001, UN Doc. S/2001/1294, and its additional report of 10 July 2002, UN Doc. S/2002/869.

142. See Paraguay's report to the CTC of 31 December 2001, UN Doc. S/2001/1293, para. XIX.

143. See Paraguay's supplementary report to the CTC of 11 July 2002, UN Doc. S/2002/878, para. 1(a).

144. See Gabon's report to the CTC of 20 December 2001, UN Doc. S/2001/1219.

145. See Ghana's additional report to the CTC of 24 September 2002, UN Doc. S/2002/708/Add.1.

146. See Jamaica's report to the CTC of 31 December 2001, UN Doc. S/2001/1314, and its additional report of 12 December 2002, UN Doc. S/2002/1369.

147. See Nigeria's report to the CTC of 14 January 2002, UN Doc. S/2002/69.

148. See Panama's report to the CTC of 17 January 2002, UN Doc. S/2002/76, and its additional report of 15 October 2002, UN Doc. S/2002/1184.

149. See Tanzania's report to the CTC of 15 July 2002, UN Doc. S/2002/765.

150. See Uruguay's additional report to the CTC of 13 June 2002, UN Doc. S/2002/676.

151. See Senegal's report to the CTC of 14 January 2002, UN Doc. S/2002/51, and its additional report of 23 October 2002, UN Doc. S/2002/1212.

152. See Rwanda's report to the CTC of 9 September 2002, UN Doc. S/2002/1028.

CONCLUSION

Security Council Resolution 1373 has clearly led member states to reconsider the effectiveness of their anti-terrorist strategies and how to facilitate international cooperation in this field. However, not all legislative measures being adopted and action taken in the name of combating terrorism are consistent with fundamental human rights principles—something which the Task Force believes the Security Council and the CTC should be mindful of. The Task Force is of the view that new laws which may restrict human rights and civil liberties should be considered carefully by legislative bodies, with emphasis placed on the likely effectiveness of such measures.

Recommendations

1) The CTC should develop strategies to promote greater compliance with the requirements of Security Council Resolution 1373, including considering seeking an extension of its mandate to include the power to impose sanctions.

2) The CTC urgently requires a greater number of experts at its disposal with a view to offering more substantive technical assistance, particularly to developing countries.

3) The CTC should undertake to include in its considerations of states reports an assessment of whether measures taken to comply with Security Council Resolution 1373 are consistent with international human rights obligations. Further, it should publish guidelines i) requiring states to report on measures taken to implement Resolution 1373 in light of human rights standards; and ii) advising on the adoption of anti-terrorist measures which are consistent with human rights obligations.

4) States should not use the fight against terrorism as a pretext to adopt measures which unlawfully restrict the rights to freedom of expression, religion, opinion and belief, nor the rights of minorities.

5) Any anti-terrorist laws which have the potential to infringe upon human rights and civil liberties should be considered carefully by legislative bodies, taking account of the relevant requirements established by international human rights law and the jurisprudence of international human rights bodies.

CHAPTER 4

UPHOLDING HUMAN RIGHTS AND CIVIL LIBERTIES IN THE FIGHT AGAINST TERRORISM

4.1 INTRODUCTION

Under international human rights law, states have a duty to protect the lives of their citizens and to prevent and punish human rights abuses both by representatives of the state and by non-state actors, including terrorists.[1] But public security should not be pursued without regard to the rights guaranteed by human rights treaties. The UN Commission on Human Rights has stated that 'all measures to counter terrorism must be in strict conformity with international law, including international human rights standards.'[2]

The Task Force believes that there is nothing contradictory between firmly countering terrorism and upholding human rights. States may, however, need to balance individual rights with community protection. In this task they are assisted by human rights treaties which take into account those situations in which national security is threatened. States are permitted to restrict a number of human rights[3] provided that those restrictions meet the following requirements: i) they are provided by a law of general application;[4] ii) pursue a legitimate aim;[5] iii) are

---

1.   See, for instance, Human Rights Committee, *Preliminary Observations: Peru*, 25 July 1996, UN Doc. CCPR/C/79/Add.67, para. 3, where the Committee affirmed 'the right and duty of the State party to take firm measures to protect its population against terror.'

2.   UN Commission on Human Rights, Resolution 2001/37 of 23 April 2001, UN Doc. E/CN.4/RES/2001/37, preambular para. 20.

3.   Human rights that are subject to restrictions include the freedom of expression and the freedom of assembly and association. See, for example, Article 19(3)(b) and Articles 21 and 22(2) of the International Covenant on Civil and Political Rights (ICCPR).

4.   See, for instance, Article 19(3) of the ICCPR which requires that restrictions of the freedom of expression must be provided by law.

5.   The interests of national security and public safety are recognised as legitimate aims in all major human rights treaties. For example, Article 19(3) of the ICCPR permits restrictions of the freedom of expression which are necessary for respect of the rights or

necessary[6]; and iv) are proportionate to the aim pursued.[7]

In addition, most international human rights treaties allow states to derogate from certain human rights guarantees, to the extent strictly required by the situation, when there is a public emergency threatening the life of a nation.[8] But derogations are only possible under the following narrowly defined circumstances[9]: (i) there exists a public emergency which threatens the life of the nation[10]; (ii) the state of emergency must be officially proclaimed[11]; (iii) the derogating state must immediately inform the other state parties of the derogation[12]; (iv) the derogating measures must be strictly required by the exigencies of the situation[13];

---

reputations of others, for the protection of national security or public order, or of public health or morals.

6. For example, Article 22(2) of the ICCPR requires that any restrictions of the freedom of association are 'necessary in a democratic society'.

7. See Human Rights Committee General Comment No. 29, para. 4.

8. See Article 4 of the ICCPR, Article 15 of the European Convention for the Protection of Human Rights and Fundamental Freedoms (ECHR), and Article 27 of the American Convention on Human Rights (ACHR).

9. These circumstances are contained in the provisions mentioned above and have been elaborated upon by the UN Human Rights Committee in its General Comment No. 29 of 31 August 2001 and by the European Court of Human Rights in the cases mentioned in the notes below.

10. This has been defined by the European Court of Human Rights, in *Lawless v. Ireland*, Judgment (Merits), 1 July 1961, para. 28, as 'an exceptional situation of crisis or emergency which affects the whole population and constitutes a threat to the organised life of the community of which the State is composed.' The ICCPR requires that even during an armed conflict measures derogating from the Covenant are allowed only if and to the extent that the situation constitutes a threat to the life of the nation. See Human Rights Committee General Comment No. 29, para. 3. States enjoy a wide margin of appreciation to determine whether a public emergency exists. The European Court of Human Rights has held that, by reason of their direct and continuous contact with the pressing needs of the moment, it falls in the first place to the national authorities to determine whether the life of their nation is threatened by a public emergency and, if so, how far it is necessary to go in attempting to overcome the emergency. However, the court also ruled that states do not enjoy an unlimited power in this respect. The court held that it is empowered to rule on whether states have gone beyond the 'extent strictly required by the exigencies' of the crisis. See *Ireland v. United Kingdom*, Judgment (Merits and just satisfaction), 18 January 1978, para. 207, and *Brannigan and McBride v. United Kingdom*, Judgment (Merits), 26 May 1993, para. 43.

11. Everyone within a territory affected by a state of emergency must be aware of the fact that some rights are limited. The Human Rights Committee has stated that this requirement 'is essential for the maintenance of the principles of legality and rule of law at times when they are most needed. When proclaiming a state of emergency with consequences that could entail derogation from any provision of the Covenant, States must act within their constitutional and other provisions of law that govern such proclamation and the exercise of emergency powers.' See General Comment No. 29, para. 2.

12. See Article 4(3) of the ICCPR, Article 15(3) of the ECHR, and Article 27(3) of the ACHR.

13. The derogation clauses of all the human rights treaties make it clear that only

(v) these measures must not involve discrimination solely on the ground of race, colour, sex, language, religion or social origin[14]; (vi) the derogating measures must be consistent with other obligations under international law. However, a number of human rights are non-derogable, meaning that they can never be restricted or suspended, not even in times of emergency.[15] Among the rights that can be suspended are procedural guarantees. However, as explored in more detail later in this chapter, the Human Rights Committee, the body that oversees the implementation of the International Covenant on Civil and Political Rights (ICCPR), has held that the fundamental requirements of fair trial must be respected even during a state of emergency.[16]

---

measures 'to the extent strictly required by the exigencies of the situation' are permissible. See Article 4(1) of the ICCPR, Article 15(1) of the ECHR, and Article 27(1) of the ACHR. The Human Rights Committee has held that this requirement 'relates to the duration, geographical coverage and material scope of the state of emergency and any measures of derogation resorted to because of the emergency. [. . .] [T]he obligation to limit any derogations to those strictly required by the exigencies of the situation reflects the principle of proportionality which is common to derogation and limitation powers.' See General Comment No. 29, para. 4. The European Court of Human Rights has ruled that whilst it falls to each contracting state to define whether the life of its nation is threatened by a public emergency, it is for the court to determine whether states have gone beyond the 'extent strictly required by the exigencies' of the crisis. The domestic margin of appreciation is thus accompanied by a European supervision. See *Brannigan and McBride v. United Kingdom, supra* note 10, para. 43.

14. See Article 4(1) of the ICCPR and Article 27(1) of the ACHR.

15. The ICCPR, for instance, in Article 4(2), lists the following rights as non-derogable: The right to life; the prohibition of torture; the prohibition of slavery; the prohibition of imprisonment because of inability to fulfil a contractual obligation; the principle of legality in the field of criminal law; the recognition of everyone as a person before the law; the freedom of thought, conscience and religion. For the ECHR see Article 15(2), for the ACHR see Article 27(2).

16. The Human Rights Committee has made it clear for the ICCPR that the fact that some of the provisions of the Covenant have been listed in Article 4(2), as not being subject to derogation does not mean that other articles in the Covenant may be subjected to derogations at will, even where a threat to the life of the nation exists. See General Comment No. 29, para. 6. Consequently, the Committee has stated that '[i]n those provisions of the Covenant that are not listed in Article 4, paragraph 2, there are elements that in the Committee's opinion cannot be made subject to lawful derogation under Article 4.' *Id.*, para. 13. For instance, the Committee has expressed the view that 'the principles of legality and the rule of law require that fundamental requirements of fair trial must be respected during a state of emergency. Only a court of law may try and convict a person for a criminal offence. The presumption of innocence must be respected. In order to protect non-derogable rights, the right to take proceedings before a court to enable the court to decide without delay on the lawfulness of detention, must not be diminished by a State party's decision to derogate from the Covenant.' *Id.*, para. 16. Similarly, the Inter-American Court of Human Rights held that the guarantees of Articles 7(6) and 25(1) of the ACHR (*habeas corpus* and *amparo*) are judicial guarantees from which derogation is not allowed. See *Habeas Corpus in Emergency Situations*, Advisory Opinion OC-8/87, 30 January 1987, Series A No. 8.

As long as the requirements enunciated above are met, states may adopt legislation to combat threats to national security, including terrorism. However, the Task Force is concerned that the combined pressures of terrorist threats and public opinion may precipitate the adoption of legislation that contradicts recognised standards of human rights. If adopted hastily and without sufficient scrutiny, as emergency measures often are, such legislation may in fact defeat its own purpose and ultimately undermine the legitimacy and credibility of the legal system. Further, attempts to restrict the due process guarantees of terrorist suspects may eventuate in wrongful convictions, an outcome contrary to both the interests of the victims of terrorism and the public at large.

The Task Force has reviewed various legislative schemes, assessing their legality in light of international standards of law. It has considered both substantive human rights and procedural ones.[17] In international human rights law, states must adhere to customary law, regardless of any treaty obligations.[18] States are also bound by becoming parties to one of the UN conventions such as the ICCPR.[19] In addition, regional organisations may adopt human rights treaties, which are binding for the ratifying states within the region.[20] Although regional treaties do not apply outside of the specific geographical area, they help consolidate international standards and contribute to the formation of human rights law in other regions. Alongside this so-called 'hard law' a wealth of non-bind-

---

17. The substantive protections relevant for this chapter include the prohibition on torture, the right to privacy, the freedom of association, the freedom of assembly, the freedom of expression and the prohibition on discrimination. The procedural guarantees include safeguards against arbitrary arrest, e.g. access to counsel and the right to challenge the detention before a court, and fair trial rights, e.g. the presumption of innocence, the right to a competent, independent and impartial tribunal, and the right to appeal.

18. Article 38(1)(b) of the Statute of the ICJ refers to international custom 'as evidence of a general practice accepted as law.' Accordingly, most commentators hold that customary international law is made up of two elements: general practice of states and the conviction that such practice reflects law (*opinio juris*). See, for example, Cassese, Antonio, *International Law*, Oxford University Press (2001), p. 119. It is generally accepted that grave violations of human rights, when practiced as state policy, are violations of customary international law. See, for example, Third Restatement of U.S. Foreign Relations Law, Vol. 2 (1987), p. 165. The prohibition on torture is also accepted as belonging to the corpus of customary law. See the decision by the U.S. Circuit Court of Appeals, 2nd Circuit, in *Filartiga v. Pena-Irala*, 630 F 2d 876 (1980). At a much more general level, it has even been argued that the standards laid down in the Universal Declaration of Human Rights have become part of customary international law. See, for example, the Proclamation of Teheran, proclaimed by the International Conference on Human Rights at Teheran on 13 May 1968, para. 2.

19. Other UN human rights treaties relevant for the present context include the Convention against Torture and other Cruel, Inhuman or Degrading Treatment or Punishment (CAT) and the International Convention on the Elimination of All Forms of Racial Discrimination (CERD).

20. The most important regional human rights treaties include the African Charter on Human and People's Rights (African Charter), the ACHR, and the ECHR.

ing instruments, known as 'soft law', provide more detailed guidelines and standards; they are normally adopted by way of UN or regional resolutions.[21] Soft law is important because the evolution of human rights shows that commonly these standards become hard law. Finally, the jurisprudence of human rights bodies, both within the UN[22] and regional organisations,[23] as well as of international criminal tribunals[24] provides

---

21. International non-treaty standards include: the Universal Declaration of Human Rights (UDHR), adopted by the UN General Assembly in 1948; the Body of Principles for the Protection of All Persons under Any Form of Detention or Imprisonment, adopted by the UN General Assembly in 1988; the Standard Minimum Rules for the Treatment of Prisoners, adopted by the First UN Congress on the Prevention of Crime and the Treatment of Offenders in 1955; the Code of Conduct for Law Enforcement Officials, adopted by the General Assembly in 1979; the Basic Principles on the Role of Lawyers, adopted by the Eighth UN Congress on the Prevention of Crime and the Treatment of Offenders in 1990; the Guidelines on the Role of Prosecutors, adopted at the Eighth UN Congress on the Prevention of Crime and the Treatment of Offenders in 1990; the Basic Principles on the Independence of the Judiciary, adopted by the Seventh UN Congress on the Prevention of Crime and the Treatment of Offenders in 1985; the United Nations Safeguards Guaranteeing Protection of the Rights of Those Facing the Death Penalty, adopted by the UN Economic and Social Council in 1984; the Standard Minimum Rules for the Administration of Juvenile Justice ('the Beijing Rules'), adopted by the General Assembly in 1985; the General Assembly Resolution on UN Rules for the Protection of Juveniles Deprived of their Liberty of 1990; the Declaration of Basic Principles of Justice for Victims of Crime and Abuse of Power, adopted by the General Assembly in 1985. Regional non-binding standards include the European Prison Rules, adopted by the Council of Europe Committee of Ministers in 1987.

22. A distinction may be drawn between UN treaty monitoring bodies, established to monitor implementation of the treaty and to investigate complaints that the provisions of the treaty have been violated, and UN thematic mechanisms, appointed by the UN Commission on Human Rights to investigate complaints of a particular type of human rights violation in all countries, whether or not the state is bound by treaties. The body monitoring the implementation of the ICCPR is the Human Rights Committee. Its General Comments provide authoritative guidance on interpretation of the ICCPR. Further, the First Optional Protocol to the ICCPR gives the Human Rights Committee the competence to consider complaints submitted by individuals claiming that a state party to the Protocol has violated rights guaranteed by the ICCPR. Other UN treaty monitoring bodies include the Committee against Torture and the Committee on the Elimination of Racial Discrimination. UN thematic mechanisms include the Working Group on Arbitrary Detention, the Special Rapporteur on Torture and the Special Rapporteur on the Independence of Judges and Lawyers.

23. Implementation of the African Charter is monitored by the African Commission on Human and Peoples' Rights; it will be complemented by the African Court on Human and Peoples' Rights, which will be able to give advisory opinions upon the request of the commission or a state party. The Inter-American Commission on Human Rights carries out on-site visits, prepares special studies, makes recommendations to governments, and acts on complaints submitted by individuals, groups or NGOs. The Inter-American Court of Human Rights examines cases submitted by states parties to the ACHR or by the Inter-American Commission and can issue advisory opinions. The European Court of Human Rights considers complaints from individuals, groups or states alleging a violation of the ECHR.

24. See the jurisprudence of the International Criminal Tribunal for the former Yugoslavia (ICTY) and of the International Criminal Tribunal for Rwanda (ICTR). Further, the Statutes of these tribunals and their Rules of Evidence and Procedure are

important guidance on the interpretation and application of human rights law, thus constantly developing it further. Although the jurisprudence of regional bodies is, of course, only binding on states within the particular region, it often contributes to the formulation of international jurisprudence.

Bearing these distinctions as to source, applicability and relevance of human rights standards in mind, the Task Force has taken into account not only international binding standards, but also regional and 'soft law' standards. Having reviewed a number of anti-terrorist laws, the Task Force concludes that certain international standards of human rights, providing both substantive protections and procedural guarantees, have come under threat.

4.2 THE DEFINITION OF TERRORIST OFFENCES AND ORGANISATIONS

4.2.1 Introduction

Many of the world's anti-terrorist laws suffer from the endemic malaise of imprecision. The dangers of bad draftsmanship are obvious; one of the potential dangers is the criminalisation of legitimate dissent. To avoid confusion and (the sometimes unwitting) abuse of human rights, such legislation should be in accordance with the recognised principles of legality and certainty. This section considers the often vague and broad definition of terrorist offences. It then moves on to consider the designation of certain organisations as terrorist and the criminalisation of persons linked to them. The procedures for banning organisations as well as the lack of a requirement to establish a link between members and terrorist acts may raise concerns with regard to the freedom of association.

4.2.2 Defining Terrorist Offences

In order to comply with internationally recognised standards, penal law, including anti-terrorism legislation, must comply with the principle of legality formulated in the maxim *nullum crimen sine lege*, which requires that crimes be specifically proscribed by law in advance of the conduct sought to be punished.[25] This principle may not be suspended in any circumstances, including during states of emergency.[26]

---

important international standards, representing contemporary fair trial guarantees. Many of these standards have been incorporated into the Statute of the International Criminal Court (ICC).

25. See Article 11(2) of the UDHR, Article 15 of the ICCPR, Article 7 of the ECHR, Article 9 of the ACHR, and Article 7(2) of the African Charter.

26. See Article 4(2) of the ICCPR. Contrary to this principle, the new Indonesian

The principle of legality also includes that of certainty, i.e. the requirement that both criminal liability and punishment are contained within clear and precise provisions.[27] It follows that liability must, to a reasonable degree, be foreseeable from the wording of any relevant provision.[28] The Inter-American Court of Human Rights has held that crimes must be classified and described in precise and unambiguous language that narrowly defines the punishable offence, since '[a]mbiguity in describing crimes creates doubts and the opportunity for abuse of power.'[29]

As 'terrorism' can be defined in very broad terms, these principles are particularly vulnerable in the context of laws that prescribe terrorist crimes. There are examples of anti-terrorism laws which define offences in such a broad and vague manner that they lack the required specificity. Ill-defined offences are of particular concern when they can potentially be used to criminalise peaceful activities, such as legitimate political opposition.[30]

4.2.3 Proscribing Terrorist Organisations

In a number of states, laws have been adopted which allow for the designation of specific organisations as 'terrorist'. States are permitted to restrict the rights to freedom of association and assembly for reasons of national security, public safety, public order, the protection of public health and morals, or the protection of the rights and freedoms of others.[31] However, the Task Force believes that such designations as an

---

anti-terrorism regulations allow for the retroactive application for offences related to the Bali terrorist attack on 12 October 2002. See Government Regulations in-lieu of Law Numbers 1 and 2. An English translation of the regulations is available at http://www.law.u nimelb.edu.au/alc/indonesia/perpu_1.html and http://www.law.unimelb.edu.au/alc/indonesia/perpu_2.html respectively. These regulations appear to be contrary to the Indonesian Constitution which stipulates that citizens must not be prosecuted for any act that was not an offence at the time it was committed under national law. See Second Amendment to the 1945 Constitution, Article 28I, para. 1. An English translation of the Indonesian Constitution is available at http://confinder.richmond.edu/Indonesia.htm

27. See Human Rights Committee General Comment No. 29, para. 7.

28. See the decision by the European Court of Human Rights in *Kokkinakis v. Greece*, Judgment (Merits and just satisfaction), 25 May 1993, para. 52.

29. See *Castillo Petruzzi et al. Case*, Judgment, 30 May 1999, Series C No. 52, para. 121.

30. For example, Section 21 of India's Prevention of Terrorism Act (POTA) makes it an offence to 'invite support' for a 'terrorist organisation'. There is no definition of what 'inviting support' includes, making it all but impossible for individuals to foresee what acts would fall under this extremely broad term. In particular, the 'inviting of support' might include completely peaceful activities which have nothing to do with the alleged terrorist activities of a group. This provision could thus be used to restrict the exercise of the freedoms of expression and association.

31. See Articles 21 and 22 of the ICCPR, Article 11 of the ECHR, Articles 15 and 16 of the ACHR, Articles 10 and 11 of the African Charter, and Article 20 of the UDHR.

administrative function should be subject to judicial review as a safeguard against the undue restriction of organisations with peaceful and legitimate aims.

In addition, some anti-terrorism laws provide for measures against individuals linked or suspected of being linked to terrorist organisations. Consequences of membership of, or association with, proscribed organisations can be severe.[32] Governments are free to criminalise membership of such organisations, provided the banning of the organisation concerned is provided by a law of general application, pursues a legitimate aim, is necessary and proportionate, and is subject to judicial review. Further, the individual concerned must have the right to challenge the criminalisation before a court.[33] Criminalising individuals on the basis of their mere association with an organisation, whether the organisation is designated as terrorist or not, could be subject to abuse by the state and may violate a range of human rights.[34]

With regard to the right of freedom of assembly, the Task Force notes that it may be subject to the limitations noted above. However, states must ensure that peaceful meetings and the expression of alternative political views are permitted.

4.2.4   Lists

The drawing up of lists containing the names of suspected terrorist entities or individuals has become practice within the United Nations,

---

32. Under Section 20 of the Indian POTA it is an offence to belong or to profess to belong to an organisation declared as terrorist. In the United Kingdom, the Anti-Terrorism, Crime and Security Act 2001 (ATCSA) authorises the Secretary of State to certify as a 'suspected international terrorist' and detain any non-UK citizen he suspects is a member of an 'international terrorist group' or 'has links with an international terrorist group'. A person is defined as having links with an international terrorist group 'if he supports or assists it.' See Sections 21(2) and (4) of the ATCSA. In the United States, non-citizens can be deported for soliciting funds or resources for a designated terrorist organisation, soliciting an individual to join it, or providing the organisation with material support, regardless of whether they knew of the designation and regardless of whether the assistance was related to the group's alleged terrorist activity. See Section 212(a)(3)(B)(iv) of the Immigration and Nationality Act (INA) as amended by Section 411 of the USA PATRIOT Act.

33. See Articles 9(4) and 14(1) of the ICCPR.

34. Under Pakistan's amended anti-terrorism laws, the government may restrict the movement of individuals or authorise detention of any person who 'is an activist, office-bearer or an associate' of a proscribed organisation, 'or in any way concerned or suspected to be concerned with such an organisation or affiliated with any group or organisation suspected to be involved in terrorism or sectarianism.' There is no requirement that the individual is linked to the commission of a terrorist offence. It is sufficient that the person may be associated with a group or organisation suspected to be involved in terrorism, whether that group or organisation is banned or not. See Anti-Terrorism Act 1997, Section 11EE, heading 'Security for good behaviour', para. 1, as inserted by the Anti-terrorism (Amendment) Ordinance 2002.

individual states and the European Union.[35] The primary purpose of such lists is for the identification of persons and entities whose involvement in terrorism requires that their assets be frozen. In some cases individual membership of the organisation may be criminalised.[36]

The procedures under which entities or individuals are included on these lists give rise to concerns, as there is commonly no legal framework under which fundamental due process rights are protected. This could result in wrongful inclusion on a list, entailing the freezing of assets and restriction of freedom of association, without judicial remedy.[37]

4.3 INFORMATION GATHERING AND SHARING

4.3.1 Introduction

Following the attacks of September 11, several states have increased their powers of surveillance, information gathering and the sharing of personal data between government departments. The Task Force recognises the importance of these means as a proactive measure against terrorism. Such strategies allow governments to keep pace with the ever more sophisticated ways of communication employed by terrorists and other criminals. Further, it appears that citizens in general are willing to accept a certain degree of surveillance, and thus restrictions of their right to privacy, as long as they constitute an effective contribution to the prevention and investigation of crime.[38]

Nonetheless, intelligence gathering and sharing remain sensitive issues. There exists a universal right not to be subjected to arbitrary or unlawful interference with privacy, family, home or correspondence.[39] Thus, wiretapping, interception of correspondence and searches of private property would represent invasions of privacy. Conversely, regular

---

35. UN Security Council Resolution 1390, adopted on 16 January 2002, see Appendix III, reaffirms earlier resolutions and requires member states to implement a range of measures with respect to Osama bin Laden, al-Qaeda, the Taliban and associated individuals, organisations and entities named in a list created pursuant to Resolutions 1267 and 1333.

36. For example, Section 18(1) of the Indian POTA declares that certain organisations listed in a schedule are 'terrorist organisations'. The government can add other organisations to the list 'if it believes that [the organisation] is involved in terrorism.' See Section 18(3). Section 20 criminalises membership of any organisation declared as terrorist. This appears to violate Article 21 of India's Constitution which provides that no person shall be deprived of his or her liberty 'except according to procedure established by law.'

37. See Chapter 6, Section 6.5 for a detailed discussion.

38. For instance, according to a poll published in the British newspaper *The Guardian*, 72 percent of British citizens agree with the statement that giving up some privacy is necessary to fight terrorism and crime. See Stuart Millar, Privacy fears revealed, *The Guardian*, 7 September 2002.

39. See, Article 17 of the ICCPR, Article 8 of the ECHR, Article 11 of the ACHR, and Article 12 of the UDHR.

police enquiries, the use of informants and questioning of witnesses do not ordinarily constitute an infringement of privacy. The Human Rights Committee has stated that the term 'unlawful' means that an interference authorised by states can only take place on the basis of law, which itself must comply with the provisions, aims and objectives of the ICCPR.[40] Even with regard to interferences that conform to the Covenant, relevant legislation must specify the circumstances in which such interferences may be permitted.[41]

The Task Force believes that in light of threats to national security posed by terrorism there may be justification for a restriction on the right to privacy. However, it believes that information gathering and sharing powers must be clearly defined and judicial supervision maintained at all times where the right to privacy might be infringed.

Finally, the Task Force notes that despite increasing international cooperation in intelligence gathering and sharing, this area is currently unregulated in international law.

4.3.2 Information Gathering by Law Enforcement Agencies

Since September 11, there has been a notable extension of powers of surveillance in a number of jurisdictions, some of which might infringe upon the right to privacy.[42] To ensure the right to privacy is respected, it is vital that the parameters of these privacy reducing measures are clearly defined. Further, the circumstances under which authorities are able to exercise these powers must be clear and unambiguous.[43]

The Task Force is of the view that restrictions of individual human rights and civil liberties, such as the right to privacy, must always be capable of judicial review to prevent their arbitrary and unlawful use. The law should not limit the ability of judges to determine the extent to which the rights of the individual should be restricted.[44]

---

40. See Human Rights Committee General Comment No.16, para. 3.

41. *Id.*, para. 8.

42. For example, the USA PATRIOT Act grants the executive branch enhanced surveillance powers to track e-mail and Internet usage, conduct 'roving' surveillance, obtain sensitive personal records, conduct covert searches and monitor financial transactions. See Sections 201–225.

43. See Human Rights Committee General Comment No. 16, para. 8.

44. For example, the USA PATRIOT Act reduces the power of judges to ensure that the gathering of information is legally conducted. Under Section 215, by way of example, the FBI may apply for a court order requiring the production of 'any tangible things', including medical, financial or library records, from any person, upon a written statement that these items are being sought for an investigation 'to protect against international terrorism or clandestine intelligence activities.' Judges, in this case, have no authority to refuse the order once the written statement is received. Another example is Section 217, according to which internet service providers, universities and network administrators can now authorise, without a judicial order, the surveillance of anyone accessing a computer without authorisation.

4.3.3 Information Sharing Between Intelligence Agencies and Law Enforcement Agencies

Some jurisdictions permit the sharing of information between intelligence agencies and law enforcement agencies. However, in a number of jurisdictions where there has previously been a separation of these powers, that separation is being blurred.[45] Information sharing may be a valuable tool for combating terrorism, nonetheless, its use runs the inherent risk of violating the right to privacy and may lead to the introduction of evidence from secret sources, e.g. from informants, which may not be presented in full to the defendant. The potential dangers in the blurring of the separation of the roles of law enforcement and intelligence services underline the importance of ensuring that the judiciary retains the authority to determine the admissibility of evidence and its effect on due process guarantees.[46] There are concerns that where there are threats to national security, the judiciary might be more likely to respond to external pressures.

4.4 LAW ENFORCEMENT

4.4.1 Introduction

Following the attacks of September 11 there has been a proliferation of racial profiling in certain law enforcement activities,[47] undoubt-

---

45. For example, the United States Foreign Intelligence Surveillance Court of Review, ruling on new 'Intelligence Sharing Procedures' by the Attorney General, designed to permit the complete exchange of information between intelligence and law enforcement officials, overturned the decision by a lower court, which had imposed limitations on such an exchange of information. The court of review argued that the amendment to the Foreign Intelligence Surveillance Act (FISA) by the USA PATRIOT Act, allowing wiretaps and searches as long as 'a significant purpose' of the surveillance is the gathering of foreign intelligence information, eliminated any justification for balancing the relative weight the government places on criminal prosecution as compared to other counterintelligence responses. See United States Foreign Intelligence Surveillance Court of Review, *On Motions for Review of Orders of the United States Foreign Surveillance Court*, 18 November 2002.

46. The due process guarantees affected include, for example, the right of the defendant to know the case against him or her.

47. In Germany, a computerised search of millions of official records was initiated. Police and intelligence agents were looking for financially self-sufficient Muslims aged between 20 and 40 with no children and a background in technical studies. See John Hooper, German courts put terror hunt in doubt, *The Guardian*, 2 February 2002. An upper court in Frankfurt upheld objections to the use of systematic, standardised searches as a means of attempting to identify terrorist suspects, arguing that the requirement of a 'present danger' necessary to impose such a measure was not fulfilled. See decision by the Oberlandesgericht Frankfurt am Main in *Hessisches Landeskriminalamt v Herr xyz* of 21 February 2002. In the United States, the Department of Justice announced in November 2001 its intention to interview 5,000 young immigrant men, based solely on their country of origin, their age, and date of arrival. See Naftali Bendavid, Bush OKs Terror Tribunals;

edly stemming from a view that the main perpetrators of terrorism are frequently men from certain Muslim countries. This section explores the human rights issues raised by such action.

It then goes on to consider the arrest of suspected terrorists. It is noted that during threats to national security the personal liberty of non-citizens is particularly at risk. Where there is insufficient evidence to arrest a non-citizen on terrorist charges, immigration laws could be used for the arrest and detention of foreign suspected terrorists without applying the standards normally required in criminal justice procedures. This is particularly questionable where the individuals are denied the right to legally challenge the suspicion of links to terrorism.

4.4.2 Racial Profiling

Whilst the targeting of law enforcement resources on suspected groups is to be expected, any investigative methods using profiling must not violate the fundamental prohibition on discrimination.[48] Article 26 of the ICCPR prohibits discrimination 'on any ground such as race, colour, sex, language, religion, political or other opinion, national or social origin, property, birth or other status' and imposes upon states a general obligation not to enact discriminatory laws.[49] Notwithstanding this, differentiation of treatment does not necessarily constitute discrimination, if the criteria employed are reasonable and objective, and if the aim is to achieve a purpose which is legitimate under the ICCPR.[50]

Whilst the Task Force recognises that criteria such as religion, race or citizenship can be important elements in establishing the profile of suspects, it takes the view that profiling should not be based exclusively on any one of these broad factors. Instead, it should be used only when applying more detailed criteria, which must themselves be reasonable.

US seeks 5000 foreign nationals for questioning in investigations, *Chicago Tribune*, 14 November 2001. In March 2002, the Attorney General extended the programme to 3,000 more individuals 'whose passports reflect a variety of settings where there have been strong al-Qaeda presences' and who had more recently entered the United States. The Attorney General made clear that these men were not suspected of any criminal activity. Rather, they were targeted, apparently, because of their ethnic background. See press release by the US Department of Justice, Attorney General Ashcroft Addresses United States Attorney's Office for the Eastern District of Virginia, 20 March 2002.

48. The prohibition on discrimination is contained in Articles 2(1), 3 and 26 of the ICCPR, Article 14 of the ECHR, Articles 1, 8(2) and 24 of the ACHR, Articles 2 and 3 of the African Charter, the International Convention on the Elimination of All Forms of Racial Discrimination (CERD), and Articles 7 and 10 of the UDHR. Moreover, the prohibition on discrimination on the basis of race is recognised as a principle of customary international law. See the decision by the International Court of Justice (ICJ) in the *South-West Africa Cases* (Second Phase), 1966 I.C.J. 6 (18 July 1966), Dissenting Opinion Judge Tanaka, at p. 293.

49. See Human Rights Committee General Comment No. 18, para. 12.

50. *Id.*, para.13.

In order to assess the reasonableness of the criteria, the severity of the measures employed must be taken into account. For example, it might be reasonable for reasons of national security to instigate immigration screening to all male citizens from country X arriving in country Y. By contrast, it may not be reasonable to question, arrest and detain all men from country X residing in, or visiting, country Y.

The Task Force is concerned that the use of religion or citizenship as criteria for screening may, in fact, be both discriminatory and ineffective.[51] Further, people with terrorist aims who do not fulfil these criteria may not be detected.[52] The use of ethnic or religious stereotypes may well alienate the very communities whose cooperation is vital in combating terrorism.

4.4.3 Arrests

The arrest of all suspects, including suspected terrorists, must be carried out 'in accordance with such procedures as are established by law.'[53] Failure by a state to abide by its own rules, regulations and procedures renders an arrest arbitrary and in consequence violates international standards. The Human Rights Committee has held that the notion of 'arbitrariness' must not only be equated with 'against the law' but be interpreted to include elements of inappropriateness, injustice and lack of predictability.[54] In addition, the Human Rights Committee has stated that remand in custody could be considered arbitrary if it is not necessary in all the circumstances of the case, i.e. where it fails to meet the criterion of proportionality.[55] This basic guarantee applies to all detainees, whether held in connection with criminal charges or immigration law violations.[56] Further, anyone arrested must be informed at the time of

---

51. For example, of the 1,200-plus non-US citizens arrested in the weeks following September 11, as of August 2002 only three had been indicted for terrorist activity. See Danny Hakim, 4 Men Charged with Being in Terrorist Cell in Detroit Area, *New York Times*, 29 August 2002. In point of fact, many of those accused of terrorist involvement in the US were not arrested during the FBI/INS sweep, and are of either American or European citizenship. Zacarias Moussaoui, 'the twentieth' hijacker, was already in detention and is a French citizen. Jose Padilla, 'the dirty bomber', is an American citizen as is the now-convicted John Walker Lindh, 'the American Taliban'. James Ujaama, arrested in July 2002 in Denver and charged with assisting al-Qaeda and attempting to set up a terrorist training camp in Oregon, is a Muslim of US citizenship.

52. For example, British citizen Richard Reid, who did not fit the profile of suspected terrorists, was able to board a plane with a bomb in his shoe. See 'Shoe Bomber' Jailed for Life, *BBC News*, 30 January 2003.

53. See Article 9 of the ICCPR, Article 6 of the African Charter, Article 7 of the ACHR, Article 5 of the ECHR, and Article 3 of the UDHR.

54. See Human Rights Committee, *Albert Womah Mukong v. Cameroon*, Communication No. 458/1991, 21 July 1994, UN Doc. CCPR/C/51/D/458/1991, para. 9.8.

55. *Id.*

56. Human Rights Committee General Comment No. 8, para. 1.

their arrest of the reasons for their arrest[57] and must be accorded the right to challenge the lawfulness of the arrest or detention in court.[58]

At times of national emergency, non-citizens are particularly vulnerable to arrest.[59] Threats from abroad may lead law enforcement authorities to pay particular attention to certain groups of people. Arrest for violation of immigration regulations is not arbitrary provided it: i) is in accordance with normal immigration regulations; ii) is not in violation of the prohibition on discrimination; iii) is not disproportionate; and iv) can be challenged before a court. Prolonged detention of an individual arrested on the pretext of an immigration violation but who is in fact detained in connection with a terrorist investigation could be arbitrary where there is no longer a legal basis for the detention in immigration law and the individual is not given the opportunity to challenge the suspicion of terrorist activities. In addition, arrests which are based only on religion, race, or citizenship may violate the prohibition on discrimination.

4.5 DETENTION

4.5.1 Introduction

The Task Force acknowledges the difficulties states may face in obtaining sufficient evidence to charge and detain potentially dangerous individuals. In order to protect the wider community, states may feel justified in detaining suspected terrorists without charge or trial.[60] However, where states resort to administrative detention it is crucial that it is subject to judicial review. An important protection against arbitrary detention is the right of those detained to the assistance of legal counsel. There are concerns that states may deny access to counsel in cases involving suspected terrorists.

4.5.2 Arbitrary Detention

The Human Rights Committee has stated that arbitrary deprivations of liberty can never be justified, not even during a state of emergency.[61]

---

57. See Articles 9(2) and 14(3)(a) of the ICCPR, Articles 5(2) and 6(3)(a) of the ECHR, Articles 7(4) and 8(2)(b) of the ACHR, and Principle 10 of the Body of Principles for the Protection of All Persons under Any Form of Detention or Imprisonment.

58. See Article 9(4) of the ICCPR, Article 5(4) of the ECHR, Article 7(6) of the ACHR, Article 7(1)(a) of the African Charter, and Principle 32 of the Body of Principles for the Protection of All Persons under Any Form of Detention or Imprisonment.

59. In the two months following September 11, some 1,200 non-US nationals were taken into custody in the USA in connection with the events of that date. On 5 November 2001, the Department of Justice indicated that 1,182 people had been detained. On 8 November 2001, it announced that it would no longer provide a running total of all individuals detained in connection with the investigation. See *Center for National Security et al v. US Department of Justice*, 2002 US District Court, Lexis 14168 (D.D.C.2 August 2002), note 7.

60. This is commonly referred to as 'administrative detention'.

61. See Human Rights Committee General Comment No. 29, para. 11.

What is to be considered an arbitrary deprivation of liberty in armed conflict needs to be determined by reference to international humanitarian law.[62] The right to challenge the lawfulness of detention before a court has also been deemed non-derogable by the Human Rights Committee and the Inter-American Court of Human Rights.[63] Although other elements of the right to liberty are generally considered to be derogable, it has been proposed that whilst under emergency conditions it might not be possible to comply with all the aspects of the right to liberty, '[i]t cannot follow from this that the right to liberty and security of person as a whole may be rendered nugatory.'[64] Moreover, even during states of emergency, the right to liberty may only be suspended to the extent deemed necessary by the specific exigencies of the situation.

In the face of recent terrorist attacks, a number of states have deemed it necessary to adopt laws permitting administrative detention. In the United States[65]

---

62. See ICJ, *Advisory Opinion on the Legality of the Threat or Use of Nuclear Weapons*, 8 July 1996, para. 25, where the Court held that the test of what is an arbitrary deprivation of life has to be determined by the applicable *lex specialis*, namely, the law applicable in armed conflict which is designed to regulate the conduct of hostilities. Thus whether a particular loss of life, through the use of a certain weapon in warfare, had to be considered an arbitrary deprivation of life contrary to Article 6 of the Covenant could only be decided by reference to the law applicable in armed conflict and not deduced from the terms of the Covenant itself. By analogy, the same is true of arbitrary deprivations of liberty.

63. See Human Rights Committee General Comment No. 29, para. 16, and Inter-American Court of Human Rights, *Habeas Corpus in Emergency Situations, supra* note 16.

64. Rodley, *The Treatment of Prisoners under International Law*, Oxford University Press (1999), second edition, p. 256.

65. An interim regulation on custody procedures issued on 20 September 2001 allows the Immigration and Naturalization Service (INS) to detain non-citizens without charge for up to 48 hours, and for an 'additional reasonable period of time' in the event of 'emergency or other extraordinary circumstance'. See 66 Fed. Reg. 48,334, 20 September 2001 (amending 8 CFR 287.3(d)). The regulation does not require that the non-citizen's detention relate to the external circumstances. Notably, no link with alleged 'terrorism' needs to be made. Neither does the INS have to justify the delay beyond 48 hours in filing charges. Similarly, Section 412(a) of the USA PATRIOT Act gives the Attorney General wider authority to detain immigrants. The Attorney General can certify and detain non-citizens if he has 'reasonable grounds to believe' that they are or have engaged in a terrorist activity or otherwise endanger national security. The Act allows for detention for a period of seven days, after which the Attorney General must begin deportation proceedings, bring criminal charges against the detainee, or authorise his or her release. For non-citizens against whom the government initiates deportation proceedings, detention must continue until they are 'decertified' by the Attorney General. This requirement applies even if the detainee is granted relief from removal. A non-citizen whose removal is unlikely in the 'reasonably foreseeable future' may be detained for additional periods of up to six months if his or her release would 'threaten the national security of the United States or the safety of the community or any person.' The Act limits judicial review of the relevant decisions to the possibility to initiate *habeas corpus* proceedings in any district court otherwise having jurisdiction and to appeal unfavourable decisions to the US Court of Appeals for the District of Columbia. See Section 412(b). There is no guidance as to the process the Attorney General must follow in making the decision to certify an individual as a suspected terrorist, as to

and in the United Kingdom,[66] laws have been introduced which permit the detention of non-citizens without charge or trial on grounds of national security. In other countries, powers of administrative detention applying to both citizens and non-citizens have been introduced.[67]

Laws providing for administrative detention raise questions about their consistency with international law. Detained persons must be accorded the right to judicial review of their detention, enabling the court to decide, without delay, on the lawfulness of their detention and, where appropriate, order their release.[68] Detention without trial requires judicial checks and balances to ensure the right to liberty is not abused. The Human Rights Committee has expressly stated that if preventive detention is used for reasons of public security, it must still be subject to judicial review.[69] If, in addition, criminal charges are instigated, the arrested or detained person must be brought promptly before a judge or other judicial officer and is entitled to trial within a reasonable time or release.[70] Whilst the word 'promptly' is not defined, the Human Rights Committee has determined that the delay should not exceed a few days.[71]

---

the evidence the courts should use to assess the reasonableness of the Attorney General's decision, or as to whether detainees have access to the evidence.

66. Part 4 of the British ATCSA authorises the Secretary of State to certify a person as a 'suspected international terrorist' if he 'reasonably (a) believes that the person's presence in the United Kingdom is a risk to national security, and (b) suspects that the person is a terrorist.' See Section 21(1). Upon certification as a 'suspected international terrorist', a non-UK citizen can be detained without charge or trial, for an unspecified period of time, if his or her removal or deportation from the UK is prevented as a result of the UK's international obligations or for practical reasons. See Section 23.

67. In Pakistan, according to the new Anti-Terrorism (Amendment) Ordinance promulgated on 16 November 2002, any person suspected of affiliation with a 'terrorist organisation' or with any group or organisation suspected to be involved in terrorism or sectarianism, can be arrested and detained without charge for a period which may be extended for up to one year. In India, terrorist suspects can be detained for 90 days without charge or trial. See POTA Section 49(2) in connection with section 167 of the Code of Criminal Procedure. The Special Court can extend this period to 180 days on application by the Public Prosecutor. See POTA Section 49(2)(b). The Indonesian Government Regulation in Lieu of Law No. 1 permits police to detain terrorist suspects for seven days without charge, based on any intelligence reports as 'preliminary evidence', and for a further six months for investigation and prosecution. See Sections 25(2), 26(1) and 28. Such intelligence reports have to be approved by a court within three days. See Section 26(2) and (3).

68. Article 9(4) of the ICCPR, Article 7(6) of the ACHR, Article 5(4) of the ECHR, Article 7(1)(a) of the African Charter, and Principle 32 of the Body of Principles for the Protection of all Persons under Any Form of Detention of Imprisonment.

69. See Human Rights Committee General Comment No. 8, para. 4.

70. See Article 9(3) of the ICCPR, Article 7(5) of the ACHR, Article 5(3) of the ECHR, Article 59(2) of the ICC Statute, and Principle 38 Body of Principles for the Protection of all Persons under Any Form of Detention of Imprisonment.

71. See Human Rights Committee General Comment No. 8, para. 2.

Where non-nationals are detained pending removal, for example on grounds of national security, it is permissible for them to be detained without trial, subject to immigration procedures and judicial review. However, in the case of some detainees it may not be possible to deport them, either for practical reasons or because it would constitute a violation of international law.[72] In such cases it is incumbent upon states to ensure detainees have access to judicial review of their detention. Nevertheless, even with a right to judicial review, prolonged detention could still constitute a violation of the prohibition on arbitrary detention.

Even without the adoption of new laws permitting administrative detention there are concerns that existing laws may be used to arbitrarily detain suspected terrorists. As noted earlier, the use of arrest powers to bring into custody suspected terrorists on grounds other than terrorism may violate the prohibition on arbitrary detention. This is particularly true where these powers are used to circumvent the normal criminal standards applicable to arrest and where detention is prolonged.[73]

4.5.3   Access to Counsel

International human rights standards provide that all detainees and arrested persons have the right to the assistance of legal counsel of their own choice.[74] Detainees should be informed of this right[75] and given access to counsel

---

72. For example, removal or deportation to a country where the individual concerned may face the death penalty could violate Protocol No. 6 to the ECHR concerning the Abolition of the Death Penalty. Further, the European Court of Human Rights has ruled that no one can be removed to a state where he or she would face a real risk of being subjected to treatment contrary to the prohibition of torture. See *Soering v. United Kingdom*, Judgment (Merits and just satisfaction), 7 July 1989, paras. 90–91. See also *Chahal v. United Kingdom*, Judgment (Merits and just satisfaction), 15 November 1996, para. 107.

73. In an unknown number of US cases the detention of suspected terrorists has been authorised on the basis that they are 'material witnesses' to a criminal trial. In the United States, courts are authorised under federal law to issue warrants for the arrest of material witnesses where their attendance and testimony cannot be secured by any other means. See 18 USC § 3144. The Department of Justice has refused to release the number and identities of those detained on this basis. District courts have expressed concern about the use of material provisions to detain suspected terrorists who can not be charged with an offence. See *Center for National Security et al v. US Department of Justice*, 2002 US District Court (D.D.C. 2 August 2002), Lexis 14168; and *United States of America v. Osama Awadallah*, First Opinion and Order, 202 F. Supp. 2d 55 (S.D.N.Y.) 30 April 2002, *United States of America v Osama Awadallah*, Second Opinion and Order, 202 F. Supp. 2d 82 (S.D.N.Y.) 30 April 2002, and *United States of America v Awadallah*, 202 F. Supp. 2d 17 (S.D.N.Y) 31 January 2002.

74. See Principle 17(1) of the Body of Principles for the Protection of All Persons under Any Form of Detention or Imprisonment and Principle 1 of the Basic Principles on the Role of Lawyers. The Human Rights Committee has stated that 'all persons who are arrested must immediately have access to counsel.' See Concluding Observations of the Human Rights Committee: Georgia, UN Doc CCPR/C/79/Add.75, 5 May 1997, para. 27.

75. See Principle 17(1) of the Body of Principles for the Protection of All Persons

without delay after arrest.[76] If a person who is arrested, charged or detained does not have legal counsel of their own choice, he or she is entitled to have a lawyer assigned, whenever the interests of justice require it. If the person cannot afford to pay, counsel must be provided free of charge.[77] Legal representation is a crucial safeguard to enable detainees to effectively exercise their rights, in particular to challenge the legality of their detention. The Special Rapporteur on the Independence of Judges and Lawyers has stated that the presence of a lawyer is especially important during police interrogations, since the absence of legal counsel gives rise to the potential for abuse, particularly in a state of emergency where more serious criminal acts are involved.[78] In addition, access to counsel is crucial in order to protect individuals charged with a criminal offence from being compelled to testify against themselves or to confess guilt.[79]

The Task Force has noted that in cases involving national security individuals have been denied access to legal representation.[80] However, the observance of due process guarantees serves the interests of both detainees and the administration of justice. Principle 1 of the UN Basic Principles on the Role of Lawyers expressly establishes the right to assistance of a lawyer at all stages of criminal proceedings. Therefore legisla-

---

under Any Form of Detention or Imprisonment and Principle 5 of the Basic Principles on the Role of Lawyers.

76. According to Principle 7 of the Basic Principles on the Role of Lawyers persons arrested or detained must have 'prompt access to a lawyer, and in any case not later than forty-eight hours from the time of arrest or detention.' The UN Special Rapporteur on Torture has recommended that 'detainees be given access to legal counsel within 24 hours of detention.' See Report of the Special Rapporteur on Torture, UN Doc E/CN.4/1995/34, para. 926(d).

77. See Principle 17(2) of the Body of Principles for the Protection of All Persons under Any Form of Detention or Imprisonment and Principle 6 of the Basic Principles on the Role of Lawyers.

78. See Report of the Special Rapporteur on the Independence of Judges and Lawyers on the Mission to the United Kingdom of Great Britain and Northern Ireland, 5 March 1998, UN Doc. E/CN.4/1998/39Add. 4, para. 47.

79. The right not to be compelled to testify against themselves or to confess guilt is guaranteed by Article 14(3)(g) of the ICCPR, Article 8(2)(g) and 8(3) of the ACHR, and Principle 21 of the Body of Principles for the Protection of All Persons under Any Form of Detention or Imprisonment.

80. According to research conducted by Amnesty International and Human Rights Watch into the treatment of those detained in the United States following September 11, the FBI, before handing over detainees to the INS, questioned the detainees frequently without informing them of their right to a lawyer. Some are also said to have been denied their requests to contact a lawyer during initial questioning. See Amnesty International, United States of America: Amnesty International's Concerns Regarding Post September 11 Detentions in the USA, 14 March 2002, p. 16, and Human Rights Watch, United States: Presumption of Guilt: Human Rights Abuses of Post-September 11 Detainees, p. 35.

tion restricting access to counsel during any part of the investigative process violates this principle.[81]

4.6 FAIR TRIAL

4.6.1 Introduction

The right of a defendant to a fair trial must be ensured whatever the accusations and no matter how heinous the alleged crime. Some states have introduced special tribunals and removed fair trial rights to try suspected terrorists. There are a number of rights which collectively ensure a fair trial. States are therefore obliged to apply them all, without distinction as to the nature of the offence and whatever the forum.

4.6.2 The Right to a Fair Trial

The right to a fair trial is recognised across a range of regional and international treaties[82] and non-treaty standards.[83] It applies both to criminal and civil tribunals and incorporates a number of principles: the right to legal counsel; the right to equality of arms; the right to a public hearing; the right to appeal; the right to have adequate time and facilities to prepare a defence; the right to be tried without undue delay; the right to be present at trial; the right to call and examine witnesses; and the right not to be compelled to testify against oneself. Basic fair trial standards apply in any court, whether ordinary, special or military.[84]

The majority of these guarantees are derogable.[85] Nonetheless, the UN Human Rights Committee has expressed the view that 'the princi-

---

81. Section 52(4) of India's POTA guarantees the right of the arrested person 'to meet the legal practitioner representing him during the course of interrogation.' The same subsection, however, states that 'nothing in this sub-section shall entitle the legal practitioner to remain present throughout the period of interrogation.' The Task Force is of the opinion that POTA should be brought into consistence with the UN Basic Principles on the Role of Lawyers.

82. See Article 14 of the ICCPR, Article 8 of the ACHR, Article 6 of the ECHR, and Article 7 of the African Charter.

83. See Article 10 of the UDHR, the Basic Principles on the Independence of the Judiciary, the Basic Principles on the Role of Lawyers, and the Guidelines on the Role of Prosecutors.

84. See Human Rights Committee General Comment No. 13, para. 4.

85. The ACHR extends non-derogable status to 'judicial guarantees essential for the protection of [the non-derogable] rights.' See Article 27(2) of the AHCR. The Inter-American Court has ruled that the judicial guarantees of *habeas corpus* and *amparo* are non-derogable. See Inter-American Court of Human Rights, *Habeas Corpus in Emergency Situations*, *supra* note 16. The UN Commission on Human Rights has called on all states 'to establish a procedure such as *habeas corpus* or a similar procedure as a personal right not subject to derogation, including during states of emergency.' See UN Commission on Human Rights, Resolution 1994/32 on the question of arbitrary detention, 4 March 1994, UN Doc. E/CN.4/RES/1994/32, para. 16.

ples of legality and the rule of law require that fundamental requirements of fair trial must be respected during a state of emergency. Only a court of law may try and convict a person for a criminal offence. The presumption of innocence must be respected.'[86]

4.6.3 The Right to Equality Before the Law and Courts

Equality before the law[87] and the courts[88] is a universal entitlement. As the Human Rights Committee has specified 'once aliens are allowed to enter the territory of a State party they are entitled to the rights set out in the Covenant',[89] and therefore, *inter alia,* to the right to equality before the courts and tribunals.[90] Any attempt to treat suspected international terrorists differently on grounds of their nationality will call into question the legitimacy of the legal proceedings and could serve to undermine the credibility of the administration of justice.

4.6.4 The Presumption of Innocence

Everyone has the right to be presumed innocent and treated as innocent unless or until convicted according to law.[91] This right has been identified by the Human Rights Committee as a non-derogable component of the right to a fair trial[92] and as a principle of customary international law.[93]

There are a number of important consequences of the presumption of innocence. Rules of evidence and conduct of the trial must ensure that the burden of proof rests with the prosecution and that the accused has the benefit of doubt. Further, the presumption of innocence applies not only to treatment in court and the evaluation of evidence, but also to pretrial treatment.

Terrorist cases arouse strong public sentiments and attract media scrutiny, increasing the temptation for public officials to comment upon the presumed guilt of suspects. For obvious reasons it is imperative that

---

86. Human Rights Committee General Comment No. 29, para. 16.

87. See Articles 2(1), 3 and 26 of the ICCPR, Article 14 of the ECHR, Articles 1(1) and 24 of the ACHR, and Articles 2 and 3 of the African Charter.

88. See Article 14(1) of the ICCPR, Article 8(2) of the ACHR, and Article 5(a) of CERD.

89. See Human Rights Committee General Comment No. 15, para. 6.

90. *Id.*, para. 7.

91. This principle is found in Article 14(2) of the ICCPR, Article 8(2) of the ACHR, Article 6(2) of the ECHR, Article 7(1)(b) of the African Charter, Article 11 of the UDHR, Principle 36(1) of the Body of Principles for the Protection of All Persons under Any Form of Detention or Imprisonment, and Rule 84(2) of the Standard Minimum Rules for the Treatment of Prisoners. The presumption of innocence is also guaranteed in times of armed conflict. See Article 75(4)(d) of the First Additional Protocol to the Geneva Conventions.

92. See Human Rights Committee General Comment No. 29, para. 11.

93. See Human Rights Committee General Comment No. 24, para. 8.

not only judges and juries, but also all other public authorities, should refrain from prejudgement.[94]

4.6.5 The Right Not to Be Compelled to Testify Against Oneself or Confess Guilt

It is a principle of international law that defendants may not be compelled to testify against themselves or to confess guilt.[95] In the spirit of this principle, authorities are not permitted to engage in coercion, to disrespect the dignity of the individual, or to impose judicial sanctions to compel the accused to testify. Inherent in the right not to be compelled to testify against oneself or confess guilt is the right to remain silent during police questioning and at trial.[96] Whether adverse inferences can be drawn from the fact that the accused remains silent differs from jurisdiction to jurisdiction. In a case concerning a suspected terrorist the European Court of Human Rights held that, having regard to all the circumstances of the case, such as the weight attached to the silence and the degree of compulsion, adverse inferences may be drawn against the accused who remained silent.[97]

4.6.6 The Right to Be Tried by a Competent, Independent and Impartial Tribunal Established by Law

At the heart of the due process of law is the right of an individual to trial in a competent, independent and impartial tribunal.[98] So important is this right that the Human Rights Committee has confirmed it is 'absolute . . . [and] may suffer no exception.'[99] Even during armed conflict, prisoners of war may only be tried by tribunals that guarantee independence and impartiality.[100]

---

94. See Human Rights Committee General Comment No. 13, para. 7.

95. Article 14(3)(g) of the ICCPR, Articles 8(2)(g) and 8(3) of the ACHR, Principle 21 of the Body of Principles for the Protection of All Persons under Any Form of Detention or Imprisonment, and Article 67(1)(g) of the ICC Statute.

96. See the decision by the European Court of Human Rights in *John Murray v. United Kingdom*, Judgment (Merits and just satisfaction), 8 February 1996, para. 45. Even persons accused of genocide, other crimes against humanity and war crimes are guaranteed the right to silence. See Article 55(2)(b) of the ICC Statute.

97. See *John Murray v. United Kingdom, id.*, para. 47.

98. See Article 14(1) of the ICCPR, Article 8(1) of the ACHR, Article 6(1) of the ECHR, and Article 7(1) of the African Charter. See also Article 10 of the UDHR and the Basic Principles on the Independence of the Judiciary.

99. See Human Rights Committee, *González del Río v. Peru*, Communication No. 263/1987, 28 October 1992, UN Doc. CCPR/C/46/D/263/1987, para. 5.2.

100. See Articles 84 and 130 of the Third Geneva Convention and Article 75(4) of Additional Protocol 1.

The requirement that the court must be *competent* is interpreted to mean that it has, by law, jurisdiction to hear the case. The *independence* of the tribunal is understood to mean that the decision-makers must be free to decide matters before them without any interference or pressure from any branch of government. The two controlling principles of the independence of the judiciary are impartiality and fairness. The requirement of *impartiality* means that judges and jurors have no personal interest in the matter before them and harbour no preconceptions on the merits of the case. The principle of fairness obliges the judiciary to ensure that the proceedings are carried out fairly and the rights of the relevant parties are respected. Adherence to these standards is fundamental in maintaining respect for the administration of justice. These standards might be at a particular risk where, in a political climate generated by fear of terrorism, judges are subject to a host of pressures which might endanger their impartiality.[101]

Principles which have to be taken into account by states in order to secure the independence of the judiciary have been formulated in the UN Basic Principles on the Independence of the Judiciary, endorsed by the UN General Assembly in 1985. These include: protecting the judiciary from interference or influence from the executive branch, and safeguards such as the security of tenure for judges. Principle 5 of the Basic Principles states that everyone shall have the right to be tried by ordinary courts or tribunals using established legal procedures. According to this principle, tribunals that use procedures not in accordance with the established due process guarantees shall not be created to displace the jurisdiction belonging to the ordinary courts or judicial tribunals. This may be especially pertinent in cases involving suspected terrorists where states may wish, in the interests of national security, to circumvent certain of the due process rights. However, the ICCPR does not prevent states from creating special courts in exceptional circumstances provided they 'genuinely afford the full guarantees stipulated in Article 14.'[102]

Where special tribunals or military commissions are created to try suspected terrorists,[103] particular consideration must be given to the principle of impartiality. Military justice systems differ from country to country. In some legal systems the appointment of judges equates with the system used in civilian courts. In others, judges are appointed from within

---

101. See Chapter 1, Section 1.7.

102. Human Rights Committee General Comment No. 13, para. 4.

103. In the United States, military commissions have been established under a new Military Order. See Chapter 5, Section 5.4 for details. In Pakistan, special anti-terrorism courts haven been established under the Anti-Terrorism Act 1997. The Act was amended on 31 January 2002, providing for new courts consisting of a judge, a magistrate and an army officer. In India, Section 23 of POTA authorises the central government or a state government to constitute special anti-terrorism courts for certain notified areas or groups of cases.

the military by officers of superior rank. In the latter case, judges may be subject to 'command influence', implying that the impartiality of judges may be threatened by superior officers who have already indicated their own views on the case or who have the ability to influence the career of the appointed judge. A trial where the military judge is under command influence and is not therefore impartial would be a violation of the right to appear before an independent court.

4.6.7 The Right to a Public Hearing

Like the independence of the judiciary, the right to a public hearing protects the impartiality and fairness of court proceedings.[104] Public hearings have long been recognised as essential safeguards to the integrity of the justice system, serving to protect defendants from abuse of process. International human rights law provides for public court hearings in the determination of any criminal charges or 'rights and obligations in a suit at law.'[105] The presence of members of the public and media helps ensure that the judges and prosecutors carry out their functions with professionalism and impartiality. Public scrutiny may also facilitate accurate fact-finding, ensuring that witnesses sense a greater obligation to speak the truth.[106] In addition, public hearings serve to educate the public and inspire confidence in the judicial system. Conversely, where hearings are held *in camera*, there is a greater likelihood of allegations of unfairness. Such allegations could undermine the credibility of the administration of justice which is not in the interest of the parties concerned, including the victims of terrorism and their families.

In a number of narrowly defined exceptions, however, the court may decide that the hearing should be closed to the press and public. These exceptions include the protection of national security[107] and the interests of victims and witnesses,[108] which have to be balanced against the right of an accused to public trial. The European Court of Human Rights has stated that all the evidence must normally be produced at a public hearing, in the presence of the accused, with a view to adversarial argu-

---

104. The right to a public hearing is guaranteed by Article 14(1) of the ICCPR, Article 6(1) of the ECHR, and Article 8(5) of the ACHR. See also Articles 64(7) and 67(1) of the ICC Statute, Articles 10 and 11 of the UDHR, and Principle 36(1) of the Body of Principles for the Protection of All Persons under Any Form of Detention or Imprisonment.

105. See Article 14(1) of the ICCPR. The Human Rights Committee has broadly interpreted the term 'suit at law'. See Nowak, Manfred, *U.N. Covenant on Civil and Political Rights: CCPR Commentary*, 1993, p. 242.

106. Weissbrodt, International Trial Observers, 18 *Stanford Journal of International Law* 1 (1982), p. 19.

107. See Article 14(1) of the ICCPR and Article 6(1) of the ECHR.

108. For example, Article 20(1) of the ICTY Statute requires that due regard be given for the protection of victims and witnesses.

ment.[109] Thus, when a court closes a hearing to the public, it must do so only in the most exceptional situations.[110]

In terrorist cases, the protection of national security will normally only make it necessary to hold *in camera* those parts of a trial where sensitive information is presented.[111] Only in very exceptional situations should the entire trial be closed to the public.

In cases involving threats to the integrity of witnesses, the right to public trial may be restricted. The International Criminal Tribunal for the Former Yugoslavia concluded, when balancing these competing interests, that 'there is a growing acceptance in domestic jurisprudence of the need to protect the identity of victims and witnesses from the public when a special interest is involved.'[112] It is increasingly clear that states have a duty to organise their criminal proceedings in such a way that the interests of victims and witnesses are not unjustifiably imperilled.[113]

4.6.8 The Right to Defend Oneself in Person or Through Counsel

Those charged with a criminal offence must be afforded the right to defend themselves, in person or through a lawyer.[114] The assistance of counsel is a primary means of ensuring a fair trial. Given the importance

---

109. See *Van Mechelen and others v. the Netherlands*, Judgment (Merits and just satisfaction), 23 April 1997, para. 51.

110. In the United States, a number of immigration hearings have now been closed to the public, based on an internal memorandum by the Chief Immigration Judge of 21 September 2001, which requires immigration judges to hold 'special interest' cases *in camera*. See Internal Memorandum by the Chief Immigration Judge, *Cases Requiring Special Procedures: Internal Memorandum*, 21 September 2001, available at http://news.findlaw.com/hdocs/docs/aclu/creppy092101memo.pdf. Two district courts have ruled the closure of an immigration hearing to the public to be unconstitutional. See *Detroit Free Press et al. v. John Ashcroft et al.*, 195 F. Supp 2d 948 (E.D. Mich.) (3 April 2002), which was confirmed by the Court of Appeals for the Sixth Circuit in *Detroit Free Press et al. v. John Ashcroft et al.*, 2002 FED App. 0291P (6th Cir.) (26 August 2002). In the case of *North Jersey Media Group v. Ashcroft* another federal district court, upon a complaint by a media group, also declared the blanket secrecy to be unlawful. See *North Jersey Media Group v. Ashcroft*, 205 F. Supp. 2d 288 (D.N.J.) (28 May 2002). However, on appeal by the Justice Department the Court of Appeals for the 3rd Circuit reversed the district court's decision. See *North Jersey Media Group v. Ashcroft*, 308 F. 3d 198 (3rd Cir.) (8 October 2002).

111. Article 64(7) of the ICC Statute provides that certain proceedings can be held in closed session to protect confidential or sensitive information to be given in evidence.

112. See *Prosecutor v. Dusko Tadic A/K/A 'Dule'*, Case No. IT-94-1, *Decision on the prosecutor's motion requesting protective measures for victims and witnesses*, 10 August 1995, para. 39.

113. See the decision by the European Court of Human Rights in *Doorson v. The Netherlands*, Judgment (Merits), 26 March 1996, para. 70.

114. See Article 14(3)(d) of the ICCPR, Article 7(1)(c) of the African Charter, Article 8(2)(d) and (e) of the ACHR, and Article 6(3)(c) of the ECHR. See also Article 11(1) of the UDHR and Principle 1 of the Basic Principles on the Role of Lawyers. The right to have access to counsel also applies to prisoners of war. See Article 99 of the Third Geneva Convention.

of the relationship of trust between client and lawyer, it is expected that the defendant should be able to appoint counsel of choice.[115] But a number of recent anti-terrorist laws have restricted the right of the accused to choose their own legal representation.[116] The rationale behind these restrictions would appear to be the risk that defendants may pass information through legal counsel to terrorist contacts. Yet even with these concerns, the interests of security must still be balanced against the right of the accused to choose counsel, as counsel appointed on behalf of defendant may lack the requisite impartiality and independence. Where legal representatives are liable to come under 'command influence', this may be particularly true. For this reason, it is proposed that methods for selecting independent counsel be established, for example by enlisting the support and assistance of the relevant law society or bar association.

4.6.9   The Right to Confidential Communication with Counsel

Under international human rights law the authorities are required to respect the confidentiality of the communications and consultations between lawyers and their clients.[117] Further, lawyers should be able to perform all of their professional functions without intimidation, hindrance, harassment or improper interference.[118] The right to confidential communication with a lawyer applies equally to those who are arrested or detained, whether or not charged with a criminal offence.[119] To balance the right to confidentiality with public security, consultations may take place within sight, but not within the hearing, of law enforcement officials.[120]

---

115. See Article 14(3)(d) of the ICCPR, Article 7(1)(c) of the African Charter, Article 8(2)(d) of the ACHR, Article 6(3)(c) of the ECHR, and Principle 1 of the Basic Principles on the Role of Lawyers.

116. See, for example, the US Military Order and the DOD Order, which restrict this right in trials before the US military commissions. See Chapter 5, Section 5.5.5 for a detailed discussion.

117. See Article 14(3)(b) of the ICCPR. The Human Rights Committee has stated that this provision requires counsel to communicate with the accused in conditions giving full respect for the confidentiality of their communications. See General Comment No. 13, para. 9. See also Principle 22 of the Basic Principles on the Role of Lawyers, Rule 93 of the UN Standard Minimum Rules for the Treatment of Prisoners, and Rule 93 of the European Prison Rules.

118. See Human Rights Committee General Comment No. 13, para. 9, and Principle 16(a) of the Basic Principles on the Role of Lawyers.

119. See Principle 18 of the Body of Principles for the Protection of All Persons under Any Form of Detention or Imprisonment, and Principles 8 and 22 of the Basic Principles on the Role of Lawyers.

120. See Principle 18(4) of the Body of Principles for the Protection of All Persons under Any Form of Detention or Imprisonment, Rule 93 of the Standard Minimum Rules for the Treatment of Prisoners, and Principle 8 of the Basic Principles on the Role of Lawyers.

Sound legal advice is dependant on the disclosure of all relevant information. Clients concerned by potential breaches of confidentiality are less likely to be frank with their legal representatives. An absence of all the facts through fear of a lack of confidentiality is likely to hinder lawyers in effectively carrying out their professional duty.

Yet in cases involving threats to national security, authorities will be keen to obtain all information relevant to the protection of the community by whatever means. Currently, with increased fears of terrorism, rules protecting client/lawyer communication appear under greater threat. If there are ever any circumstances where there is a reasonable suspicion that counsel will divulge information in breach of national security, it is preferable for alternative counsel to be provided, and respect for the confidentiality of lawyer/client communications maintained.[121]

An issue connected to the right of confidentiality is whether lawyers are, under certain circumstances, obliged to reveal information given to them by their clients. In civil law systems, there is generally no such requirement. In common law countries, legal counsel are so required, albeit to a limited extent. The proposed Code of Professional Conduct for Counsel before the ICC provides that lawyers may reveal information, *inter alia*, to prevent a criminal act that may result in death or substantial bodily harm to any person.[122] Where in exceptional circumstances a state is considering imposing a duty on lawyers to reveal to the authorities information in terrorist cases, this must be subject to certain limitations: i) any such requirement must be agreed by organisations representing the legal profession, and ii) the duty only applies in the prevention of a terrorist act which may result in death or substantial bodily harm to any person.

4.6.10 The Right to Adequate Time and Facilities for the Preparation of the Defence

The right to adequate time and facilities to prepare a defence[123] includes the requirement that the defendant and their counsel must be granted access to appropriate information.[124] This is not an absolute right.

---

121. Contrary to this, a new rule of the US Department of Justice, published on 31 October 2001, authorises the Attorney General to direct the Bureau of Prisons to monitor all communications between persons in federal custody and their lawyers where he certifies 'that reasonable suspicion exists to believe that a particular inmate may use communications with attorneys or their agents to further or facilitate acts of violence or terrorism.' See Department of Justice Rule of 31 October 2001, 66 Fed. Reg. 55061 (Attorney General Order No. 2529-2001 amending 28 CFR Parts 500 and 501).

122. See Article 7(3)(d). The proposed Code of Conduct is available at http://www.ibanet.org/pdf/ICC_CoC_IBA.pdf

123. This right is guaranteed by Article 14(3)(b) of the ICCPR, Article 6(3)(b) of the ECHR, and Article 8(2)(c) of the ACHR.

124. See Principle 21 of the Basic Principles of the Role of Lawyers, which requires

In criminal proceedings, competing interests such as national security must be weighed against the rights of the accused.[125] However, restrictions on these rights are only permissible where strictly necessary. It is for the court to weigh up the rights of the defendant against the needs of national security after hearing argument for both the prosecution and the defence.[126]

As a general rule, where the defendant is denied access to evidence, access should nonetheless be granted to the defendant's counsel. But it is commonly the defendant who is in the best position to refute the evidence against them. Failure to disclose the prosecution's case may disrupt the equality of arms between the parties, to the detriment of a fair trial. Where the defendant has appointed counsel of choice, the authorities may be reluctant to reveal security sensitive information to the lawyer. It may be argued that this impasse can be alleviated by the appointment of special security vetted lawyers to handle cases involving national security. However, such action conflicts with the right of the defendant to appoint their counsel of choice. Ultimately, it will be for the court to weigh up the competing interests of the defendant's rights and national security.

4.6.11 The Right to Call and Examine Witnesses

A fundamental element of the right of defence is the right of the accused to call and to question witnesses.[127] This right also stems from the principle of equality of arms and guarantees to the accused 'the same legal powers of compelling the attendance of witnesses and of examining or cross-examining any witnesses as are available to the prosecution.'[128] However, the right to a fair trial must be balanced against the rights of victims and witnesses to be protected from intimidation and retaliation.

The right to call and examine witnesses includes the right of a defendant to know the identity of a witness. The identity of the witness may be crucial to the ability of defendants to refute the evidence against them. In some situations it may be the defendant alone whose knowledge of a witness's identity enables him or her to rebut the evidence. In cases involving suspected terrorists it might be argued that the protection of the personal integrity of a witness justifies keeping secret his or her identity. Nonetheless, only in the most exceptional circumstances may the court

---

the authorities to ensure lawyers have access to appropriate information, files and documents in their possession.

125. See the decision of the European Court of Human Rights in *Rowe and Davis v. United Kingdom,* Judgment (Merits and just satisfaction), 16 February 2000, para. 61.

126. *Id.*, paras. 61–66.

127. This right is guaranteed by Article 14(3)(e) of the ICCPR, Article 8(2)(f) of the ACHR, and Article 6(3)(d) of the ECHR. See also Article 67(1)(e) of the ICC Statute.

128. See Human Rights Committee General Comment No. 13, para. 12.

determine that the right of the defendant to examine witnesses be over-ridden by the calling of anonymous witnesses.

Authorities differ as to whether the calling of anonymous witnesses *necessarily* constitutes a violation of defendants' rights. The Human Rights Committee held that the system in Colombia, which provided for face-less judges and anonymous witnesses, did not comply with paragraph 3(b) and (e) of Article 14 of the ICCPR.[129] By contrast, the European Court of Human Rights has not ruled out the use of anonymous witnesses in all cases.[130] However, the European Court has stated that if the anonymity of prosecution witnesses is maintained, the position of the defence will be hampered. Accordingly, the handicaps under which the defence labours should be sufficiently counterbalanced by the procedures followed by the judicial authorities.[131] The court held that, as a general rule, the ECHR requires defendants to be given an adequate and proper opportunity to challenge and question prosecution witnesses, either when making statements or at a later stage.[132]

In the Statute of the ICTY, Article 22 provides for protective measures on behalf of witnesses.[133] Under Rule 75 of the ICTY Rules of Procedure and Evidence a judge or chamber is permitted to order appropriate measures for the privacy and protection of victims and witnesses, provided that the measures are consistent with the rights of the accused. In *Prosecutor v. Dusko Tadic* the Trial Chamber ruled that, subject to certain conditions, the identity of witnesses could be withheld and their evidence not given before the defendant.[134]

---

129. See *Concluding Observations by the Human Rights Committee: Colombia,* 5 May 1997, UN Doc. CCPR/C/79/Add.76, para. 21.

130. See the decision in *Doorson v. The Netherlands, supra* note 113, para. 69.

131. *Id.,* para. 72.

132. See *Kostovski v. The Netherlands,* Judgment (Merits), 20 November 1989, para. 41.

133. Similarly, Article 68 of the ICC Statute provides that the court shall take appropriate measures to protect the safety, physical and psychological well-being, dignity and privacy of witnesses.

134. See *Prosecutor v. Dusko Tadic A/K/A 'Dule', Decision on the prosecutor's motion requesting protective measures for victims and witnesses, supra* note 112, paras. 53–86. The conditions stipulated by the Trial Chamber are that i) there must be a real fear for the safety of the witness or his or her family, ii) the testimony of the particular witness must be important to the prosecutor's case, iii) the Trial Chamber must be satisfied that there is no *prima facie* evidence that the witness is untrustworthy, iv) the witness is not part of an effective witness protection programme, and v) any measures taken must be strictly necessary. *Id.,* paras. 62–66. The Trial Chamber went on to establish the following guidelines that must be followed to ensure a fair trial: i) the judges must be able to observe the demeanour of the witness in order to assess the reliability of the testimony, ii) the judges must be aware of the identity of the witness, in order to test the reliability of the witness, and iii) the defence must be allowed ample opportunity to question the witness on issues unrelated to his or her identity, or current whereabouts, such as how the witness was able to obtain the incrim-

The Task Force has considered the use of anonymous witnesses in terrorist cases and has concluded that the practice should be restricted to cases where there is a threat to the personal integrity of the witness, or his or her family, provided some or all of the following conditions are considered: i) the evidence must be important to the prosecutor's case; ii) no suitable witnesses protection schemes are available; iii) the witness in question is testifying as to facts which are verifiable and in part corroborated by other evidence; iv) the identity of the witness is not especially relevant to the ability of the defendant to cross-examine him or her; v) there is no *prima facie* evidence of the untrustworthiness of the witness; and vi) any protective measures should be strictly necessary.

4.6.12 The Rights of Victims and Witnesses

International human rights standards are being developed which grant victims and witnesses opportunities to play an active role in the administration of justice. The Declaration of Basic Principles of Justice for Victims of Crime and Abuse of Power states that victims are entitled to access the mechanisms of justice, and to prompt redress for harm they have suffered.[135] They should be informed of the proceedings and of the disposition of their cases and be provided with proper assistance throughout the legal process.[136] They should be allowed to present their views and concerns at appropriate stages of the proceedings where their personal interests are affected.[137] States should ensure that inconvenience to victims is kept to a minimum, their privacy is protected, and safety from intimidation and retaliation is guaranteed. These protections should be extended to families of victims, and those testifying on their behalf.[138] In the context of criminal proceedings against suspected terrorists, measures to protect victims and witnesses gain special importance. Such measures taken by courts may include closing all or parts of the proceedings to the public and allowing the presentation of evidence by electronic or other special means.

Other, more established, standards protecting the personal integrity of victims and witnesses have been developed by the European Court of

---

inating information. *Id.*, para. 71. However, in a dissenting opinion, Judge Stephen held that the ICTY Statute did not intend that the defence and the accused should be denied the right to see and hear witnesses give evidence as this would adversely affect the right of the accused to a fair trial. See *Prosecutor v. Dusko Tadic A/K/A 'Dule', Separate Opinion of Judge Stephen on the Prosecutor's Motion Requesting Protective Measures for Victims and Witnesses*, 10 August 1995.

135. See Article 4 of the *Declaration of Basic Principles of Justice for Victims of Crime and Abuse of Power*, adopted by UN General Assembly Resolution 40/34 of 29 November 1985.

136. *Id.*, Article 6(c).

137. *Id.*, Article 6(b).

138. *Id.*, Article 6(d).

Human Rights, which has held that substantive provisions of the ECHR, such as those protecting life, liberty and security, and the right to privacy, imply that states should organise their criminal proceedings in such a way that the interests of witnesses in general, and those of testifying victims in particular, are not imperilled without justification.[139] The Statute of the ICC includes several provisions designed to ensure the protection of witnesses before the new court: Article 43(6) of the ICC Statute provides for the establishment of a Victims and Witnesses Unit, which will provide protective measures and security arrangements, counselling and other appropriate assistance for witnesses and victims. Article 68(1) instructs the Court to 'take appropriate measures to protect the safety, physical and psychological well-being, dignity and privacy of victims and witnesses.'

However, the rights of victims and witnesses to be protected from intimidation and retaliation have to be balanced against the right of the accused to a fair trial. As the European Court of Human Rights has stated, the right to the fair administration of justice requires that any measures restricting the rights of the defence must be strictly necessary.[140] The ICC Statute attempts to balance the rights of witnesses and defendants by stating that '[t]he Trial Chamber shall ensure that a trial is fair and expeditious and is conducted with full respect for the rights of the accused and due regard for the protection of victims and witnesses.'[141] It further provides that none of the witness protection measures shall be prejudicial to, or inconsistent with, the rights of the accused and a fair and impartial trial.[142] Balancing these sets of fair trial rights is particularly relevant in the context of the right to a public hearing, and the right to examine witnesses.

4.6.13 Protection of Journalists' Sources

Where a journalist is in possession of information relating to terrorist activities, the question arises as to whether he or she has a duty to disclose the source and may be compelled to testify in any terrorist trial regardless of the circumstances.

The protection of journalists' sources is one of the basic conditions for press freedom. In *Goodwin v. the United Kingdom* the European Court of Human Rights held that '[w]ithout such protection, sources may be deterred from assisting the press in informing the public on matters of public interest. As a result the vital public-watchdog role of the press may be undermined and the ability of the press to provide accurate and reli-

---

139. See *Doorson v The Netherlands, supra* note 113, para. 70.
140. See *Van Mechelen and others v The Netherlands, supra* note 109, para. 58.
141. See Article 64(2).
142. See Article 68(1).

able information may be adversely affected.'[143] Consequently, the court concluded that an order requiring a journalist to reveal his source violated Article 10 of the ECHR.[144]

The Task Force believes that there are inherent dangers in enacting an automatic duty of disclosure of information relating to acts of terrorism, preferring that a balance be struck between the protection of the freedom of media organisations and national security in all cases. By carefully weighing up these competing interests, the dangers to journalists of exposing their sources can be taken into account. If journalists are forced to be witnesses and required to disclose the names of confidential sources in cases against terrorist suspects, they might be put at risk of greater danger and it would become more difficult for them to conduct terrorism-related investigations. Thus, journalists might find themselves in a similar situation as humanitarian workers who enjoy a qualified privilege before the ICC.[145]

The Appeals Chamber of the ICTY, aware of the requirement to strike a balance, held that society's interest in protecting the integrity of the newsgathering process was particularly important in the case of war correspondents, as they play 'a vital role in bringing to the attention of the international community the horrors and reality of conflict.'[146] The case concerned the Washington Post reporter Jonathan Randal who refused to give evidence about an interview with the Bosnian Serb Radoslav Drdjanin. The Appeals Chamber took the view that 'compelling war correspondents to testify before the International Tribunal on a routine basis may have a significant impact upon their ability to obtain information and thus their ability to inform the public on issues of general concern.'[147] Consequently, the Appeals Chamber set aside the subpoena against Randal, reasoning that war correspondents may only be compelled to testify if the evidence sought is 'direct and important to the core issues of the case' and is not reasonably available from other sources.[148]

The Task Force believes that the deliberations of the ICTY Appeals Chamber could also have some relevance in terrorist trials. An approach which balances the interests of public security on the one hand and protection of the personal integrity of journalists and the role of the media on the other, is to be preferred over measures requiring automatic disclosure.

---

143. See *Goodwin v. the United Kingdom,* Judgment (Merits and just satisfaction), 27 March 1996, para. 39.

144. *Id.,* para. 46.

145. See Rule 73(4)–(6) of the ICC Rules of Procedure and Evidence.

146. See *Prosecutor v. Radoslav Brdjanin and Momir Talic,* Decision on Interlocutory Appeal, 11 December 2002, para. 36.

147. *Id.,* para. 44.

148. *Id.,* paras. 48–49.

4.6.14 The Right to Appeal

The right of those convicted of a criminal offence to a review of the conviction and sentence by a higher tribunal is guaranteed by a number of human rights treaties[149] and has been confirmed by the Human Rights Committee.[150] The right to a fair and public trial must be observed during appeal proceedings. Its components include, *inter alia*, the right to counsel, the right to equality of arms, and the right to a hearing before a competent, independent and impartial tribunal established by law within a reasonable time.[151] The Inter-American Commission has stated that appeals to courts which lack independence are incompatible with the right to a fair trial.[152]

Where special tribunals are created to try suspected terrorists, in order for there to be a meaningful appeal, a higher independent tribunal applying all fair trial standards must be established.

4.7 ASYLUM

Security Council Resolution 1373 requires states to ensure that those who have participated in or planned terrorist acts are not granted refugee status.[153] There are concerns that states could interpret this to the detriment of protections under the 1951 Convention relating to the Status of Refugees (Refugee Convention).

The cornerstone of the system of international refugee protection is the right of refugees not to be returned to a country where their lives or freedoms are threatened (the principle of *non-refoulement*). This principle is enshrined in Article 33(1) of the Refugee Convention[154] and is now generally recognised as being part of customary international law.[155] The principle of *non-refoulement*, while central to refugee law, has also

---

149. See Article 14(5) of the ICCPR, Article 8(2)(h) of the ACHR, Article 7(1)(a) of the African Charter, and Article 2 of Protocol No. 7 to the ECHR.

150. See *Salgar de Montejo v. Colombia*, Communication No. 64/1979, 24 March 1982, UN Doc. CCPR/C/15/D/64/1979, paras. 10.4 and 11.

151. See the decision by the European Court of Human Rights in *Melin v. France*, Judgment (Merits), 22 June 1993, para. 23, where the court, although finding no violation of the ECHR, noted that certain fair trial rights apply during appeal proceedings.

152. See Inter-American Commission on Human Rights, Report on the Situation of Human Rights in Chile, OEA/Ser.L/V/II.66, Doc. 17, 9 September 1985, Chapter VIII.

153. See UN Security Council Resolution 1373, adopted 28 September 2001, see Appendix IV, para. 3(f).

154. Article 33(1) states: 'No Contracting State shall expel or return ('refouler') a refugee in any manner whatsoever to the frontiers of territories where his life or freedom would be threatened on account of his race, religion, nationality, membership of a particular social group or political opinion.'

155. See Goodwin-Gill, Guy, *International Law and the Movement of Persons between States*, Clarendon Press (1978), pp. 141–142 and 219.

become part of general human rights law. For example, the Convention against Torture prevents the expulsion, return or extradition of a person to a state 'where there are substantial grounds for believing that he would be in danger of being subjected to torture.'[156]

Contained within the Universal Declaration of Human Rights (UDHR) is the provision that '[e]veryone has the right to seek and to enjoy in other countries asylum from persecution.'[157] This right might be jeopardised where individuals cannot access fair and impartial asylum determination procedures, due to visa requirements, security checks, and other barriers to entry that effectively prevent persons from applying for asylum. Yet it is incumbent upon states to give substantive consideration to the individual claims of those seeking refuge within their territory. Thus, automatic bars to accessing an asylum procedure, even of suspected criminals, for example by means of rejection at border crossings, without the provision of access to an asylum procedure, could result in *refoulement*.[158]

At the same time, the Refugee Convention makes extensive provision for national security and public order concerns. It is thus difficult to identify a security issue relating to refugees and asylum-seekers that cannot be addressed in a rights-sensitive way through application of the Convention. Several provisions of the Convention are of particular importance to security and public order issues. First, the Convention permits the determining state to exclude perpetrators of gross human rights violations and serious non-political crimes from protection under the refugee regime.[159]

---

156. See Article 3 of the Convention against Torture and Other Cruel, Inhuman or Degrading Treatment or Punishment. Similarly, the Human Rights Committee, in General Comment No. 20, para. 9, has held that 'States parties must not expose individuals to the danger of torture or cruel, inhuman or degrading treatment or punishment upon return to another country by way of their extradition, expulsion or refoulement.' The European Court of Human Rights held in a case concerning an alleged Sikh terrorist seeking asylum in the United Kingdom that when there are substantial grounds for believing that the individual in question would face a real risk of being subjected to treatment contrary to the prohibition on torture and other cruel and inhuman treatment if removed to another state, his or her activities, however undesirable or dangerous, cannot be a material consideration. The protection afforded by Article 3 of the ECHR was thus wider than the one provided by the Refugee Convention. See *Chahal v. United Kingdom*, Judgment (Merits and just satisfaction), 15 November 1996, para. 80.

157. See Article 14(1) of the UDHR.

158. The United Nations High Commissioner for Refugees (UNHCR) has stated: 'All persons have the right to seek asylum and to undergo individual refugee status determination. Each claim, even where there is a suspicion of involvement in grave criminal acts, must be determined on its own merits, and not against negative and discriminatory presumptions deriving from the nationality, ethnic origin or religious faith of the claimant. The refugee definition, properly applied, should lead to the exclusion of those responsible for serious criminal, including terrorist, acts.' See UNHCR, *Addressing Security Concerns without Undermining Refugee Protection: UNHCR's perspective*, 29 November 2001, para. 6.

159. Article 1(F) states that refugee status cannot be granted to any person with

Second, while Article 31 of the Refugee Convention states that refugees shall not be penalised on account of their illegal entry, it is recognised that detention may be resorted to if necessary for reasons of national security or public order.[160] Finally, once a refugee has been recognised and admitted to the host state, protection against expulsion can be withdrawn in cases where he or she has committed a serious crime, including terrorist acts, in the territory of the country of refuge.[161]

However, one of the principles underlying the Refugee Convention is the presumption of inclusion on the basis of a full review of all the relevant facts surrounding an individual's asylum claim before evidence is adduced of past criminal activity that would exclude an individual from being granted refugee status: the principle of 'inclusion before exclusion.'[162] There might be a temptation for governments to reverse this approach in the case of suspected terrorists.[163]

---

respect to whom 'there are serious reasons for considering that: (a) he has committed a crime against peace, a war crime, or a crime against humanity, as defined in the international instruments drawn up to make provision in respect of such crimes; (b) he has committed a serious non-political crime outside the country of refuge prior to his admission to that country as a refugee; (c) he has been guilty of acts contrary to the purposes and principles of the United Nations.' From the perspective of international terrorism, Article 1F(b) is central. 'Serious non-political crimes' would generally encompass acts of terrorism as defined in relevant international conventions, notwithstanding any political motives behind such acts. This follows from the fact that the extradition clauses of these conventions have abolished the political offence exemption. Moreover, especially violent acts of terrorism are likely to fail the proportionality test used in many jurisdictions to define political offences. See UNHCR, *Addressing Security Concerns without Undermining Refugee Protection,* *supra* note 158, para. 15. Moreover, the September 11 attacks on the World Trade Center arguably constituted a crime against humanity and therefore those involved in the attacks would fall within the scope of Article 1F(a).

160. See Executive Committee of the UNHCR, Conclusion No. 44, *Detention of Refugees and Asylum-Seekers*, 13 October 1986.

161. Article 32(1) of the Refugee Convention states that states parties are allowed to expel a refugee lawfully in their territory on grounds of national security or public order. Article 33(2) provides an exception to the principle of *non-refoulement* by stating that this principle may not be claimed 'by a refugee whom there are reasonable grounds for regarding as a danger to the security of the country in which he is, or who, having been convicted by a final judgement of a particularly serious crime, constitutes a danger to the community of that country.'

162. See UNHCR, *Handbook on Procedures and Criteria for Determining Refugee Status under the 1951 Convention and the 1967 Protocol relating to the Status of Refugees*, HCR/IP/4/Eng/REV.1, January 1992, para. 141. See also UNHCR Standing Committee, *UNHCR Note on the Exclusion Clauses*, 30 May 1997, EC/47/SC/CRP.29, in particular paras. 4–6 and 14–15, and Lisbon Expert Roundtable, *Summary Conclusions—Exclusion from Refugee Status*, 30 May 2001, EC/GC/01/2Track/1.

163. Section 33(1) of the British ATCSA authorises the Secretary of State to certify that a person is not entitled to the protection of the *non-refoulement* principle by virtue of the application of Article 1(F) or 33(2) of the Refugee Convention, and because removal from the UK would be conducive to the public good. Where such a certificate is made, the

When a state is considering applying the exclusion clause to an individual asylum-seeker it will need to strike a balance between the nature of the offence and the degree of feared persecution.[164] Where it is determined that the exclusion clause applies, the asylum-seeker can legitimately be returned to his or her home country. An exception to this is where it is established that an asylum-seeker on being returned to their country of origin will face torture and possibly other ill-treatment.[165] In such circumstances expulsion would not be possible.

Whilst it is legitimate for states to consider excluding suspected terrorists from the refugee system, common sense dictates that persons with terrorist intent are unlikely to bring themselves under the scrutiny of the authorities by applying for asylum. Yet the focus on refugee protection schemes in the fight against terrorism has the potential to undermine the principal aims of the Refugee Convention and to cause distrust amongst host communities.

CONCLUSION

Human rights treaties allow for a balance to be struck between the rights of individuals and protecting the wider community. Further, during extreme threats to the nation many treaties permit the suspension of certain human rights to the extent strictly required. However, governments might be tempted to use threats to national security to justify human rights restrictions that go further than required and may fail to respect fundamental guarantees that can not be derogated from under any circumstances. Moreover, there is a danger that restrictions of human rights applied to suspected terrorists will be in place for longer than strictly necessary, allowing such procedures to be embedded in the general fabric of the law. This in turn could lead to the expansion of such restrictive measures to other areas of criminal law.

Procedural rights such as those protecting from arbitrary arrest and unfair trial are particularly at risk when a state faces terrorist threats. Whilst human rights treaties allow for the restriction of procedural rights, certain fundamental guarantees must be respected at all times. Failure to apply these fundamental protections may result in miscarriages of justice. Such an outcome is of great concern for the following reasons: i)

Special Immigration Appeals Commission (SIAC) must, in deliberating upon the asylum appeal, consider only statements made in that certificate, and is not able to consider whether there exists a sustainable claim to refugee status on the basis of a well-founded fear of persecution. See Sections 33(3)–(5) of the ATCSA. In effect, this provision empowers the Secretary of State to make a determination that an individual does not have the right to substantive consideration of his or her application for asylum if he considers this person a danger to national security.

164. See UNHCR Handbook, *supra* note 162, para. 156.

165. See *supra* note 156.

innocent individuals will be convicted; ii) the perpetrators will go unpunished; iii) the victims and their relatives will be denied justice; and iv) the credibility of the justice system will be undermined.

Restrictions of substantive rights, such as the freedom of association and assembly, might be used by states to suppress legitimate political dissent. Not only could such action generate greater animosity towards the state, it also constitutes a blunt instrument which may have little effect in combating threats to national security. Similarly, overbroad measures which target asylum-seekers or citizens of certain states may be both discriminatory and ineffective.

Yet these concerns do not necessarily conflict with the ability of states to take preventative and effective measures to protect themselves from threats to national security, including terrorism. The Task Force believes that in order to both respect human rights and be effective, any anti-terrorist activity should be based on sound investigative and intelligence gathering methods, thus promoting a targeted approach over sweeping measures. Such an approach would require, amongst other things, sufficient resourcing of relevant investigative agencies, international cooperation in information sharing and penal matters, and, where necessary, international technical assistance.[166]

Recommendations

1) When states intend not to comply with certain obligations contained within human rights treaties to which they are parties, they can only do so for reasons of national emergency and provided the criteria for derogating are observed. Further, the suspension of human rights should be regularly reviewed and must be limited in time.

2) Where states introduce specific terrorist offences these must be defined with precision and clarity.

3) For profiling to be effective and not fall foul of the prohibition on discrimination, it must operate under more detailed criteria than either race, religion, or citizenship alone.

4) All restrictions of substantive human rights must be expressly provided by law, must be necessary and proportionate, and must not exclude the possibility of judicial review.

5) At all times arrested or detained individuals must be accorded the right to promptly challenge the actions of the state before a court. Nobody should be held in administrative detention indefinitely.

6) Even during states of emergency the fundamental principles of the right to a fair trial must be respected. This necessitates at

---

166. See Chapter 7 for a detailed discussion of these issues.

the least protecting the presumption of innocence, the right to be tried by an independent and impartial court, access to counsel and the right to appeal. Without providing these rights a state runs the risk of discrediting its own justice system. Upholding these fair trial guarantees is even more crucial in cases attracting the death penalty.

7) Even those suspected of terrorist acts must be granted access to counsel at the earliest opportunity to help ensure due process rights are guaranteed.

8) States must give substantive consideration to individual asylum claims of all refugees, including those seeking entry to claim asylum and those suspected of crimes, including terrorism.

CHAPTER 5

TERRORISM AND INTERNATIONAL HUMANITARIAN LAW

5.1 INTRODUCTION

When encountering terrorist groups in an armed conflict situation, states may be tempted not to apply the standards of international humanitarian law to the fighters captured. Terrorist organisations commonly do not apply the laws and customs of war and thus opposing armed forces may feel reluctant to apply standards of treatment that will not be reciprocated. There may, in addition, be a sense that, as perpetrators of criminal acts, terrorists have no right to be treated in accordance with international humanitarian law.

International humanitarian law consists of a number of treaties negotiated over more than a century,[1] many provisions of which are now recognised as customary law.[2] All states are therefore bound by obligations

---

1. International humanitarian law (IHL) is the body of rules which, during armed conflict, protects people who are not or are no longer participating in the hostilities and restricts the means and methods of warfare. Its central purpose is to limit and prevent human suffering in times of armed conflict. The rules are to be observed not only by governments and their armed forces, but also by armed opposition groups and any other parties to a conflict. The four Geneva Conventions of 1949 and their two Additional Protocols of 1977 are the principal instruments of humanitarian law. The Geneva Conventions are: the Convention for the Amelioration of the Condition of the Wounded and Sick in Armed Forces in the Field; the Convention for the Amelioration of the Condition of Wounded, Sick and Shipwrecked Members of Armed Forces at Sea; the Convention Relative to the Treatment of Prisoners of War; and the Convention Relative to the Protection of Civilian Persons in Time of War. The two Additional Protocols are: the Protocol Additional to the Geneva Conventions relating to the Protection of Victims of International Armed Conflict (Protocol I) and the Protocol Additional to the Geneva Conventions relating to the Protection of Victims of Non-International Armed Conflict (Protocol II).

2. For a discussion of international humanitarian law as customary see Meron, *Human Rights and Humanitarian Norms as Customary Law*, Clarendon (1985). See also Greenwood, Customary Law Status of the 1977 Additional Protocols in *Humanitarian Law of Armed Conflict: Challenges Ahead*, Delissen and Tanja (Eds.) Martinus Nijhoff Publishers (1991), 93.

arising from customary law[3] and those treaties to which they are a party. Thus, when a state as powerful as the United States professes to misgivings in applying international humanitarian law, as it has done over the captured Taliban and al-Qaeda fighters held in Guantánamo Bay, Cuba, and elsewhere, this is naturally subject to debate and criticism. Yet the United States is not alone in questioning the applicability of the Geneva Conventions or the humanitarian law regime.[4] Neither is it the only country accused of violating international humanitarian law.[5]

In support of its position, the United States has argued that aspects of international humanitarian law are no longer relevant in the current 'war against terrorism' and that those captured are highly dangerous individuals who must be brought to justice.[6] However, international humanitarian law was designed to apply to armed conflict however it is conducted and, notably, prohibits any form of terrorism committed in an armed conflict.[7] In the

---

3. However, states which have persistently objected to a rule which ultimately becomes customary international law are not bound by it.

4. For example, during its military involvement in Lebanon, Israel opposed granting prisoner of war (POW) status to any of its alleged terrorist detainees on the basis that they were not entitled. Their subsequent detention at various centres under the Israel defence forces was subject to international criticism as it failed to abide by fundamental standards of humanity. See Roberts, Counter-terrorism, Armed Force and the Laws of War, 44 *Survival*, journal of the International Institute for Strategic Studies, Spring 2002, pp. 13–14.

5. The Russian armed forces are accused of having violated humanitarian law in the internal armed conflict in Chechnya. See Crimes of War Project, *Chechnya and the Laws of War*, October 1999, available at http://www.crimesofwar.org/expert/chechnya.html and, for example, Human Rights Watch, *Civilian Killings in Staropromyslovski District of Grozny*, 1 February 2000. Iraq allegedly used poison gas in the Iraq-Iran war. See Stockholm International Peace Research Institute, Robinson and Goldblat, *Chemical Warfare in the Iraq-Iran War*, May 1984. French forces are accused of having committed war crimes and crimes against humanity in the Algerian war in the 1950s. See Human Rights Watch, *France Must Investigate Alleged War Crimes*, 16 May 2001. Members of the Italian contingent of the multi-national task force operating in Somalia allegedly tortured Somali prisoners in 1993. See Amnesty International, AI Index EUR 01/06/97, *Concerns in Europe: January–June 1997*, 1 September 1997.

6. The United States President's press spokesman, Ari Fleischer said: 'So as this nation, the United States, deals with a new type of war, we're also dealing with a new type of detention system—people in Cuba. And that means it's much more complicated than a simple reading of the Geneva Convention would imply. And that's why, frankly, I think it's a healthy process that's underway, where the lawyers are having a discussion about exactly how do you apply—[sic]the Geneva Convention was written in a very different era, following world war—to apply to the war on terrorism, where people don't wear uniforms, they are unlawful combatants and they come from 30 different nations, not any one recognized nation with whom the United States is fighting a war.' See White House press briefing of 28 January 2002.

7. The right to use force and commit acts of violence is confined to the armed forces of the parties to a conflict against other members of armed forces and military targets. Further there is no right to use unlimited means and methods of warfare. International humanitarian law specifically protects civilians from terrorism. Article 33 of the Fourth

words of the President of the International Committee of the Red Cross (ICRC), '[t]he Geneva Conventions and their Additional Protocols are not an obstacle to Justice. They merely require that due process of law be applied in dealing with alleged offenders.'[8] Indeed, they call for the prosecution of those (including terrorists) that commit grave breaches of the Geneva Conventions and do not prevent prosecution for acts committed prior to the hostilities.[9] It is the view of the Task Force that international humanitarian law remains as applicable and important today as it was prior to September 11. Suggestions that international humanitarian law is no longer relevant to situations involving terrorists, together with the failure to abide by its principles, only serve to undermine the binding force of international humanitarian law.

Similarly, when bringing suspected terrorists, whether captured in armed conflict or not, to trial, states appear to be reluctant to grant them the full range of fair trial rights under international humanitarian law and human rights law. A number of states have established special or military tribunals which have jurisdiction to try civilians for crimes against national security. Often exceptional procedures, restricting the normal fair trial rights of the defendant, apply before these tribunals. Further, the establishment of special or military tribunals may raise concerns as to their independence and impartiality.

One of the most recent, and most disputed, examples of the establishment of such tribunals was the decision of the United States administration to set up Military Commissions to try certain civilians as a reaction

---

Geneva Convention prohibits 'all measures of intimidation or of terrorism.' Article 51 (2) of Additional Protocol I, which deals with the protection of the civilian population, similarly provides that '[a]cts or threats of violence the primary purpose of which is to spread terror among the civilian population are prohibited.'

8.   Statement by the President of the International Committee of the Red Cross, Jakob Kellenberger, to the 59th Annual session of the UN Commission on Human Rights, Geneva 18 March 2003.

9.   See Articles 129 and 130 of the Third Geneva Convention, and Articles 146 and 147 of the Fourth Geneva Convention. Article 130 of the Third Geneva Convention defines 'grave breaches' as 'any of the following acts, if committed against persons or property protected by the Convention: wilful killing, torture or inhuman treatment, including biological experiment, wilfully causing great suffering or serious injury to body or health, compelling a prisoner of war to serve in the forces of the hostile Power, or wilfully depriving a prisoner of war of the rights of fair and regular trial prescribed in this Convention.' Article 147 of the Fourth Geneva Convention defines 'grave breaches' as 'any of the following acts, if committed against persons or property protected by the Convention: wilful killing, torture or inhuman treatment, including biological experiments, wilfully causing great suffering or serious injury to body or health, unlawful deportation or transfer or unlawful confinement of a protected person, compelling a protected person to serve in the forces of a hostile Power, or wilfully depriving a protected person of the rights of fair and regular trial prescribed in the present Convention, taking of hostages and extensive destruction and appropriation of property, not justified by military necessity and carried out unlawfully and wantonly.'

to the events of September 11. The military order entitled 'Detention, Treatment, and Trial of Certain Non-Citizens in the War Against Terrorism'[10] (Military Order), issued by the United States President on 13 November 2001, stipulates that suspected al-Qaeda members or other international terrorists may be tried by these commissions. The Task Force is concerned that any forthcoming trials before the Military Commissions could fail to meet a number of due process guarantees found both in international humanitarian law and human rights law. The Task Force believes that the United States as the most powerful country in the world should be encouraged to set an example to other states by adhering to the relevant international standards when trying suspected terrorists.

5.2 STATUS OF CAPTURED COMBATANTS

International law recognises a distinction between lawful and unlawful combatants.[11] The former are those who have a legal right to take part in hostilities, such as members of the armed forces. Upon capture they must be granted prisoner of war (POW) status and treated in accordance with the Third Geneva Convention, which regulates the treatment of POWs. Lawful combatants may not be prosecuted for taking part in a conflict, unless they have committed a violation of the Geneva Conventions. By contrast, unlawful or illegal combatants are fighters who are not members of the armed forces or any voluntary or militia corps belonging to a party to the conflict, and as such have no right to participate in the conflict. Whilst they do not qualify for POW status, the Fourth Geneva Convention will nonetheless apply.[12] Unlike lawful combatants, the authorities are free to prosecute them for taking part in a conflict and for any crimes that may have been committed in that regard. They are, however, entitled to the judicial guarantees set out within the Fourth Geneva Convention should they be prosecuted for their actions.[13] Thus all those who take part in an international armed conflict, including fighters described as 'unlawful', 'illegal' or 'terrorist', cannot be detained without reference to the Geneva Conventions.

To help distinguish between lawful and unlawful combatants, Article 4(A) of the Third Geneva Convention sets out the categories of persons who, having fallen into the hands of the enemy, qualify as POWs. They include members of the armed forces of a party to the conflict, including members of militias or volunteer corps forming part of such armed

---

10. 66 Fed. Reg. 57,833, 16 November 2001.

11. These terms are often also referred to as 'privileged' and 'unprivileged' combatants.

12. See Gasser, 84 *ICRC Review*, September 2002, 547, p.566. The Fourth Geneva Convention applies to 'protected persons', defined as those who find themselves in the hands of a party to the conflict of which they are not nationals.

13. *Id.*

forces.[14] Members of other militias or volunteer corps belonging to a party to the conflict are also included, subject to the conditions that they: (i) are commanded by a person responsible for his subordinates; (ii) have a distinctive sign recognisable at distance; (iii) carry their arms openly; and (iv) conduct their operations in accordance with the laws and customs of war.[15]

The classification of combatants must be made strictly in accordance with Article 4 and will not be dependant upon any alternative designation by a state. Further, where lawful combatants have carried out acts such as the targeting of civilians or protected property, prohibited under international humanitarian law, their classification will not be altered, although they should be held accountable for their acts as grave breaches of the Geneva Conventions.

In any situation where there is uncertainty as to the status of captured combatants, Article 5 of the Third Geneva Convention applies. This article states:

> 'Should any doubt arise as to whether persons, having committed a belligerent act and having fallen into the hands of the enemy, belong to any of the categories enumerated in Article 4, such persons shall enjoy the protection of the present Convention until such time as their status has been determined by a competent tribunal.'

The classification of those captured and held at Guantánamo Bay (and elsewhere) by United States forces, following the military campaign in Afghanistan, has been the subject of much debate.[16] In October 2001

---

14. Article 4(A)(1). Members of regular armed forces are entitled to prisoner of war status even if they belong to a party not recognised by their adversaries; see Article 4(A)(3).

15. Article 4(A)(2).

16. In a press release of 8 February 2002, the International Committee of the Red Cross (ICRC) acknowledged that there were 'divergent views between the United States and the ICRC on the procedures which apply on how to determine that the persons detained are not entitled to prisoner of war status.' ICRC Press release, 9 February 2002 available at http://www.icrc.org/Web/Eng/siteeng0.nsf/iwpList74/26D99836026EA80DC1256B6600610C90. On 16 January 2003 the UN High Commissioner for Human Rights issued a statement in which she reminded the detaining powers of their obligation to treat prisoners humanely and expressed the view that where the status of the detainees is disputed a competent tribunal should make the determination. Statement available at http://www.unog.ch/news/documents/newsen/hr02004e.htm. The United States' decision was also considered by the Inter-American Commission on Human Rights, which ordered the US to 'take the urgent measures necessary to have the legal status of the detainees at Guantánamo Bay determined by a competent tribunal.' The Commission considered that in the absence of clarification of the legal status of the detainees, 'the rights and protections to which they may be entitled under international or domestic law cannot be said to be the subject of effective legal protection by the State.' See Annual Report 2002, Inter-American Commission

the United States forces, assisted by the armed forces from other states, launched military operations in Afghanistan, attacking the armed forces of the Taliban regime. The Taliban controlled all but a small part of Afghanistan at that time and was thus its effective government. In these circumstances, there was an international armed conflict between the United States (and its allies) and Afghanistan.[17] Consequently, international humanitarian law, and in particular the four Geneva Conventions, to which both the United States and Afghanistan are party, became applicable. In the course of the engagement the United States army captured a considerable number of combatants belonging to the Taliban and al-Qaeda. On 10 January 2002, United States forces began flying suspected Taliban and al-Qaeda fighters to the US Naval Station at Guantánamo Bay, Cuba.[18] By May 2003 there were around 680 detainees in Guantánamo.[19] As they were almost all captured during an international armed conflict, questions arose as to their legal status and the protection to which they might be entitled. The government of the United States determined that: i) the Geneva Convention Relative to the Treatment of Prisoners of War (the 'Third Geneva Convention') applies to the Taliban detainees, but not to the al-Qaeda detainees; ii) neither the Taliban nor the al-Qaeda detainees are entitled to prisoner of war (POW) status[20]; iii) nevertheless, all Taliban and al-Qaeda detainees in Guantánamo Bay are to be treated humanely and consistent with the principles of the Third Geneva Convention.[21]

Given that the Taliban government was in effective control of most of Afghanistan it seems reasonable to conclude that the Taliban soldiers represented the armed forces of Afghanistan. Therefore upon capture they would be entitled to POW status. However, the United States government did not take this view, claiming instead that as the Taliban had not effectively distinguished themselves from civilians nor conducted their operations in accordance with the laws and customs of war, they did

---

on Human Rights, *Detainees at Guantanamo Bay, Cuba; Decision on Request for Precautionary Measures*, 12 March 2002.

17. Greenwood, International Law and the 'War against Terrorism', 78 *International Affairs*, 301 (2002), p. 314.

18. James Dao, US Is Taking War Captives to Cuba Base, *New York Times*, 11 January 2002. Whilst many were transported directly from the combat zone, six Algerian men are reported to have been transported from Bosnia Herzegovina on 18 January 2002, and there are allegations that others have been transferred from countries neighbouring Afghanistan. See Amnesty International, *United States of America: Memorandum to the US Government on the rights of people in US custody in Afghanistan and Guantanamo Bay*, 15 April 2002, pp. 12–13.

19. Julian Borger, US frees 13, but detains another 30, *The Guardian*, 10 May 2003.

20. As the Third Geneva Convention deals exclusively with POWs it is unclear as to how the United States proposes to apply the Convention to the Taliban without granting them POW status.

21. White House fact Sheet, Status of detainees at Guantanamo, 7 February 2002.

not fulfil the conditions set out in Article 4(A)(2) and therefore would not be entitled to POW status.[22] Yet the text of Article 4(A) indicates that members of the armed forces, unlike militia and volunteer corps, do not need to fulfil these four requirements to qualify for POW status.[23]

For al-Qaeda fighters the position is somewhat different. As a clandestine organisation, composed of persons based in various countries, al-Qaeda seems unlikely to have formed part of the armed forces of the Taliban government. However, they might be 'members of other militias or volunteer corps belonging to' the Taliban side. To qualify for POW status, they would then be required to fulfil the four criteria cited above. Yet from their past activities it is reasonable to surmise that they did not conduct their operations in accordance with the laws and customs of war. Thus, it would appear (although this cannot be determined conclusively) that members of al-Qaeda did not qualify as POWs.

It must be acknowledged that determining the status of combatants is not necessarily an easy or clear-cut exercise. However, as reference should be made to the facts in each individual case, a blanket refusal to grant POW status can never be accepted conduct. Failure to apply the Geneva Conventions by one state party could undermine the principle of reciprocity and even the humanitarian law regime itself.

5.3 MINIMUM STANDARDS

Whatever the status of captives in an armed conflict they cannot be held in a legal vacuum, even those guilty or suspected of carrying out terrorist acts.[24] Those who do not qualify as POWs may fall under the Fourth

---

22. Statement from the White House Press Secretary, Ari Fleischer in which he said 'The Taliban have not effectively distinguished themselves from the civilian population of Afghanistan. Moreover, they have not conducted their operations in accordance with the laws and customs of war. Instead, they have knowingly adopted and provided support to the unlawful terrorist objectives of the al Qaeda.' Available at Lexis Library, legal >Federal legal -US>Individual Legal news. http://www.lexis.com/research/retrieve/frames?_m= f477da84097b1f41eb180cc0fc2c7eb8&csvc=bl&cform=bool&_fmtstr=FULL&doc-num=1&_startdoc=1&wchp=dGLbVtb-lSlWt&_md5=a9d85d0d2cb8f01671e05045ea2cbf95, para. 5.

23. See ICRC Commentary to Article 4 of the Third Geneva Convention, available at http://www.icrc.org/ihl.nsf/b466ed681ddfcfd241256739003e6368/eca76fa4dae5b32ec12563c d00425040?OpenDocument, which confirms that during the 1949 Diplomatic Conference on the Geneva Conventions it was stated that the four conditions 'apply to militia and corps of volunteers not forming part of the regular armed forces' and not to regular armed forces.

24. The ICRC commentary to Article 4 of the Fourth Geneva Convention states: 'Every person in enemy hands must have some status under international law: he is either a prisoner of war and, as such, covered by the Third Convention, a civilian covered by the Fourth Convention, or again, a member of the medical personnel of the armed forces who is covered by the First Convention. There is no intermediate status; nobody in enemy hands can be outside the law. We feel that that is a satisfactory solution—not only satisfying to the mind, but also, and above all, satisfactory from the humanitarian point of view.' Available

Geneva Convention.[25] In addition, captives have certain fundamental rights under customary international law and human rights law. The International Criminal Tribunal for the Former Yugoslavia (ICTY) has held in the *Furundzija* case that the general principle of respect for human dignity is the 'basic underpinning' of human rights and humanitarian law:

> 'The essence of the whole corpus of international humanitarian law as well as human rights law lies in the protection of the human dignity of every person, whatever his or her gender. The general principle of respect for human dignity is the basic underpinning and indeed the very *raison d'être* of international humanitarian law and human rights law; indeed in modern times it has become of such paramount importance as to permeate the whole body of international law. This principle is intended to shield human beings from outrages upon their personal dignity, whether such outrages are carried out by unlawfully attacking the body or by humiliating and debasing the honour, the self-respect or the mental well being of a person.'[26]

The most basic requirement, established under the so-called Martens clause, found in the preamble to the Hague Conventions of 1899 and 1907, is that during armed conflict all persons, no matter what their status, must be treated with humanity.[27] Article 3, common to all Geneva Conventions (common Article 3), and Article 75 of Additional Protocol I are also recognised as reflecting customary international law.[28] They set

---

at http://www.icrc.org/ihl.nsf/b466ed681ddfcfd241256739003e6368/18e3ccde8be7e2f8c12563cd0042a50b?OpenDocument

25. The Fourth Geneva Convention applies to 'protected persons', defined as those who find themselves in the hands of a party to the conflict of which they are not nationals. Even those who by virtue of their nationality would not fall under this definition, may still qualify as protected persons in situations where they may be assimilated to enemy nationality, in this case Afghanistan. See Cerone, Status of Detainees in International Armed Conflict, and their Protection in the Course of Criminal Proceedings, *American Society of International Law*, (2002), available at http://www.asil.org/insights/insigh81.htm

26. *Prosecutor v. Anto Furundzija* (Judgment), Case No. IT/95-17/1-T, 10 December 1998, para. 183.

27. The Martens Clause first appeared in the preamble to the 1899 Hague Convention. It reads: '[u]ntil a more complete code of the laws of war has been issued, the High Contracting Parties deem it expedient to declare that, in cases not included in the Regulations adopted by them, the inhabitants and the belligerents remain under the protection and the rule of the principles of the law of nations, as they result from the usages established among civilized peoples, from the laws of humanity, and the dictates of the public conscience.' The International Court of Justice has recognised these humanitarian requirements as customary. See International Court of Justice, *Corfu Channel Case*, Merits, ICJ Reports (1949), 4, p. 22.

28. The ICJ held in the *Case concerning Military and Paramilitary Activities in and against Nicaragua (Nicaragua v. United States of America) (Merits)* that Article 3, common to all four

out a range of minimum standards requiring persons in the hands of a party to the conflict to be treated humanely and without discrimination. Moreover, they prohibit the passing of sentences and the imposition of penalties without a fair trial before an impartial and regularly constituted court.

Fundamental human rights standards must also be respected. While in humanitarian law the obligations of states vary according to the classification of the conflict and the individuals involved, these categories are not relevant in human rights law. Human rights protections are increasingly important where the nature of the conflict has changed or may be drawing to a close. Thus non-derogable human rights and international humanitarian norms constitute the minimum standards applicable in an armed conflict. According to the Human Rights Committee, even during an armed conflict measures derogating from the ICCPR are allowed only if and to the extent that the situation constitutes a threat to the life of a nation.[29] Thus, the minimum standards set out below, flowing from both international human rights and humanitarian law, apply to the treatment of all detainees, irrespective of their status.

5.4 TREATMENT OF DETAINEES NOT DESIGNATED AS POWS

The treatment of individuals captured during an armed conflict but who are not designated as POWs must at all times conform to fundamental standards of international humanitarian law and basic human rights.

5.4.1 Prolonged Detention

According to the Human Rights Committee, arbitrary deprivations of liberty can never be justified, not even in states of emergency.[30] During armed conflict, deprivations of liberty are governed by international

---

Geneva Conventions 1949, constitutes the minimum yardstick in both non-international and international conflict. See ICJ Reports, June 1986, para. 218. For the acceptance of these provisions as customary by the US government see United States Army, *Operational Law Handbook*, JA 422, 1997, p. 266, available at http://www.cdmha.org/toolkit/cdmha-rltk/PUBLICATIONS/oplaw-ja97.pdf, and Remarks by M. Matheson in The Sixth Annual American Red Cross-Washington College of Law on International Humanitarian Law: A Workshop on Customary International Law and the 1977 Protocols Additional to the 1949 Geneva Conventions, 2 *American University Journal of International Law and Policy*, 415 (Fall 1987), at p. 427. See also Greenwood, *supra* note 2, at p. 103.

29. See Human Rights Committee General Comment No. 29, para. 3. On 14 September 2001, President George W. Bush issued Presidential Proclamation 7463 declaring that a national emergency exists by reason of the terrorist attacks, available http://www.defenselink.mil/ra/mobil/pdf/proclamation.pdf. However, the United States has not formally announced the intention to derogate from the terms of the ICCPR and has not filed a derogation notice as required under Article 4(3) of the ICCPR.

30. See Human Rights Committee General Comment No 29, para 11. See also Chapter 4, section 4.5.2.

humanitarian law,[31] which permits detention for the duration of the armed conflict save for those who are awaiting criminal proceedings or who are serving a sentence.[32] From this time, those still detained must have the opportunity to challenge their detention before a court.

Regrettably, the prompt return of POWs at the cessation of hostilities is not always observed.[33] There are concerns that the individuals detained in Guantánamo Bay are likely to be held beyond the cessation of the hostilities in Afghanistan,[34] which would subject them to prolonged and arbitrary detention. They are also unlikely to obtain any judicial review of their detention within the jurisdiction of the United States. This is of particular concern given that the right to challenge the lawfulness

---

31. See ICJ, *Advisory Opinion on the Legality of the Threat or Use of Nuclear Weapons*, 8 July 1996, para. 25, where the Court held that an arbitrary deprivation of life has to be determined by the applicable *lex specialis*, namely, the law applicable in armed conflict which is designed to regulate the conduct of hostilities. Thus, whether a particular loss of life, through the use of a certain weapon in warfare, had to be considered an arbitrary deprivation of life contrary to Article 6 of the Covenant could only be decided by reference to the law applicable in armed conflict and not deduced from the terms of the Covenant itself. By analogy, the same could be said to be true of arbitrary deprivations of liberty.

32. Article 118 of the Third Geneva Convention provides that POWs must be released and repatriated without delay after the cessation of active hostilities. Article 119 states that POWs against whom criminal proceedings are pending may be detained until the end of such proceedings and, if necessary, until the completion of their punishment. The same applies to 'protected persons' who are not eligible for POW status, see Article 133 of the Fourth Geneva Convention.

33. More than a decade after the end of the Iran/Iraq war, several thousand Iraqi POWs were still being detained by the Iranian authorities. See *Aftermath of the Iran/Iraq War*, ICRC annual report, 1998 available http://www.icrc.org/Web/Eng/siteeng0.nsf/iwpList165/6E4EBDD1CCB96B29C1256B890033D66A. Following the end of fighting between Eritrea and Ethiopia, POWs on both sides were not promptly repatriated. See Emma Jane Kirby, Ethiopia and Eritrea to free all POWS, *BBC News*, 23 August 2002, available http://news.bbc.co.uk/1/hi/world/africa/2212159.stm

34. The Secretary of Defense has declared: 'I think that the way I would characterize the end of the conflict is when we feel that there are not effective global terrorist networks functioning in the world that these people would be likely to go back to and begin again their terrorist activities.' See Department of Defense, *News Briefing*, 28 March 2002. The United States Military Order of 13 November 2001, Detention, Treatment, and Trial of Certain Non-Citizens in the War Against Terrorism', issued by President George W. Bush on 13 November 2001; 66 Fed. Reg. 57,833 (16 November 2001) under which these individual may be held, permits detention of persons for whom there is 'reason to believe' that they are, or were, members of al-Qaeda, have engaged in international terrorism against the United States, or have knowingly harboured an individual falling into these categories. See Military Order § 2(a)(1). This Order is unclear as to the purpose and length of the detention, as it does not require that all individuals subject to it be brought to trial. See § 2(b) of the Military Order which states: '. . . the Secretary of Defense shall take all necessary measures to ensure that any individual subject to this order is detained in accordance with section 3, and, *if the individual is to be tried*, that such individual is tried only in accordance with section 4' (emphasis added).

of detention before a court has been deemed non-derogable.[35] Yet when two *habeas corpus* applications brought on behalf of the detainees held in Guantánamo Bay came before United States courts, they were dismissed on the grounds that the courts lacked jurisdiction.[36] In one of these cases the appeals court concluded that the detainees were beyond its jurisdiction as they are not United States citizens and are not held on United States territory. Thus they were not permitted to bring claims under the United States Constitution. Even where it was argued that US law incorporated customary international law, the court was not swayed.[37] The effect of this decision has been to remove any possibility of the detainees claiming a breach of their human rights within United States courts.[38] Yet states are not permitted to perpetrate violations of human rights on the territory of another state and may be held liable for the violation of rights committed by their agents abroad.[39] The Special Rapporteur on the independence of judges and lawyers has expressed concern that the United States court has in effect evaded application of domestic and international law, thus denying suspects their legal rights.[40]

---

35. See Human Rights Committee, General Comment No. 29, para. 16, and Inter-American Court of Human Rights, *Habeas Corpus in Emergency Situation*, Advisory Opinion, OC-8/87, Inter-Am.Ct.H.R. (Ser. A) No. 8 (1987), paras. 40–42.

36. See the District Court decision in *Coalition of Clergy v. Bush*, 189 F. Supp. 2d 1036 (CD. Cal. 2002), 21 February 2002, which was upheld by Federal Appeals Court in *Coalition of Clergy v. Bush*, 310 F. 3d 1153 C.A.9, 18 November 2002. Certiorari was subsequently denied by the United States Supreme Court in *Coalition of Clergy v. Bush*. May 2003, US Lexis, 3702. The second case, *Rasul et al v Bush*, 215 F. Supp 2d 55, was first determined by the District Court on 30 July 2002 and the decision confirmed on 11 March 2003 in *Al Odah Khaled A.F. v USA*, 312 F.3d 1134, US DC Circuit Court of Appeals, 11 March 2003.

37. *Id.Al Odah Khaled A.F. v USA*, 312 F.3d 1134, US DC Circuit Court of Appeals at 1144 and 1145.

38. US soldiers could, however, be subject to disciplinary or criminal procedures under US military law for maltreatment of the detainees.

39. See Human Rights Committee, *Delia Saldias de Lopez v Uruguay*, 29 July 1981, Communication No.52/1979,UN Doc CCPR/C/13/D/52/1979, where the Human Rights Committee concluded that Uruguay had violated the ICCPR when its security forces abducted and tortured a Uruguayan citizen in Argentina. Similarly, the European Court of Human Rights in *Loizidou v Turkey*, Series A, No. 310, 23 February 1995, found a violation of the ECHR by Turkish armed forces stationed in northern Cyprus. The court found that Turkey had effective or overall control over these armed forces and was therefore liable for the human rights violations committed by them. The Inter-American Commission for Human Rights in *Coard et al v USA*, Case No. 10.951, Report No. 109/99, 29 September 1999, held the United States to have violated the American Declaration on the Rights and Duties of Man for its mistreatment of Grenadian nationals during the armed forces' invasion in Grenada. It was accepted that the United States was responsible for upholding the rights of any person subject to its jurisdiction and that the Grenadians were subject to its authority and control.

40. See UN press release, *US Court Decision on Guantanamo Detainees has Serious Implications for Rule of Law, Says UN Rights Expert*, 12 March 2003. The Special Rapporteur said that the decision 'appears to imply that a government of a sovereign State could lease

5.4.2 Access to Counsel

International humanitarian law does not provide for access to counsel, unless a charge is brought against a detainee.[41] Article 75(4) of Additional Protocol I to the Geneva Conventions stipulates that detainees have to be informed without delay of the particulars of an offence alleged against them and be afforded all necessary rights and means of defence. Implicit in this is a right to legal counsel. To assist detainees with all necessary means of defence they should be granted counsel at the earliest opportunity, likely to be at the instigation of criminal charges. Not only does this assist in bringing about a fair trial, it also serves both the administration of justice and the detaining power by helping to ensure that the trial is not undermined by criticism of abuse of process.

For the Guantánamo Bay detainees who have been or are being interrogated for purposes of law enforcement,[42] it follows that access to legal counsel should be provided at the latest when a charge is brought.[43] Early access to legal counsel is crucial to ensure detainees are aware of the right not to give self-incriminating evidence as part of the fundamental principle of the presumption of innocence. Access to counsel does not necessarily compromise questioning for law enforcement purposes.

5.4.3 Conditions of Detention

Both international humanitarian law and human rights law provide for the humane treatment of detainees.[44] Torture and other cruel, inhu-

---

a piece of land from a neighboring State, set up a detention camp, fully operate and control it, arrest suspects of terrorism from other jurisdictions, send them to this camp, deny them their legal rights—including principles of due process generally granted to its own citizens—on grounds that the camp is physically outside its jurisdiction.'

41. Article 105 of the Third Geneva Convention provides that a POW is entitled to be defended 'by a qualified advocate or counsel of his own choice.' Similarly, Article 72 of the Fourth Geneva Convention provides that accused persons 'shall have the right to be assisted by a qualified advocate or counsel of choice.'

42. On 27 February 2002 the US Secretary of Defense stated that all 'except for one or two' of those held at Guantánamo Bay had been questioned and interrogated for intelligence gathering purposes. He added 'We're now starting the process of doing a series of interrogations that involve law enforcement. That is to say to determine exactly what these individuals have done. Not what they know of an intelligence standpoint, but what they've done from a law enforcement standpoint. That process is underway.' See Department of Defense, *Rumsfeld Interview with KSTP-ABC, St. Paul, Minn.*, News Transcript, 27 February 2002

43. Nevertheless, at time of writing, none of the detainees have as yet been charged with an offence, nor granted access to legal counsel. On 19 February 2002, a petition for writ of habeas corpus filed by several detainees asserted that their relatives had been unable to arrange provision of legal advice. The detainees had neither been provided with legal counsel, nor with the means to contact legal counsel. See Petition for Writ of Habeas Corpus in the case of *Rasul .v Bush, supra* note 36.

44. See Common Article 3 to the Geneva Conventions, Article 75(1) of the Additional Protocol I, Article 13 of the Third Geneva Convention, Article 27 of the Fourth Geneva

man or degrading treatment are absolutely prohibited, even during armed conflict.[45] Violations of this prohibition are considered so serious as to warrant individual and state responsibility. Under international humanitarian law an individual can be tried for war crimes or, under certain conditions, for crimes against humanity. During peacetime a violation could also be considered a crime against humanity.

In accordance with the prohibition on torture and other ill-treatment, states have a duty to ensure minimum standards of detention and imprisonment.[46] The Human Rights Committee has found that incommunicado detention, i.e. detention without access to the outside world, may constitute inhumane treatment and a violation of the prohibition on torture and other ill-treatment.[47] The Committee has also stated that '[p]rovisions should be made against incommunicado detention' as a means of preventing cases of torture and ill-treatment.[48] Even where, in the most extreme circumstances, incommunicado detention is deemed necessary by the exigencies of the situation, the right to access to a court (and concurrently the right to legal counsel) must be upheld in order to ensure that the detaining authorities are not abusing their power.[49]

Convention. See Human Rights Committee General Comment No. 21, para. 4., which describes Article 10(1) of the ICCPR as a 'fundamental and universally applicable rule.' Rodley, *Treatment of Prisoners under International Law*, Oxford University Press (1999), p. 279, describes Article 10(1) as a rule of general international law.

45. See Common Article 31(a) to the Geneva Conventions, which prohibits 'violence to life and person, in particular murder of all kinds, mutilation, cruel treatment and torture,' and Article 75(2)(a)(ii) of the Additional Protocol I, which prohibits both physical and mental torture. See also Article 13 of the Third Geneva Convention and Article 32 of the Fourth Geneva Convention. The prohibition on torture and other cruel, inhuman or degrading treatment is also recognised as non-derogable in human rights law. See Article 4 (2) of the ICCPR, Article 2 (2) of the Convention against Torture, Article 27 (2) of the ACHR, Article 15 (2) of the ECHR. Article 1 of the Convention Against Torture and Other Cruel, Inhuman or Degrading Treatment or Punishment defines 'torture' as 'any act by which severe pain or suffering whether physical or mental, is intentionally inflicted on a person for such purposes as obtaining from him or a third person information or a confession, punishing him for an act he or a third person has committed or is suspected of having committed, or intimidating or coercing him or a third person, for any reason based on discrimination of any kind, when such pain or suffering is inflicted by or at the instigation of or with the consent or acquiescence of a public official or other person acting in an official capacity'.

46. See Human Rights Committee, General Comment No. 21, para 3.

47. See *Mukong v. Cameroon*, 21 July 1994, Communication No. 458/1991, UN Doc. CCPR/C/51/D/458/1991, para. 9.4. *El-Megreisi v Libyan Arab Jamahiriya*, Communication No. 440/1990, UN Doc. CCPR/C/50/D/440/1990, para. 5.4.

48. See Human Rights Committee General Comment No. 20, para. 11.

49. Article 71 of the Third Geneva Convention provides that prisoners are allowed to send and receive letters. Similarly, Article 107 of the Fourth Geneva Convention permits internees to correspond with their family.

Like incommunicado detention, solitary confinement, if prolonged, may amount to a violation of the prohibition against torture and ill-treatment.[50] One factor that may be taken into account is 'whether the enforcement of isolation is more extreme than necessary to achieve disciplinary objectives or protection of the prisoner from other inmates.'[51] The Human Rights Committee has held on one occasion that total isolation for a year constitutes inhuman treatment in violation of Article 7 and 10(1) of the ICCPR.[52]

5.5 TRIAL OF SUSPECTED TERRORISTS BEFORE MILITARY TRIBUNALS

5.5.1 Introduction

In a number of countries, military or special courts or tribunals have jurisdiction to try civilians for certain non-military offences, in particular for crimes against national security.[53] While the practice of trying civilians in military courts is not prohibited by international standards, it raises fair trial issues. Often the reason for the establishment of such courts is to enable special procedures to be applied which do not comply with normal standards of justice.[54] Accordingly, the Human Rights Committee has held that the trial of civilians in such courts should be very exceptional and may only take place under conditions which genuinely afford the fair trial guarantees of Article 14 of the ICCPR.[55]

Following the attacks of September 11, the United States government has introduced legislation providing for the trial of certain civilians before military tribunals. The Military Order stipulates that non-US citizen may be tried by Military Commissions after the United States President has determined that there is 'reason to believe' that the indi-

---

50. See Human Rights Committee, General Comment No. 20, para 6.

51. *Supra* note 44, Rodley p 295

52. See *Poloy Campos v Peru*, 9 January 1998, Communication No. 577/1994 UN DocCCPR/C/61/D/577/1994.

53. For example, in Lebanon, according to this state's periodic report to the Human Rights Committee of 1996, 'persons who commit acts which endanger security' are to be referred to the military courts. See *Second Periodic Report*, 22 November 1996, UN Doc CCPR/C/42/Add.14, para. 23. The Human Rights Committee expressed concern about the broad scope of the jurisdiction of military courts in Lebanon, especially the procedures adopted and its application to civilians. See *Concluding Observations of the Human Rights Committee: Lebanon*, 1 April 1997, UN Doc CCPR/C/79/Add.78, para. 14. Similarly, the Inter-American Commission on Human Rights has recommended that the jurisdiction of the military justice system in Colombia be limited to crimes truly related to military service. See Inter-American Commission on Human Rights, *Third Report on the Human Rights Situation in Colombia*, 26 February 1999, OEA/Ser.L/V/II.102, Chapter V, Recommendation No. 6.

54. See Human Rights Committee General Comment No. 13, para. 4.

55. *Id.*

viduals are, or were, members of al-Qaeda, have engaged in international terrorism against the United States, or have knowingly harboured an individual falling into these categories.[56] Further, it authorises the Military Commissions to sit 'at any time and any place.'[57] They have exclusive jurisdiction with respect to the offences alleged to have been commited by the accused.[58] The Secretary of Defense is authorised to issue orders and regulations as may be necessary to carry out trials.[59] He did so on 21 March 2002 by issuing a first set of procedures for trials by Military Commissions.[60] There are concerns that any forthcoming trials could fail to meet the fair trial guarantees set out below, found both in international humanitarian law and human rights law, as well as those in US law.

Although the right to a fair trial is derogable, the Human Rights Committee has acknowledged:

> 'As certain elements of the right to a fair trial are explicitly guaranteed under international humanitarian law during armed conflict, the Committee finds no justification for derogation from these guarantees during other emergency situations.'[61]

The Task Force is concerned at the possible obstacles to the lawful trial by Military Commissions created under the Military Order. First, Article 102 of the Third Geneva Convention provides that POWs can only be sentenced by the same courts and according to the same procedures as members of the armed forces of the detaining power. Thus, should any of the Guantánamo detainees subsequently be granted POW status, they would not be eligible for trial under the Military Commissions.

A second obstacle to the lawfulness of Military Commission trials is that the Military Order is applicable to non-citizens only and that it fails to grant the same due process guarantees as are provided to United States citizens taking part in an armed conflict. This may constitute a denial of equal treatment in violation of the norms of customary international law.[62]

---

56. See Military Order § 2(a)(1).

57. *Id.*, § 4(c)(1).

58. *Id*, § 7(b)(1).

59. *Id.*, § 4(b).

60. Department of Defense Military Commission Order No. 1 of 21 March 2002 (hereinafter DOD Order).

61. See Human Rights Committee General Comment No 29, para. 16.

62. See Article 75(1) of the Additional Protocol I, which prohibits discrimination based upon, *inter alia*, national origin. Common Article 3 (1) provides that detainees must be treated without adverse distinction founded on race, colour, religion or faith, sex, birth or wealth or any other similar criteria.

Third, Article 75(4) of Additional Protocol I stipulates that sentences can only be passed by a regularly constituted court. A 'regularly constituted court' is one which administers justice impartially and in accordance with the fair trial guarantees listed in Article 75(4) of the Additional Protocol I.[63] Similarly, common Article 3(1)(d) stipulates that sentences must be passed by regularly constituted courts, affording judicial guarantees. As explored below, there are concerns that the Military Commissions established under the Military Order may not be impartial and may fail to meet these fair trial guarantees.

5.5.2 The Right to Be Tried by a Competent, Independent and Impartial Tribunal Established by Law

The right to be tried by a competent, independent and impartial tribunal is absolute and may suffer no exception.[64] Even during armed con-

---

63. See ICRC Commentary to Article 75 of Additional Protocol I, para. 3084, available at http://www.icrc.org/ihl.nsf/b466ed681ddfcfd241256739003e6368/e46340b132 ac1b86c12563cd004367bf?OpenDocument. Article 75 (4) states:

'No sentence may be passed and no penalty may be executed on a person found guilty of a penal offence related to the armed conflict except pursuant to a conviction pronounced by an impartial and regularly constituted court respecting the generally recognized principles of regular judicial procedure, which include the following:

(a) the procedure shall provide for an accused to be informed without delay of the particulars of the offence alleged against him and shall afford the accused before and during his trial all necessary rights and means of defence;

(b) no one shall be convicted of an offence except on the basis of individual penal responsibility;

(c) no one shall be accused or convicted of a criminal offence on account of any act or omission which did not constitute a criminal offence under the national or international law to which he was subject at the time when it was committed; nor shall a heavier penalty be imposed than that which was applicable at the time when the criminal offence was committed; if, after the commission of the offence, provision is made by law for the imposition of a lighter penalty, the offender shall benefit thereby;

(d) anyone charged with an offence is presumed innocent until proved guilty according to law;

(e) anyone charged with an offence shall have the right to be tried in his presence;

(f) no one shall be compelled to testify against himself or to confess guilt;

(g) anyone charged with an offence shall have the right to examine, or have examined, the witnesses against him and to obtain the attendance and examination of witnesses on his behalf under the same conditions as witnesses against him;

(h) no one shall be prosecuted or punished by the same Party for an offence in respect of which a final judgement acquitting or convicting that person has been previously pronounced under the same law and judicial procedure;

(i) anyone prosecuted for an offence shall have the right to have the judgement pronounced publicly; and

(j) a convicted person shall be advised on conviction of his judicial and other remedies and of the time-limits within which they may be exercised.'

64. See Human Rights Committee, *González del Río v Peru*, 28 October 1992, Communication No. 263/1987, UN Doc. CCPR/C/46/D/263/1987.

flict, POWs can only be tried by tribunals that guarantee independence and impartiality.[65]

As in the case of many other special military tribunals,[66] the establishment of the United States Military Commissions raises concerns as to their independence and impartiality. Under the Military Order, the President and the Secretary of Defense have the power to create and shape the Military Commissions and to determine who shall be tried before them. The executive has almost unfettered discretionary power. For instance, the Secretary of Defense (or his designee) has the power to appoint the members of the commissions,[67] to remove them,[68] to designate a presiding officer,[69] to decide which parts of the proceedings should be held *in camera*,[70] and to appoint the panel who review the record of trial.[71] The President or, if designated by the President, the Secretary of Defense makes the final decision on any appeal.[72] The Commissioners are military officers who are ultimately answerable to the Secretary of Defense and the President. Further, the Secretary of Defense has the power to remove Commissioners 'for good cause'.[73] Given that the United States President and the Secretary of Defense have made public comments on the guilt of those detained under the Military Order,[74] the military Commissioners could be subject to 'command influence', seriously jeopardising the impartiality and independence of the trial process.[75]

Moreover, the Human Rights Committee has stated that the jurisdiction of special courts should be strictly defined by law.[76] The Military Order, however, provides for military jurisdiction over a broadly defined category of individuals and is not time limited. All these shortcomings are of particular concern given that the Military Commissions have the authority to pass death sentences.[77] In capital punishment cases the duty

---

65. See Article 75(4) of Additional Protocol I.

66. For example, the Inter-American Commission on Human Rights noted in its special report on Peru, that its military courts 'can only be applied to members of the military who have committed service-related offenses, and that military courts do not have the necessary independence and impartiality for sitting in judgment of civilians.' OEA/Ser.L/V/II.106, Doc. 59 Rev June 2002, para 155.

67. § 4(A)(1) of the DOD Order.

68. *Id*, § 4(A)(3).

69. *Id*, § 4(A)(4).

70. *Id*, § 6(B)(3).

71. *Id*, § 6(H)(4).

72. *Id*, §§ 6(H)(2) and (6) and Military Order § 4(8).

73. *Id*, § 4(A)(3).

74. See *infra* Section 5.5.6 on the presumption of innocence.

75. See Chapter 4, section 4.6.6.

76. See Human Rights Committee, Concluding Observations: Iraq, 19 November 1997, UN Doc CCPR/C/79/Add.84, para 15.

77. See § 4(a) of the Military Order and § 6(F) and (G) of the DOD Order. The Orders do not exempt juveniles from the death penalty. According to the US authorities,

of states to observe rigorously all the guarantees of a fair trial is imperative.[78] Consequently, the UN Special Rapporteur on the independence of judges and lawyers sent representations regarding the Military Order, expressing concerns as to the implications of the order and the Military Commissions for the rule of law.[79]

5.5.3 The Right to a Public Hearing

In proceedings before the new US Military Commissions, the Secretary of Defense (or his designee) and the Presiding Officer have the power to order closed hearings. The hearings may be closed to the public, *inter alia*, to protect classified information, to ensure witness safety, to protect intelligence and law enforcement sources, methods, or activities, and for 'other national security interests'.[80]

Clearly, the government has a duty to guard state secrets and protect witnesses. Nonetheless, procedures already exist in the US courts that safeguard those interests without sacrificing public scrutiny of the proceedings.[81] Concerns with the broadly-defined circumstances under which trials before the Military Commissions may be closed is heightened by the fact that the decision to close trials is vested in the hands of the executive rather than the judiciary.

5.5.4 Right to Equality of Arms

Not only can the trials before the Military Commissions be closed to the public, the defendant may be excluded from parts of the trial for the same reasons as can any non-military defence counsel and, under certain

---

several juveniles are among the Guantánamo detainees. See Jane Sutton, U.S. Says Juveniles Among Guantánamo Prisoners, *Reuters*, 23 April 2003. See also Amnesty International, United States: Rights of Children Must be Respected, 25 April 2003.

78. *Supra* note 44, pp. 227–229.

79. See Report of the Special Rapporteur on the independence of judges and lawyers to the 58th Session of the UN Commission on Human Rights, 11 February 2002, UN Doc E/CN.4/2002/72, para. 208.

80. § 6 B(3) of the DOD Order.

81. Rule 16(d)(1) of the United States Federal Rules of Criminal Procedure, for instance, allows judges to issue protective orders to deny, restrict or defer discovery of evidence upon a sufficient showing. The Classified Information Procedures Act, 18 U.S.C. app. §3(1999), authorises the government to delete specified items of classified information from documents to be made available to the defendant through discovery under the Federal Rules of Criminal Procedure, to substitute a summary of the information for such classified documents, or to substitute a statement admitting relevant facts that the classified information would tend to prove. See also the Federal Witness Protection Program, 18 U.S.C. §§ 3521–3528 Supp IV 1986, according to which the Attorney General may provide for the relocation and other protection of a witness or a potential witness in an official proceeding concerning an organised criminal activity or other serious offence.

circumstances, the military defence counsel.[82] Given that defendants may be in the best position to refute evidence against them, questions are raised regarding the equality of arms and the right of the defendant to know the case against him or her.[83]

Associated with the principle of equality of arms is the right of the accused to call and to question witnesses. Article 75(4)(g) of Additional Protocol I expressly provides for the right of the accused to examine prosecution witnesses and to obtain the attendance and examination of witnesses on their behalf under the same conditions as witnesses against them. Yet those appearing before the new Military Commissions would be denied the right to confrontation or examination of all the witnesses called. Only witnesses who appear before the Commissions can be cross-examined.[84] Therefore, witnesses who provide testimony 'by telephone, audiovisual means, or other means' cannot be cross-examined.[85] Furthermore, confrontation and cross-examination are also restricted by the allowance of witness testimony by sworn or unsworn written statements, testimony from prior trials and proceedings, and reports.[86] The use of alternative means to provide witness testimony is not restricted to cases where it is required for the protection of witnesses, but is at the discretion of the Commission. This blanket authorisation would appear to be contrary to Article 75(4)(g) of Additional Protocol I, as well as to the spirit of the rules of procedure in a number of international tribunals, including the ITCY, which, though allowing depositions, hold that as a general rule witnesses must be physically present before the Tribunal.[87]

5.5.5 The Right to Defend Oneself in Person or Through Counsel

Even in armed conflict situations defendants must be afforded 'all necessary rights and means of defence', which implies the right to the assistance of legal counsel.[88] The appointment of counsel is a primary means of ensuring protection by means of a fair trial.

---

82. § 6 B(3) of the DOD Order.

83. Article 75(4)(a) of the Additional Protocol I provides that the defendant shall be afforded all the necessary rights and means of defence. According to Article 75(4)(e) anyone charged with an offence shall have the right to be tried in his presence.

84. §§ 5(I) and 6(D)(2)(c) of the DOD order.

85. *Id*, § 6(D)(2)(a).

86. *Id*, § 6(D)(3).

87. See Rule 71 of the ICTY Rules of Procedure and Evidence which provides that depositions may be used 'where it is in the interests of justice to do so.' The motion for the taking of a deposition has to indicate the circumstances justifying it; the accused 'shall have the right to attend the taking of the deposition and cross-examine the person whose deposition is being taken'; the Presiding Officer has to ensure that 'the deposition is taken in accordance with the Rules and that a record is made of the deposition, including cross-examination and objections raised by either party for decision by the Trial Chamber.'

88. See Article 75 (4)(a) of the Additional Protocol I. For POWs, Article 105 of the

In the Military Commissions, the Chief Defense Counsel appoints (or the accused can choose) a military officer to act as counsel.[89] The accused can appoint, at his or her own expense, a civilian lawyer, providing the latter is a US citizen and receives the necessary security clearance.[90] However, where a civilian lawyer is appointed, the defendant will still be represented by the military lawyer, even against the defendant's wishes.[91] Moreover, military co-counsel are authorised to have access to certain classified information denied to the civilian lawyer and the accused.[92] It is the view of the Task Force that there is no reason to compel defendants to accept representation by military counsel, given the necessity for civilian counsel to receive security clearance. The Human Rights Committee has found in a similar case that the right to choose defence counsel was violated when an accused was forced to accept appointed military counsel, despite there being a civilian lawyer willing to represent him.[93]

5.5.6 Presumption of Innocence

Even in armed conflict everyone has the right to be presumed innocent and treated as innocent unless or until convicted according to law.[94] This right is guaranteed even to those facing charges of genocide, crimes against humanity and war crimes under the Statute of the International Criminal Court,[95] and has been identified by the Human Rights Committee as a non-derogable component of the right to a fair trial.[96] It has been argued that it amounts to a principle of customary international law.[97]

If those detained at Guantánamo Bay come to trial before the Military Commissions, the presumption of their innocence will already have been damaged. Numerous United States officials, most notably those having overall control over the Military Commissions, the President[98] and the

---

Third Geneva Convention expressly provides for the right to assistance by a legal counsel of own choice. Article 72 of the Fourth Geneva Convention makes similar provision for internees.

89. §§ 4(C)(2) and 4 (C)(3)(a) of the DOD Order.

90. *Id.*, § 4(C)(3)(b).

91. *Id.*

92. *Id.*, §§ 4(C)(3)(b) and 6(B)(3).

93. See *Acosta v Uruguay*, Communication No 1 10/1981, 29 March 1984, UN Doc. CCPR/C/21/D/110/1981, paras. 13.2 and 15.

94. See Article 75(4)(d) of the First Additional Protocol to the Geneva Conventions.

95. See Article 66 of the ICC Statute.

96. See Human Rights Committee General Comment No. 29, para. 11.

97. See Human Rights Committee General Comment No. 24, para. 8.

98. The President has referred to those held in Guantánamo as 'these killers' and as 'terrorists.' See The White House new release, *President Meets with Afghan Interim Authority Chairman; Remarks by the President and Chairman of the Afghan Interim Authority Hamid Karzai,* 28 January 2002. Similarly, in the State of the Union address of 29 January 2002 he said: 'Terrorists who once occupied Afghanistan now occupy cells at Guantanamo Bay.'

Secretary of Defense,[99] have made public comments on their presumed guilt. These public comments run counter to the duty of public authorities to refrain from prejudging the outcome of a trial, In the light of such public declarations it may be difficult to effectively guarantee the presumption of innocence.

5.5.7   Right to Appeal

The right of those convicted of a criminal offence to a review of the conviction and sentence by a higher tribunal is confirmed by the Human Rights Committee[100] and the Geneva Conventions.[101] The right to appeal will be particularly important where the offence can attract the death penalty. The Human Rights Committee has confirmed that in death penalty cases the procedural guarantees prescribed by Article 6 of the ICCPR must be observed, including the right to a fair hearing by an independent tribunal, and the right to review by a higher tribunal.[102]

According to § 7(b)(2) of the Military Order, convicted individuals 'shall not be privileged to seek any remedy or maintain any proceeding, directly or indirectly, or to have any such remedy or proceeding sought on the individual's behalf, in (i) any court of the United States, or any State thereof; (ii) any court of any foreign nation; or (iii) any international tribunal.' Instead, convictions will be reviewed by a three-member panel of military officers, appointed by the Secretary of Defense.[103] The authority of the panel is limited to reviewing the record of the trial. The panel will then forward the case with a recommendation to the Secretary of Defense, who will then review the record of the trial and the panel's recommendation.[104] The final decision on the case resides with the President,[105] who, it will be recalled, designates the individuals subject to the Military Order, or the Secretary of Defense, who may personally select the suspects for trial by the Military Commissions.[106] The UN Special

---

99. The Secretary of Defence described the Guantánamo detainees as being 'among the most dangerous, best-trained, vicious killers on the face of the earth.' See American Forces Information Service, new release, *Rumsfeld visits, thanks US troops at Camp X-Ray in Cuba*, 27 January 2002.

100. *Salgar de Montejo v Colombia*, 24 March 1982, communication no. 64/79UN Doc CCPR/C/15/D/64/1979. paras. 129–130.

101. However, the right to appeal is not absolute. Article 106 of the Third Geneva Convention provides for a right of appeal where the armed forces of the detaining powers are also accorded this right. Similarly, Article 73 of the Fourth Geneva Convention provides that a convicted person shall have the right to appeal provided for by the laws applied by the court of the detaining power.

102. See Human Rights Committee General Comment No. 6, para. 7.

103. § 6(H)(4) of the DOD Order.

104. *Id.*, § 6(H)(5).

105. §6(H)(6). He may designate the Secretary of Defense to make the final decision.

106. § 6(A)(l) and (2).

Rapporteur on the independence of judges and lawyers has expressed concerns about the establishment of an executive review process to replace the right to appeal, the conviction and sentence to a higher tribunal, as well as the exclusion of jurisdiction of any other courts and international tribunals.[107]

5.6 'ENEMY COMBATANTS'

In addition to the detention of non-citizens under the Military Order, the United States has classified a number of citizens as 'enemy combatants' as part of its 'war against terrorism'.[108] Yet the proclamation of a 'war against terrorism' does not automatically imply the existence of a state of emergency and permit the suspension of human rights obligations and constitutional guarantees. Where there is an armed conflict in existence then the protections contained within international humanitarian law must be applied.[109]

Whilst the term 'enemy combatant' is not one recognised in international law, any state is at liberty to create legal categories for its citizens, provided the designated citizens are treated in accordance with international standards. However, the legal consequences of being classified as an 'enemy combatant' in the United States raise a number of concerns. Not only has there been a lack of official notification as to who qualifies as an 'enemy combatant',[110] but further there is uncertainty as to the legal ramifications of this categorisation. In practice, persons designated as 'enemy combatants' have been detained without charge, denied access to legal counsel[111]

---

107. *Supra* note 79, para. 208.

108. Two United States citizens have been designated as enemy combatants. Yaser Hamdi was captured in Afghanistan and transferred to Guantánamo, where US officials realised that he was a US citizen. As a result, he was transferred to a US military base in Virginia, where he was still being held at the time of writing, without charge or trial. Jose Padilla was arrested in Chicago and originally held as a material witness in connection with an alleged conspiracy to create and use against an American target a radioactive 'dirty bomb'. Before a district court in New York could rule on motions contesting the legality of Padilla's detention, he was designated an 'enemy combatant'. See Department of Defense News Article, 10 June 2002. Consequently, he was transferred to military custody in South Carolina, where he was still being held in a naval brig at the time of writing.

109. See Article 2 Common to the Geneva Conventions and Article 1 of the Additional Protocol II, both of which set out the circumstances in which the treaties apply.

110. The criteria being used to assess whether individuals should be held as 'enemy combatants' or should be charged before ordinary courts are unclear. While the United States citizens Hamdi and Padilla have been designated as 'enemy combatants', their fellow citizens Lindh and Ujaama, and even the French '20th hijacker' Moussaoui and the British 'shoe bomber' Reid have not. The case of Padilla appears to be particularly striking, given that he is a US citizen arrested on American soil, far from any battlefield or combat arena.

111. Hamdi has been denied access to legal representation since his capture in Afghanistan in autumn 2001. An appeal court reversed the order of a district court to allow

and the right to challenge the lawfulness of their detention.[112]

Granting the government the authority to designate citizens as 'enemy combatants' and to detain them without charge or trial could lead to the circumvention of normally applicable due process guarantees. Even where states deem it necessary, for reasons of national security, to detain people without charge, the detention must still be subject to judicial review.[113] Further, legal representation is a crucial safeguard to enable detainees to exercise this right. Therefore, they should be given access to legal counsel without delay after arrest.[114] These due process guarantees, which are part of international human rights law, should be respected regardless of the categorisation of individuals in domestic law.

---

a public defender access to Hamdi. See *Hamdi v Rumsfeld*, 294 F. 3d 598 (C.A.4 (Va.), 2002), 26 June 2002, p. 600. Upon a second filing by Hamdi's father, the district court ordered again that Hamdi be given access to a public defender. See *Hamdi v Rumsfeld*, District Court for the Eastern District of Virginia, 11 June 2002. The government appealed against the order and the court of appeals remanded the case for further proceedings. See *Hamdi v Rumsfeld*, 296 F. 3d 278 (C.A.4 (Va.), 2002), 12 July 2002. Padilla was represented by an attorney during his detention as a material witness in New York, but has been denied further access to legal counsel since his transfer to military custody in June 2002. In December 2002, a district judge ruled that he must be granted access to a lawyer to challenge his detention as an enemy combatant. See *Padilla v Bush*, District Court for the Southern District of New York, 4 December 2002, p. 101. However, in March 2003 the conditions under which Padilla could be allowed to consult with counsel were still not agreed upon. See *Padilla v Rumsfeld*, District Court for the Southern District of New York, 11 March 2003.

112. In the case of Hamdi, the government has effectively taken the position that 'with no meaningful judicial review, any American citizen alleged to be an enemy combatant could be detained indefinitely without charges or counsel on the government's say-so.' See decision by the Court of Appeals for the Fourth Circuit in *Hamdi v Rumsfeld*, 296 F. 3d 278, C.A.4 (Va.), 12 July 2002, p. 283. The Court of Appeals remanded the case to the district court for further proceedings, in particular for reconsideration as to whether Hamdi is an 'enemy combatant'. In the case of Padilla, a district judge held that the US President was authorised under the constitution and by law to direct the military to detain enemy combatants, such that Padilla's detention was not *per se* unlawful. See *Padilla v Bush*, District Court for the Southern District of New York, 4 December 2002, p. 101.

113. See Article 9(4) of the ICCPR, Article 7(6) of the ACHR, Article 5(4) of the ECHR, Article 7(1)(a) of the African Charter, Principle 32 (1) of the Body of Principles for the Protection of all Persons under Any Form of Detention of Imprisonment. See also Human Rights Committee General Comment No. 8, para. 4 and General, Comment No. 29, para. 16, and Inter-American Court of Human Rights, *Habeas Corpus in Emergency Situation*, Advisory Opinion of 1987, *supra* note 35.

114. Principle 17(1) of the Body of Principles for the Protection of All Persons under Any Form of Detention or Imprisonment, Principle 1 of the Basic Principles on the Role of Lawyers. The Human Rights Committee has stated that 'all persons who are arrested must immediately have access to counsel', see Concluding Observations of the Human Rights Committee: Georgia, UN Doc. CCPRIC/79/Add.75, 5 May 1997, para. 27.

CONCLUSION

Whilst the Task Force recognises the threat posed by international terrorism to the security of nations, it is troubled by certain failures to take into account and apply fundamental principles of international humanitarian law. The consequences of such action are grave and may undermine the binding force of the humanitarian law regime. It is vital that the treatment of those captured during armed conflict conforms to both international humanitarian law and fundamental human rights standards, regardless of the scenario in which they were captured and suspicions as to their criminal activities. Similarly, those prosecuted for acts committed before or during an armed conflict must be afforded fundamental fair trial guarantees. To do otherwise would undermine the very standards that the international community established after the Second World War.

It must be acknowledged, however, that states might find it difficult to apply international humanitarian law to combatants who themselves do not comply with the same provisions. In addition, the humanitarian law regime is not without ambiguity, gaps or flaws. Yet in dealing with new situations, states should act in accordance with the spirit and fundamental objectives of international humanitarian law and, in this regard, take due note of the views of the ICRC, which is assigned a special role in this process. Greater adherence to all treaties in the area of international humanitarian law would constitute a significant improvement in the protection of all those affected by armed conflict, most notably civilians.

Recommendations

1) Without exception the determination of POW status must continue to be made strictly in accordance with Article 4 of the Third Geneva Convention.

2) Where there is any doubt as to the status of captured combatants, a state must convene a competent tribunal. It is not only for the detaining power to determine whether or not there is doubt as to the status of the captured combatants. Doubt may be expressed by interested state parties and the international community.

3) States can not hold detainees, for which they are responsible, outside of the jurisdiction of all independent courts or tribunals competent to determine the legality of their detention. All detainees must have the right to challenge their detention before an independent court or tribunal.

4) Access to counsel should be made available to all those detained in an armed conflict and charged with a criminal offence at the earliest possible moment. This is particularly important to ensure

detainees are aware of their right not to give self-incriminating evidence, which is part of the fundamental right to the presumption of innocence.

5) Treatment in detention must comply with fundamental standards. Detainees must never be held in prolonged incommunicado detention or solitary confinement.

6) The fundamental due process guarantees must be accorded those facing trial, whether before a military tribunal or regularly constituted court, at times of peace and during armed conflict. All detainees must be treated in accordance with these standards regardless of their nationality.

CHAPTER 6

PREVENTING THE FINANCING OF TERRORISM

6.1 INTRODUCTION

This chapter examines the phenomenon of 'terrorist financing', that is to say the means by which funds reach those who aim to carry out terrorist acts, and the international response to this problem. Although the financing of terrorist activities has come into the spotlight following September 11, it is part of a long existing global criminal problem in which illegitimate funds cross international borders.

Following the adoption of UN Security Council Resolution 1373 states have been required to take measures freezing the assets of terrorist individuals. In practice, the freezing of assets of individuals who have not been convicted of terrorist activities is likely to engender serious human rights concerns. Yet there is a notable absence of any review procedures or appeal mechanisms to ensure that such action does not adversely affect the rights of innocent individuals.

Since the terrorist attacks in the United States, the rise of state imposed control mechanisms in the area of financial transactions has been swift, affecting both business and individuals. These controls take two basic forms. Firstly, the introduction and implementation of identification and record-keeping requirements to an acceptable standard and, secondly, the monitoring and reporting of suspicious transactions. Such controls can obviously be useful tools in the fight against terrorism and in efforts to restrict or prevent terrorist financing. To ensure maximum effectiveness of control mechanisms, they must be consistently and proportionately enforced throughout the international community. As explored in this chapter, greater cooperation is a necessity but at present risks failure through lack of a sufficiently empowered international regulatory body.

6.2 PROBLEMS IN IDENTIFYING 'TERRORIST FINANCE'

Not all acts of terrorism require significant financial support; often all that is needed is enough money to cover the living expenses of the perpetrators.[1] Some terrorist acts may also be furthered by the mere provision of goods and services. Terrorism finance may be derived from apparently legitimate sources such as registered charities, legitimate businesses or individual donations. For these reasons it is not sufficient for financial institutions to only monitor the legality of the source or the activities of the recipient, they should also focus on monitoring suspicious transactions. The Financial Action Task Force on Money Laundering (FATF)[2] has commented:

> 'It should be acknowledged as well that financial institutions will probably be unable to detect terrorist financing as such. Indeed, the only time that financial institutions might clearly identify terrorist financing as distinct from other criminal misuse of the financial system is when a known terrorist or terrorist organisation has opened an account. [. . .] For this reason, financial institutions do not necessarily need to determine the legality of the source or destination of the funds. Instead, they should ascertain whether transactions are unusual, suspicious or otherwise indicative of criminal or terrorist activity.'[3]

Yet determining whether financial transactions are suspicious is fraught with difficulty. Firstly, it is not obvious how terrorist finance can be distinguished either from legitimate transactions or from other types of illegitimate financial activity. The only way transactions may be specifically linked to terrorist activities is when one of the parties involved in the financial transaction is a known or suspected terrorist or terrorist organisation.

Secondly, as noted above, acts of terrorism do not necessarily require large sums of money or involve specific forms of transaction which attract the attention of financial institutions.

---

1. A study of the September 11 attacks apparently revealed mainly small wire transfers of less than US$10,000 which were explicable as tuition fees and living expenses for students, which was the cover the attackers used; it has been said that 'those active in terrorist operations are unlikely to be caught only by following a trail of suspicious transactions.' See Molloy, Timon, Terrorism, typologies and non-cooperation, *Money Laundering Bulletin*, February 2002, p. 2.

2. The FATF is an inter-governmental body, established by the G7 in 1989, whose purpose is the development and promotion of policies, both at national and international levels, to combat money laundering.

3. See FATF, Guidance for Financial Institutions in Detecting Terrorist Financing, 24 April 2002, para. 9.

Thirdly, with unofficial banking or alternative transmission services operating in many countries, terrorists can easily evade attention by transferring funds through such sources. Since September 11, two types of funding activities, charitable relief organisations and the informal money exchange system known as Hawala, have been the focus of international attention. Both are reported to have been used to provide money to suspected terrorists, although it is important to acknowledge that by far the vast majority of transactions are not related to terrorist activities. Some charities can have a dual purpose: collecting money to provide actual humanitarian relief on the one hand and providing logistical, political and monetary support to a particular organisation on the other. Hawala is effectively an independent international money exchange system operating largely outside the boundaries of mainstream financial business, commonly where formal international transfer services do not operate.[4] It can take a large variety of forms, and few, if any, records are kept. Recently, some jurisdictions[5] have begun to require that 'hawaladars' register with the authorities in the same way as other money transfer systems, for example bureaux de change. It is questionable whether this approach will do anything other than make unregistered hawala transactions even more difficult to detect.

Finally, as financial authorities will potentially be required to investigate a huge number of suspicious transactions there will be considerable resource implications. This will be particularly true given the inability of financial monitors to distinguish suspicious transactions connected to terrorism from ordinary criminal activity, therefore requiring monitoring bodies to treat each case as a priority.

6.3 MEASURES IN PLACE TO SUPPRESS TERRORIST FINANCING

6.3.1 UN Security Council Resolutions

Probably the most important Security Council Resolution adopted following September 11 is Resolution 1373,[6] calling for states to prevent and suppress the financing of terrorism[7] and to criminalise the wilful provision or collection of funds for such acts. Further, terrorist funds, finan-

---

4.   For a general introduction to Hawala, see Jost and Sandhu, The Hawala alternative remittance system and its role in money laundering, Interpol General Secretariat, January 2000, available at http://www.interpol.int/Public/FinancialCrime/MoneyLaundering/hawala/default.asp.

5.   For example the United Kingdom, the United States and Saudi Arabia.

6.   Security Council Resolution 1373, adopted on 28 September 2001, UN Doc. S/RES/1373 (2001). See Appendix IV. Most recently reaffirmed in Security Council Resolution 1440 of 24 October 2002, UN Doc. S/RES/1440 (2002).

7.   *Id.*, para. 1(a).

cial assets and economic resources are to be frozen without delay.[8]

> Paragraph 1(d) is particularly important as it requires states to: '[p]rohibit their nationals or any other persons and entities within their territories from making funds, financial assets or economic resources or financial or other related services available, directly or indirectly, for the benefit of persons who commit or attempt to commit or facilitate or participate in the commission of terrorist acts . . .'.

To monitor states' compliance with its requirements, Resolution 1373 creates the Counter-Terrorism Committee (CTC). States are required to report to the CTC on measures taken to implement Resolution 1373. The CTC's published guidance requests states to act quickly to freeze the assets of terrorists and terrorist groups and suggests that this can be achieved by (i) the adoption of generic legislation, and (ii) the creation of lists, which might be based on information provided by other states or international or regional organisations, thus removing the requirement of the need to have first-hand information.[9]

Resolution 1390, adopted on 16 January 2002,[10] reaffirms Security Council Resolution 1373 and recalls Resolutions 1267[11] and 1333.[12] Resolution 1267 set up a committee tasked with collating a list of Taliban entities, including those owned or controlled, directly or indirectly, by the Taliban. Under this resolution states are required to freeze the funds and other financial resources of those listed.[13] This was extended by Resolution 1333 to include the funds and financial assets of Osama bin Laden and individuals and entities associated with him, including those in the al-Qaeda organisation.[14] Referring to the list created pursuant to Resolutions 1267 and 1333, Resolution 1390 requires states to freeze funds and other financial assets or economic resources of the named individuals or entities connected with Osama bin Laden or the Taliban.[15]

---

8. Para. 1(c) requires states to 'Freeze without delay funds and other financial assets or economic resources of persons who commit, or attempt to commit, terrorist acts or participate in or facilitate the commission of terrorist acts; of entities owned or controlled directly or indirectly by such persons; and of persons and entities acting on behalf of, or at the direction of such persons and entities, including funds derived or generated from property owned or controlled directly or indirectly by such persons and associated persons and entities.'

9. See letter by J.W. Wainwright, expert adviser to the CTC, to the Chairman of the CTC, 11 November 2002. Available at http://www.un.org/Docs/sc/committees/1373/.

10. See Appendix III.

11. Adopted by the Security Council on 15 October 1999.

12. Adopted by the Security Council on 19 December 2000.

13. See para. 4(b).

14. See para. 8(c).

15. See para. 2.

6.3.2 International Convention for the Suppression of the Financing of Terrorism

This Convention was opened for signature in 1999. Prior to 11 September, just four countries had ratified it. A further 22 ratifications took place after that date and the Convention entered into force on 10 April 2002. Article 2(1) of the Convention establishes an offence which reads as follows:

> 'Any person commits an offence within the meaning of this Convention if that person by any means, directly or indirectly, unlawfully and wilfully, provides or collects funds with the intention that they should be used or in the knowledge that they are to be used, in full or in part, in order to carry out:
> (a) An act which constitutes an offence within the scope of and as defined in one of the treaties listed in the annex[16]; or
> (b) Any other act intended to cause death or serious bodily injury to a civilian, or to any other person not taking an active part in the hostilities in a situation of armed conflict, when the purpose of such act, by its nature or context, is to intimidate a population, or to compel a government or an international organization to do or to abstain from doing any act.'

The Convention provides that states should take 'appropriate measures' for the detection and freezing, seizure or forfeiture of any funds used or allocated for the purposes of committing the offences.[17]

6.3.3 The Financial Action Task Force on Money Laundering (FATF)

The Paris-based FATF was established by the G-7 Summit held in 1989. In 1990 it issued a framework for combating international money laundering, commonly known as the 'Forty Recommendations'. Amended in 1996, they set out certain basic requirements to combat money laun-

---

16. The Annex lists the following nine UN instruments on terrorism: Convention for the Suppression of Unlawful Seizure of Aircraft (1970), Convention for the Suppression of Unlawful Acts against the Safety of Civil Aviation (1971), Convention on the Prevention and Punishment of Crimes against Internationally Protected Persons including Diplomatic Agents (1973), International Convention against the Taking of Hostages (1979), Convention on the Physical Protection of Nuclear Material (1980), Protocol for the Suppression of Unlawful Acts of Violence at Airports Serving International Civil Aviation, supplementary to the Convention of Unlawful Acts against the Safety of Civil Aviation (1988), Convention for the Suppression of Unlawful Acts against the Safety of Maritime Navigation (1988), Protocol for the Suppression of Unlawful Acts against the Safety of Fixed Platforms located on the Continental Shelf (1988), International Convention for the Suppression of Terrorist Bombing (1997).
17. See Article 8 of the Convention.

dering, including criminalisation of the laundering of the proceeds of serious crime, obligations on financial institutions to identify clients to an acceptable standard, and adequate control and supervision of such financial institutions.[18]

In October 2001 FATF expanded its mission to include measures to combat terrorist financing, and issued a further eight special recommendations in that regard. Briefly, these are: i) ratification and implementation of UN instruments; ii) criminalising the financing of terrorism and associated money laundering; iii) freezing and confiscating terrorist assets; iv) reporting suspicious transactions related to terrorism; v) international cooperation; vi) licensing or registrating 'alternative remittance' agents; vii) inclusion of accurate and meaningful information on wire transfers; and viii) reviewing the adequacy of laws and regulations that relate to entities that can be abused for the financing of terrorism, particularly non-profit entities.[19] However, these recommendations are not legally binding.

Probably the most important contribution of FATF to combating international money laundering and terrorist financing has been through its programme of multilateral monitoring and peer review. In particular, its designation of certain countries as a Non-Cooperative Country or Territory (NCCT) has generally proved reasonably effective in persuading that particular country to adopt anti-money laundering measures. Countries are expected to be particularly vigilant in dealing with transactions from NCCTs.[20]

FATF has singled out a number of red flags for the creation of a suspicion of terrorist involvement in account activity.[21] They include: i) accounts that receive periodical deposits and are dormant at other periods; ii) a dormant account containing a minimal sum suddenly receives a deposit or series of deposits followed by daily cash withdrawals that continue until the transferred sum has been removed; iii) where a customer refuses to provide information or provides misleading information on account opening; iv) where several persons having signature authority over accounts but no apparent business or family relationship otherwise;

18. See FATF, *The Forty Recommendations*, available at http://www1.oecd.org/fatf/40Recs_en.htm

19. See *Special Recommendations on Terrorist Financing*, 31 October 2001, available at http://www1.oecd.org/fatf/SRecsTF_en.htm

20. Recommendation 21 of the FATF Forty Recommendations advises financial institutions to give 'special attention' to transactions with such countries. Further 'countermeasures' can then be taken, including 'enhanced surveillance and reporting' of financial transactions and raising due diligence requirements for clients from such a territory available, *supra* note 17.

21. See FATF publication *Guidance for Financial Institutions in Detecting Terrorist Financing*, annex I, 24 April 2002.

v) a legal entity or organisation with the same address as other organisations, or the same person as a signature authority with no apparent reason; vi) a recently formed legal entity with higher level of deposits than expected in comparison with the income of the founders; and vii) the opening of multiple accounts by one person with numerous small deposits not commensurate with income. However, it should be noted that the existence or absence of all or any of these red flags does not reasonably point towards or away from terrorist funding. Indeed, these red flags may indicate some other form of delinquent activity, e.g. ordinary criminal conduct, the laundering of bribes etc., or none at all.

6.3.4 The International Monetary Fund (IMF)

The IMF has also become increasingly concerned with terrorism financing. Not only has it endorsed the FATF recommendations[22] but has added Anti-Money Laundering and Combating the Financing of Terrorism (AML/CFT) to the list of areas in respect of which countries are assessed by the IMF under its Report of Standards and Codes (ROSC) regime.[23] The IMF assessment criteria include reviewing measures to implement international criminal justice cooperation, criminalisation of the relevant activity, the existence of preventative measures for financial institutions and mechanisms for the monitoring or reporting of large currency and cross-border transactions.[24] It has drawn these criteria not only from the FATF recommendations but also through including relevant elements from United Nations Security Council Resolutions and international conventions, and from supervisory/regulatory standards for the banking, insurance and securities sectors.[25] In addition, it is providing technical assistance to member countries on combating terrorist finance.[26]

The IMF has clearly understood the magnitude of the task faced by it and any other international organisations trying to encourage and enforce compliance in financial systems, as indicated by its description of the measures required below:

'A truly effective AML/CFT system requires that other conditions not covered by the AML/CFT assessment criteria also be

---

22. See *Report on the Outcome of the FATF Plenary Meeting and Proposal for the Endorsement of the Methodology for Assessing Compliance with Anti-Money Laundering and Combating the Financing of Terrorism (AML/CFT) Standard*, 8 November 2002. Available http://www.imf.org/external/np/mae/aml/2002/eng/110802.pdf

23. The IMF country Reports on the Observance of Standards and Codes (ROSCs) can be found at http://www.imf.org/external/np/rosc/rosc.asp

24. *Id.*, Annex II, p. 6.

25. *Id.*, p. 3.

26. See IMF fact sheet on technical assistance available on http://www.imf.org/external/np/exr/facts/tech.htm

in place. These include sound and sustainable financial sector policies and a well-developed public sector infrastructure. In particular, effectiveness depends on a proper culture of deterrence shared and reinforced by government, financial institutions, other providers of financial services, industry trade groups, and self-regulatory organisations (SROs). The infrastructure requires ethical and professional lawyers, examiners, accountants, auditors, police officers, prosecutors, and judges, etc., and a reasonably efficient court system whose decisions are enforceable. An essential aspect of assessing the adequacy of these conditions is the existence of a system for ensuring the ethical and professional behaviour on the part of examiners, accountants and auditors, and lawyers, including the existence of codes of conduct and good practices, as well as methods to ensure compliance such as registration, licensing, and supervisory bodies.'[27]

6.4 PROBLEMS OF ENFORCEMENT AND COOPERATION

With the opportunities created by the global financial and communications market, suppressing the financing of terrorism requires an all-encompassing, international approach to have any chance of success. Therefore, *all* states must put in place effective measures restricting terrorist financing.

One advancement in international cooperation has been the coming into force of the 1999 International Convention for the Suppression of the Financing of Terrorism (Terrorism Finance Convention). However, this convention only criminalises the financing of activities which are covered by one of the other UN conventions. Thus, the applicability of the Terrorism Finance Convention is dependent upon states ratifying the other UN conventions. Wide ratification of these conventions would therefore enhance international cooperation in combating the financing of terrorism, as would agreement on a common definition of terrorism, either as part of a new convention on terrorist finance or a comprehensive convention on terrorism.

The recommendations by the FATF are a good starting point for governments and could serve as a common framework on standards for combating terrorist financing. In particular, it is to be welcomed that the FATF calls on countries to enhance international cooperation and to afford each other the greatest possible assistance. However, there is no central international organisation or body which could coordinate the efforts of the different international and regional bodies and monitor the implementation of existing standards. Although Security Council Resolution

---

27. *Supra* note 22, Annex II, p. 5.

1373 is binding, the CTC itself has a purely advisory role and is not empowered to penalise non-compliant countries. In the future more coercive methods may need to be adopted by the Security Council including the naming of non-compliant states and the imposition of penalties.

Further, it is unclear to what extent the CTC is able to provide technical assistance to those states which lack sufficient legislative and implementing structures in place to monitor terrorism finance. Ideally, a high level of expertise should be offered to the considerable number of states that require such assistance. The Task Force considers such technical assistance crucial if Resolution 1373 is to be consistently implemented.

The lack of consistent enforcement throughout the international community could result in some states becoming safe havens for illegitimate financial transactions, including for terrorist financing. It would only take a small number of states without a sufficient regulatory framework for terrorist organisations to circumvent international control mechanisms.

The lack of coordination in combating terrorist financing is also demonstrated by the variety of lists designating individuals and organisations suspected of being involved in terrorist activities. There is an increasing number of such lists created by individual states, groups of states, regional bodies and international organisations. These lists often overlap and are shared with other states and organisations. But no single international list has been compiled to a single standard embodying all the necessary information. Without such a list, it is difficult to fashion a global framework to regulate its compilation and indeed the removal of names found to be erroneously included.

6.5 IMPACTS ON RIGHTS OF INDIVIDUALS

Security Council Resolution 1373 requires states to freeze the financial assets of individuals or entities engaged in terrorist activities. Neither the text of the resolution nor the CTC experts offer any indication of legal safeguards that must be applied in the process of freezing assets.

In their efforts to restrict terrorism finance some governments have adopted anti-terrorism legislation which is drawn extremely widely. A particular example can be found in the UK Anti Terrorism Crime and Security Act, section 4. The Treasury may make a 'freezing order' against an account if it reasonably believes 'that action to the detriment of the United Kingdom's economy (or part of it) has been or is likely to be taken by a person or persons.' The only restriction on this is that the person or persons believed to have taken or be likely to take the action must be either the government of, or a resident of, a country or territory outside the United Kingdom.

Another means by which the assets of individuals or entities can be frozen is their inclusion on already mentioned lists of those engaged in terrorism. Since September 11 states have collated and shared lists, detailing not just entities connected with the Taliban and al-Qaeda, as required by the Security Council Resolutions 1267, 1333 and 1390, but also individuals and organisations suspected of being involved in other terrorist organisations.[28] Citizens are usually prohibited from dealing with or providing financial services to listed persons or entities, or are required to make suspicious transaction reports in respect of any dealings they have.

The effect on the rights of individuals whose assets are frozen either through specific legislation or inclusion on a list is profound. Therefore, it is of particular concern that neither the relevant Security Council resolutions nor the guidelines published by the CTC establish a minimum legal framework regulating the process of asset freezing. In effect, states that introduce these measures often protect the secrecy of the information they possess. The opportunity to challenge the state's action is therefore restricted as persons affected by freezing orders and the like simply have no information as to the basis of the order, and are thus disadvantaged in any challenge they make to the orders affecting them. Whilst it is accepted that there may be security reasons for failing to provide certain information, this must be balanced by the need of individuals to protect themselves from such draconian measures. Only a court should decide whether national security requirements outweigh individual interests. Yet there are no requirements to provide for any judicial review or right of appeal to an individual or entity whose assets are incorrectly frozen.

---

28. In the United States, for example, on 24 September 2001, the United States President signed Executive Order (EO) 13224, Blocking Property and Prohibiting Transactions with Persons who Commit, Threaten to Commit, or Support Terrorism. The order lists a number of individuals and organisations in the annexe and then declares that all property and interests in property of such persons in the United States now or in the future are blocked. Thus blocking extends to persons who assist, sponsor or provide financial material or technological support or are otherwise associated with anyone on the list. More significantly, Section 2 (a) states 'any transaction or dealing by United States persons or within the United States in interests in property blocked pursuant to this order is prohibited . . ." In addition, any transaction for the purpose of evading or avoiding the prohibitions is also in itself prohibited. Many of its provisions apply to 'United States persons', meaning any United States citizen, permanent resident alien, entity organised under the laws of the United States (including foreign branches) or any person in the United States. See Section 3(c). Pursuant to Section 1 (d) of the Order the Secretary of State, in consultation with the Secretary of the Treasury and the Attorney General and, if he deems necessary, any foreign authorities, may designate those who assist, sponsor or provide financial material or technological support to named persons as being persons subject to the order. This would indicate that the Order has an extra-territorial effect. In addition, the Office of Foreign Assets Control (OFAC), a department of the Treasury, has published a list of 'Specially designated Nationals (SDN) and blocked persons' on its website. See http://www.treas.gov/offices/enforcement/ofac/sdn/index.html. Regulations for various industries then encourage the blocking of transactions with such persons. The regulations for the banking industry, for instance, encourage the use of 'interdict software', i.e. programs which automatically block transactions which include a name of an SDN.

The freezing of assets has the potential to irreparably damage financial interests, as well as to stigmatise a person's name and reputation. Further, there is a great potential for innocent parties such as shareholders and other co-owners to be adversely affected by freezing orders and it is for this reason that closer attention should be paid to the effect of such lists and legislation. Matters are made worse when lists are shared with other states or regional organisations.

The Task Force believes it is essential that certain due process guarantees and safeguards should be in place where freezing of assets or other action is taken. Such guarantees should include: i) judicial supervision of such procedures; ii) respect for fundamental due process guarantees; iii) the establishment of a *prima facie* case; and iv) sufficient financial provision for living necessities to be provided for from frozen funds.

CONCLUSION

Ultimately, the effectiveness of legislation against terrorist financing can only be determined by evaluating its success in frustrating, deterring or preventing an act of terrorism. The problem lies in assessing such effectiveness—a thwarted terrorist act will probably only be known as such if it is prevented very shortly before it is carried out, in which case the probability is that the terrorists were able to access funds to get as far as they did. Effective restriction of funding to terrorists should mean that any planned activity is stifled early, and it is therefore difficult to truly measure the efficacy of anti-terrorist finance legislation.

Further, it should not be assumed that all terrorist acts can be prevented by blocking funds belonging to or intended for terrorists. Not all such funds flow through the regulated financial systems and those that do are often extremely difficult to identify, even when using suspicious transaction criteria. In any event, a terrorist act does not necessarily require significant quantities of funding to be perpetrated.

The efforts of those international organisations combating terrorist finance have been most effective in identifying areas or countries of concern and bringing pressure to bear on jurisdictions to tighten money laundering controls. However, international cooperation could be slowed down by the CTC's lack of any regulatory teeth. An internationally agreed definition of terrorism would constitute an important component in improving international cooperation in combating the financing of terrorism.

International efforts to eradicate terrorism finance have unfortunately led some states to implement measures which can significantly erode the rights of individuals. The lack of a legal framework regulating the seizure and freezing of assets commonly leaves those affected without means of obtaining the evidence against them or legally challenging the actions of the state. As a matter of urgency the international community should agree upon certain minimum evidential and due process requirements.

Recommendations

1) In order to tackle terrorism finance globally, all states must put in place measures to detect and suppress funds used to support terrorist activities. Such measures must be consistently and universally enforced, taking account of guidelines developed by international expert bodies.

2) States lacking sufficient technical expertise and/or resources to adopt and enforce measures to detect and suppress terrorism finance must be given sufficient support, including, where necessary, financial. The central banks of such states may need particular assistance to implement the required control mechanisms. The Task Force believes that the creation of specialised regional bodies under the auspices of international financial organisations may be the best way of providing the necessary support.

3) Greater opportunities for cooperation between states in sharing information about suspected terrorists and their financiers should be created, ideally within a regulated international framework.

4) The system of asset seizure must be placed within a more regulated framework, in particular to ensure transparency and protect due process guarantees.

CHAPTER 7

INTERNATIONAL COOPERATION IN COMBATING TERRORISM

7.1 INTRODUCTION

Terrorist organisations, impervious to international borders, capable of utilising sophisticated communications technology, present a renewed challenge to the international community. Nation states, regardless of region and/or political ideology have a duty to cooperate more closely, to improve their shared information systems if they are to face this challenge effectively. As the world perceives the terrorist threat to be increasing in severity and breadth, there is a corresponding imperative to look at and evaluate existing mechanisms of cooperation. And yet, for the reasons noted elsewhere in this report, each step toward countering terrorism is accompanied by a corresponding duty to respect human rights—principles of non-discrimination, freedom of association, freedom of religion—as well as those judicial safeguards—the presumption of innocence, right to a defence, and right to be tried by an independent and impartial tribunal—that are the hallmarks of the rule of law.

International cooperation between states takes the form of eight modalities which apply to all types of international, transnational and domestic criminality. They are therefore not limited to terrorism, nor are there any modalities more appropriate to terrorism than others. The weaknesses and strength of these modalities thus have an impact on the effectiveness of combating terrorism.

These modalities are: extradition, legal assistance, execution of foreign penal sentences, recognition of foreign penal judgments, transfer of criminal proceedings, freezing and seizing of assets deriving from criminal conduct, intelligence and law enforcement information gathering and sharing, and regional and sub-regional 'judicial spaces'. These modalities depend on legislative authority, administrative and prosecutorial competencies, and judicial oversight. They must therefore observe the due process of law, yet be unencumbered by too many formalities that can impede their effectiveness.

These modalities are contained in specialised treaties which deal, however, with only one or the other of such modalities. They are also contained, though only with respect to some of them, in regional multilateral treaties. National legislation also includes some of these modalities, but the number of states having such legislation is estimated at less than half of the world's states, and among those, less than half cover more than one of these modalities. Not one of these sources of law encompasses all of these eight modalities, and only three states deal with them in a comprehensive manner.

7.2 EXISTING MODALITIES OF INTERNATIONAL COOPERATION

There is no multilateral comprehensive convention encompassing all of these modalities. Instead, there are some regional conventions developed by the Council of Europe,[1] the Organization of American States,[2] and the League of Arab States[3] that cover separately extradition, mutual legal assistance and money laundering. The Council of Europe conven-

---

1. European Convention on Extradition, ETS No. 024 (13 December 1957); Additional Protocol to the European Convention on Extradition, ETS No. 086 (15 October 1975); Second Additional Protocol to the European Convention on Extradition, ETS No. 098 (17 March 1978); European Convention on Mutual Assistance in Criminal Matters, ETS No. 030 (20 April 1959); Additional Protocol to the European Convention on Mutual Assistance in Criminal Matters, ETS No. 099 (17 March 1978); Second Additional Protocol to the European Convention on Mutual Assistance in Criminal Matters, ETS No. 182 (8 November 2001); European Convention on the International Validity of Criminal Judgments, ETS No. 070 (28 May 1970); European Convention on the Transfer of Proceedings in Criminal Matters, ETS No. 073 (15 May 1972); Convention on the Transfer of Sentenced Persons, ETS No. 112 (21 March 1983); Additional Protocol to the Convention on the Transfer of Sentenced Persons, ETS No. 167 (18 December 1997); Convention on Laundering, Search, Seizure, and Confiscation of the Proceeds from Crime, ETS No. 141 (8 November 1990).

2. Inter-American Convention on Mutual Assistance in Criminal Matters (23 May 1992); Optional Protocol Related to the Inter-American Convention on Mutual Assistance in Criminal Matters (11 June 1993); Inter-American Convention on Extraterritorial Validity of Foreign Judgments and Arbitral Awards (8 May 1979); Inter-American Convention on Proof of and Information on Foreign Law (8 May 1979); Inter-American Convention on the Taking of Evidence Abroad (30 January 1975); Additional Protocol to the Inter-American Convention on the Taking of Evidence Abroad (24 May 1984); Inter-American Convention on Extradition O.A.S.T.S. No. 60 (25 February 1981); International American Convention on Mutual Assistance in Criminal Matters O.A.S.T.S. No. 75 (23 May 1992); Inter-American Convention on Jurisdiction in the International Sphere for the Extraterritorial Validity of Foreign Judgments (24 May 1984); Inter-American Convention on Serving Criminal Sentences Abroad (9 June 1993). *See* http://www.oas.org/juridico/english/treaties.html.

3. Arab League Extradition Agreement, Sept. 14, 1951, in *League of Arab States Collection of Treaties and Agreements* 95 (1978) See also the Arab League Agreement on Extradition and Judicial Cooperation of 1983 (commonly referred to as the Riyadh Agreement), which has been ratified by sixteen Arab states. It includes the 1951 Arab League Agreement on Extradition and 1951 Arab League Agreement on Judicial Cooperation.

tions, however, encompass (though separately), transfer of sentenced persons, transfer of criminal proceedings and recognition of foreign penal judgments.[4]

At the level of national legislation, only a few countries have a comprehensive section in their codes of criminal procedure which includes international cooperation. They are: Austria, Germany, Italy and Switzerland.[5] Even so, these codes, with the exception of Germany's 2003 Code of International Criminal Cooperation,[6] deal with only four to six of the eight modalities listed above. None includes as part of their legislation on international cooperation in penal matters intelligence and law enforcement cooperation in the gathering and sharing of information, or 'judicial spaces'.[7]

Of the fifteen treaties applicable to international terrorism,[8] none

---

4. European Convention on Transfer of Sentenced Persons, Strasbourg, 21 Mar. 1983, E.T.S. 112. See also Epp, Transfer of Prisoners: The European Convention, in 2 *International Criminal Law: Procedural and Enforcement Mechanisms* 751 (M. Cherif Bassiouni ed., 2nd rev. ed., 1999); The European Convention on the International Validity of Criminal Judgments, 28 May 1970, E.T.S. 70.

5. Only three countries have developed integrated national legislation on international cooperation. They are Austria, Switzerland, and Germany. Austrian Law on Mutual Assistance in Criminal Matters, *Bundesgesets vom 4 December 1979 Uber alle Auslieferung und die Rechtshilfe in Strafsachen* (Auslieferungs—und Rechtshilfegesetz—ARGH), BGBl, Nr. 529/1979. See also Robert Linke, Et Alinternationales Stafrecht (1981), Klaus Schwaighofer, Auslieferung und Internationales Strarecht (1988). Swiss Federal Law on International Mutual Assistance in Criminal Matters, Entraide Internationale en Matière Penal of 20 March 1981, amended 1996. Germany has, in connection with its ratification of the ICC, adopted a new comprehensive legislation on international cooperation in penal matters. See German ICC Cooperation Act of 21 June 2002, 1BGBI 2144 (Federal Gazette)(2002).

6. *Id.*

7. This may, however, change in 2004 with the entry into effect of the EU's European Arrest Warrant. See Council Framework Decision of 13 June 2002 on the European Arrest Warrant & the Surrender Procedures Between Member States; (2002/584/JHA), *Offical Journal of European Communities*, 1–20, L190 of 18, July 2002. See also Giuliano Vassalli, Mandato d'arresto e pricipio d'equalianza, Il Guisto Processo, 129, No. 3, Sept.–Oct. 2002.

8. They are: Convention on the High Seas, UN Doc. A/Conf. 13/L. 52–55 or 52 & 56 & 58 (1958); Convention on Offenses and Certain Other Acts Committed on Board Aircraft [hereinafter Tokyo Hijacking Convention], *opened for signature* Sept. 14, 1963, 704 U.N.T.S. 219; Convention for the Suppression of Unlawful Seizure of Aircraft, *opened for signature* Dec. 16, 1970, 860 U.N.T.S. 105 [hereinafter Hague Hijacking Convention]; Convention for the Suppression of Unlawful Acts Against the Safety of Civil Aviation, *opened for signature* Sept. 23, 1971, 974 U.N.T.S. 177 [hereinafter Montreal Hijacking Convention]; Convention on the Prevention and Punishment of Crimes Against Internationally Protected Persons, including Diplomatic Agents, *opened for signature* Dec. 14, 1973, 1035 U.N.T.S. 167; International Convention Against the Taking of Hostages, UN Doc. A/Res/34/146 (1979); Convention on the Physical Protection of Nuclear Material, IAEA Doc.IFCIRC/225 (Mar. 3, 1980); 1456 U.N.T.S. 125; Convention on the Law of the Sea, UN Doc. A/Conf. 62/122 or 13/51 & 45 (1982); Protocol for the Suppression of Unlawful Acts of Violence at Airports Serving International Civil Aviation, ICAO Doc. 9518 (Feb. 24, 1988); Convention for the Suppression of Unlawful Acts Against the Safety of Maritime Navigation, IMO Doc.

contains all of these modalities.[9] Most of them contain provisions on extradition and mutual legal assistance but even these provisions are sketchy.[10] Most of them, at best, include two or three lines identifying a given modality and briefly describing it, leaving it to the states parties to develop specificity in their national legislation. Yet these treaties provide that states may rely on these provisions in lieu of bilateral treaties, and by implication they offer states the opportunity to rely on these provisions if national legislation is inexistent.

These fifteen conventions deal with different subjects (such as hijacking of airplanes, taking civilian hostages, attacks upon internationally protected persons, bombings, etc.). There is so far no comprehensive convention which focuses on the combination of the perpetrators' intentions, the means employed and the outcomes. Instead, the conventions focus on the protected persons or protected targets or prohibit violence

---

Sua/Conf/15.Rev.1 (1988); Protocol for the Suppression of Unlawful Acts Against the Safety of Fixed Platforms Located on the Continental Shelf, IMO Doc. Sua/Conf/16/Rev.2 (1988); Convention on the Marking of Plastic Explosives for the Purpose of Detection, S/22393 & Corr.1 (Mar. 1, 1991); Convention on the Safety of United Nations and Associated Personnel, U.N. Doc. A/49/742 (1994); International Convention for the Suppression of Terrorism Bombings, U.N. Doc. A/Res/52/164 (1998); International Convention for the Suppression of the Financing of Terrorism, G.A. Res. 109, U.N. GAOR 6th Comm., 54 Sess., 76th mtg., Agenda Item 160, U.N. Doc. A/54/109 (1999). These treaties are reprinted in International Terrorism: Multilateral Conventions (1937–2001) 135 (M. Cherif Bassiouni ed., 2001) (hereinafter Bassiouni, Terrorism Conventions). The literature on the subject commonly ignores the 1958 Geneva Convention on the Law of the Sea (Convention on the High Seas, U.N. Doc. A/Conf. 13/L. 52–55 or 52 & 56 & 58 (1958)), and the 1982 Montego Bay Convention on the Law of the Sea (Convention on the Law of the Sea, U.N. Doc. A/Conf. 62/122 or 13/51 & 45 (1982)), which have provisions on piracy, a form of terrorism, as evidenced by the case of the Achille Lauro which brought about a specialised IMO Convention, Convention for the Suppression of Unlawful Acts Against the Safety of Maritime Navigation, IMO Doc. Sua/Conf/15.Rev.1 (1988)). In addition, the literature also ignores the Universal Postal Union Convention (Constitution of the Universal Postal Union, *open for signature* July 10, 1964; Additional Protocol to the Constitution of the Universal Postal Union of July 10, 1964, Article 29 (1)(e), *opened for signature* Nov. 14, 1969, 810 U.N.T.S. 69; Second Additional Protocol to the Constitution of the Universal Postal Union of 10 July 1964, *open for signature* July 5, 1974; Third Additional Protocol to the Constitution of the universal Postal Union of July 10, 1964, *opened for signature* July 28, 1984; Fourth Additional Protocol to the Constitution of the Universal Postal Union of 10 July 1964, *opened for signature* Dec. 14, 1989; Fifth Additional Protocol to the Constitution of the Universal Postal Union of 10 July 1964, *opened for signature* Sept. 14, 1994; Universal Postal Union Postal Parcels Agreement, Article 19(a)(v), *opened for signature* Nov. 14, 1969, 810 U.N.T.S. 224; Agreement Concerning Postal Parcels, *opened for signature* Sept. 14, 1994), prohibiting the mailing of explosive and other dangerous substances. This is particularly relevant to the use of letter and package bombing, and the inclusion of substances such as Anthrax.

9.   For an analysis of which UN treaties contain which provisions on mutual legal assistance see Appendix V.

10.   *Id.*, Bassiouni, Terrorism Conventions.

by certain means.[11] Possibly as a result of this subject-matter approach, it was not possible to develop a comprehensive approach to all the modalities of cooperation. As to the text of these provisions, the drafters who are usually diplomats are not necessarily skilled in international criminal law. Thus, diplomatic lack of expertise with the subject of international cooperation in penal matters is probably what leads to the drafting of treaty provisions in the manner described above. As a consequence, states do not feel that they can rely on these provisions, and in practice, seldom rely upon them.

7.3 THE MAXIM *AUT DEDERE AUT JUDICARE*

International cooperation in penal matters is predicated on the maxim *aut dedere aut judicare*.[12] Essentially the maxim requires states to prosecute or extradite. While prosecute or extradite is more limited in scope than the range of available modalities in international cooperation in penal matters, it is understandable insofar as the maxim emerged in 1624,[13] while most of the modalities of international cooperation beyond extradition developed mostly in the last fifty years. But, even so, the maxim *aut dedere aut judicare* is flawed in respect of its application to international criminal law in general and to terrorism in particular. It is uncertain as to whether the existence of the duty to prosecute or extradite is alternative or cumulative and no international treaty which includes this obligation clarifies this legal issue. Moreover, the obligation to prosecute or extradite does not contain any qualifying criteria. Presumably, the two-pronged duty is predicated on certain unarticulated premises which are of a qualitative nature, namely that the prosecution, in the prosecuting state, is to be effective and fair, that the extradition process in the requested state is to be effective and fair, and that the prosecution, in the requesting state is also to be effective and fair. No treaty addresses the issues of effectiveness and fairness, just as no treaty addresses the issue of whether the duty to prosecute precedes that of extradition and whether the duty to prosecute or extradite are cumulative duties and not alternative ones.[14]

As a result of this lack of clarity, questions arise between states as to whether the duty to prosecute has priority over that of extradition and

---

11. This is the approach of the European Convention on Terrorism, see *supra* note 1.

12. See Bassiouni and Wise, Aut Dedere Aut Judicare: The Duty to Prosecute or Extradite in International Law (1995).

13. The maxim originated in a longer formula developed by Hugo Grotius in 1624 as '*aut dedere . . . aut punire*'. See Hugo Grotius, De Jure Belli Ac Pacis, bk II, ch. XXI secs. III and IV, in *Classics of International Law* 526–29, (James B. Scott ed., F. Kelsey trans., 1925).

14. An alternative proposition is that the state has a choice on the matter, but again the situation is unclear.

to what extent can states deny extradition on the grounds that the person requested may be treated unfairly or given an unfair trial. Conversely, a requesting state may claim that the willingness of a requested state to carry out prosecutions may be ineffective or may even be a sham.

The seminal case in point is the Lockerbie case, where for over a decade the United Kingdom and the United States challenged Libya's avowed intention to prosecute two of its nationals who were indicted for the tragic incidents of Pan Am 103's explosion over Lockerbie, Scotland, in 1988, resulting in the deaths of 259 passengers and eleven persons.[15] Libya, in reliance on Articles 7 and 8 of the Convention for the Suppression of Unlawful Acts Against the Safety of Civil Aviation (1971),[16] took the position that the duty to prosecute was stated first in the Convention and thus, because it preceded the duty to extradite, it was deemed by Libya that it had a priority right to prosecute over the secondary obligation to extradite. The United Kingdom and the United States argued that Libya was not likely to conduct an effective trial of two intelligence operatives, and Libya argued that it could not surrender its nationals to be tried in either the United States or the United Kingdom, as they would be treated unfairly. Four years into the deadlock Libya filed an action against the United Kingdom and the United States before the International Court of Justice (ICJ). To forestall the ICJ's decision on the merits, in 1992 the United States and the United Kingdom obtained from the Security Council an unprecedented resolution requiring the surrender of the two indicted persons. This Security Council action, in fact, created a new challenge for the ICJ, which resulted in a precedent, making Security Council resolutions not judicially reviewable by the ICJ.[17] As a result, there is no judicial determination as to whether the duty to prosecute has precedent over the duty to extradite or whether, under some circumstances, it is the duty to extradite which has precedence. Furthermore, it remains unclear whether the unarticulated conditions of effectiveness and fairness can be relied upon in competing claims between states. The stalemate in the Lockerbie case was, however, resolved by rely-

---

15. For application, pleadings, orders, oral arguments and judgments arising out of this incident, see generally, *Case Concerning Questions of Interpretation and Application of 1971 Montreal Convention Arising from the Aerial Incident at Lockerbie,* General List No. 88 (*Libyan Arab Jamahiriya v. United Kingdom*) (Instituted in Registry of the Court of International Justice on 3 March 1992), *available at* http://www.icj-cij.org/icjwww/idocket/iluk/iluk2 frame.html (last visited November 15, 2002). *See also* Case Concerning Questions of Interpretation and Application of 1971 Montreal Convention Arising from the Aerial Incident at Lockerbie, General List No. 89 (*Libyan Arab Jamahiriya v. United Kingdom*), (Instituted in Registry of the Court of International Justice on 3 March 1992), available at http://www.icj-cij.org/icjwww/idocket/ilus/ilusframe.html (last visited November 15, 2002).

16. Montreal Hijacking Convention, *supra* note 8.

17. See, e.g. Bedjaouri ed, *International Law: Achievements and Prospects* (1992).

ing on one of the modalities of international cooperation, namely, transfer of criminal proceedings (though in this case this was more in the nature of a change of venue, since the involved states agreed to have a case tried in the Netherlands, but in accordance with Scottish law and before Scottish judges).

There are also a number of generally recognised exceptions and defences to extradition and mutual legal assistance, which also extend, explicitly or by implication, to the other modalities. They include: the political offence exception; the exclusion of nationals; limitations in respect of states that carry certain penalties such as capital and corporal punishment, and *non bis in idem* (for civilist legal systems) and its common law counterpart of double jeopardy. As a result of these conditions, extradition occasionally fails, leaving requesting states with difficult choices, particularly in terrorism cases.[18]

7.4 ANALYSIS OF THE EFFECTIVENESS OF THE PRESENT SYSTEM OF COOPERATION

A comprehensive approach to international cooperation can minimise the weaknesses of each of the different modalities. The analogy is to a gearbox. By dealing with every modality separately, each gearbox has only one gear. By combining all the modalities together, the gearbox has multiple gears, and it is possible to shift from one to another. Thus, in the Lockerbie case, when extradition failed, the solution was to shift to the gear of transfer of the criminal proceedings to a different venue. There are many similar obstacles which can be avoided or reduced by this 'gearshifting' approach. For example, a prohibition of extradition of nationals can be overcome by a conditional extradition which requires the prosecuting state to return the person to the state of nationality for the execution of the sentence. This can also be relied upon whenever a state hesitates to grant extradition because the requesting state may inflict upon the requested person penalties or treatment that the requested state may deem cruel or inhumane. A conditional extradition, subject to the return of the person once the trial is over, and the execution of a sentence in the state of nationality, if found guilty, solves the problem. In short, using these modalities interchangeably enhances accountability without reducing the standards of due process. Instead, the present approach which is mostly due to legislative shortsightedness, produces gaps in the net of accountability that allows persons accused of terrorism to escape prosecution.

---

18. One of the choices is abduction or disguised extradition, which violates due process. See Bassiouni, *International Extradition: US Law and Practice* (4th rev. ed., 2002), at chapters 4 and 5.

The problems of international cooperation do not only arise in connection with the terrorism conventions but more so with respect to national legislation. As indicated above, there are few states that have comprehensive legislation on the modalities of international cooperation but fewer than one-half of the world's countries have any legislation at all. Most countries of the world rely on bilateral treaties which are, of course, characterised by their diversity. The absence of comprehensive national legislation and reliance on bilateral treaties, even by such developed countries, exposes the weaknesses of each of these modalities. This is particularly true with respect to extradition, which is the most important of them. But mutual legal assistance, which frequently includes freezing and seizing of assets which relate to terrorism financing, is not included in almost two-thirds of the world's national legislation, and only a few bilateral treaties contain such modalities.[19] For example, the United States has thirty-six bilateral treaties on mutual legal assistance,[20] and over one hundred treaties on extradition.[21]

Contrary to what some government officials argue, the problems of international cooperation do not stem from procedural requirements that increase the rights of the individual to the detriment of an effective legal process. Though the argument is not entirely without merit, it ignores the systemic causes which include the absence of a comprehensive multilateral convention on the modalities of international cooperation, the ineffectiveness of dealing at the national legislative level with these modalities on an uncoordinated basis, the relatively low number of states which have legislation governing these modalities, the large number of procedural technicalities which do not necessarily enhance due process but which delay cooperation and last, but not least, the ineffectiveness of domestic legal systems. Consequently, a new approach is needed.

The systemic problems of international cooperation also derive from the insistence by many governments on bilateralism over multilateralism. The reason states favour bilateralism over multilateralism is because they view international cooperation in penal matters as an extension of their political relations. Thus, governments reduce procedural barriers to international cooperation with friendly nations and the nations of those whose

---

19. The thrust of Security Council Resolution 1373 (2001), See Appendix IV concerning counter-terrorism is on money laundering. This limited focus evidences once again the myopic view of those who sponsored and supported this approach, instead of developing a broader, more comprehensive one. For reports of the Counter Terrorism Committee, see http://www.un.org/Docs/sc/committees/1373.

20. See Ellis, Pisani, and Gualtieri, United States Treaties on Mutual Assistance in *Criminal Matters, in International Criminal Law: Procedural and Enforcement Mechanisms* 549, (Bassiouni ed., 2nd rev. ed. 1999).

21. See Bassiouni, *supra* note 17, Appendix II at 925.

legal systems they respect, and increase them with less friendly ones.[22] As a result, international cooperation in penal matters has become a part of states' political accommodation processes, instead of being a legal system, based on an international *civitas maxima.*

A new approach is needed in which all the modalities of international cooperation, now applied piecemeal, are to be integrated into a unified system. In other words, the eight modalities discussed above should be part of the same gearbox in order to allow the appropriate national authorities to shift from one gear to another. Thus, if extradition fails, the alternative is not to kidnap the person, but to obtain conditional extradition subject to the return of the accused if proven guilty to serve the sentence in the originally requested state,[23] or to transfer the criminal proceedings. In an integrated comprehensive system of international cooperation, more options are available to enhance the success of the process. That can easily be accomplished by national legislation,[24] and through multilateral and bilateral treaties. Such an integrated system's goals should include: political neutrality, the preservation of international standards of legality, human rights protections, and the enhancement of effective inter-state cooperation in penal matters.

Multilateralism should serve to buttress bilateralism and *vice versa.* Moreover, harmonisation of national legislation should be sought to produce new synergies that enhance complementarity. Thus, extradition, legal assistance, transfer of execution of penal sentences, recognition of foreign penal judgments, transfer of criminal proceedings, freezing and seizing of assets derived from criminal proceeds, intelligence and law enforcement information-sharing, and regional and sub-regional 'judicial spaces' can reinforce each other without sacrificing proper legal procedures and without violating individual human rights.[25]

---

22. See Bassiouni, The 'Political Offense Exception' Revisited: Extradition Between the U.S. and the U.K.—A Choice Between Friendly Cooperation Among Allies and Sound Law and Policy, 15 *Denver Journal of International Law and Policy* 255 (1987). Another set of problems arises out of the bureaucratic divisions that burden the administration of criminal justice in almost every country, which weakens international cooperation, the limited number of experts among judges, prosecutors, and administrative officials working in this field, and the fact that such personnel must face a large volume of cases with limited resources and support.

23. I.e., execution of foreign sentences.

24. *Supra* note 5.

25. See, e.g., Trechsel, The Protection of Human Rights in Criminal Procedure, 49 *Revue Internationale de droit Pénal* 541 (1968); Resolution of Twelfth International Penal Law Congress, in International Congress in Penal Law, Actes Du XIIE Congrés International de Droit Pénal 553–64 (Hamburg, Sept. 22, 1979) (Hans-Heinrich Jescheck ed., 1980). See also Bayefsky, The UN Human Rights Treaty System: Universality at the crossroads (2001), The Protection of Human Rights I the Administration of Justice: A Compendium of United nations Norms and Standards (M. Cherif Bassiouni ed., 1994); Human Rights and the Administration of Justice (Gane & Mackarel, eds., 1997).

CONCLUSION

The present weaknesses of international cooperation include: i) failing to provide an overall framework that integrates all the applicable modalities; ii) depending almost entirely on the effectiveness of national legal systems; iii) lacking a policy that provides continuity and progressive development; iv) placing the sole duty on states to act in conformity with treaty obligations without international constraints; v) over-reliance on bilateralism; vi) failing to provide a mechanism for the resolution of conflicts that arise between states; and vii) lacking adequate safeguards to insure 'due process'. In short, the present system has all the weaknesses inherent to an incoherent system.

A priority solution is to clarify and reinforce the obligations of states under the maxim *aut dedere aut judicare*. The duties to prosecute or extradite must include the unarticulated conditions of being executed effectively and fairly and to develop a multinational integrated approach for all the modalities of international cooperation.[26] The cumbersome, costly, and lengthy bilateral approach must give way to a more effective multilateral process or at least to an integrated bilateral approach which can strive for greater national similarities.[27]

The practices of states in international cooperation in penal matters continue relatively unchanged, even though the resort to these modalities on a singular and unintegrated basis has proven to be ineffective and inadequate in coping with increased international, transnational, and national criminality, particularly with respect to organised crime,[28] drug

---

26. Resolution of the Council of Ministers of Justice in 1987. See Rec. No. R/87/1 of the Member States (adopted by Committee of Ministers of Justice, Council of Europe 19/1/87); La Cooperation Inter-Étatique Européene En Matière Penale 1695–1791 (Müller-Rappard & Bassiouni ed., 2nd rev. ed., 1991). A special Committee of Experts has since been established with the Council of Europe to work on this project. In addition, the Council of Arab Ministers of Justice developed such a modal code of inter-state penal cooperation in 1988. Regrettably, it has not received attention from the Arab governments, as those states have not yet made international penal cooperation a priority. See 2 Council of Arab Ministers of Justice: *A Collection of the Council's Documents*, 96–148 (Jan. 1988); Wilkitzki, International and Regional Developments in the Field of Inter-State Cooperation in Penal Matters: The Council of Europe, in 2 *International Criminal Law:Procedural and Enforcement Mechanisms 999* (Bassiouni ed., 2nd rev. ed. 1999).

27. There are an estimated 2,000 treaties among over 150 countries in the world regulating one or another aspect of international cooperation. The US has over one hundred bilateral extradition treaties. See Bassiouni, *supra* note 16 113–121. The US also has forty-six bilateral treaties on mutual legal assistance and nine treaties on execution of foreign penal sentences. A large number of bilateral treaties deal with inter-state cooperation in tax matters. The Council of Europe has twenty-eight multilateral treaties on inter-state cooperation in penal matters. Other regional organisations like the OAS and The League of Arab States have a number of such multilateral treaties.

28. See Bassiouni & Vetere, Organized Crime and its Transnational Manifestations, in 1 *International Criminal Law: Crimes 883* (Bassiouni ed., 2nd rev. ed. 1999).

traffiking,[29] and terrorism.[30] Consequently, international, transnational, and national criminal phenomena are not as effectively controlled as they could be, and governments find themselves attracted to either reduce the procedural safeguards of due process or to engage in questionable and even in illegal practices under their domestic laws and under international law as a way of overcoming the ineffectiveness of the system.

This state of affairs is in part due to a lack of vision on the part of responsible officials. But it is also due in part to the fact that there are insufficiently knowledgeable experts on international criminal law advising ministries of foreign affairs and justice in many countries, particularly in developing countries. Yet developed countries offer little technical legal assistance and support to developing countries. Inter-governmental organisations too, are not offering sufficient technical legal assistance and support to developing countries. Moreover, administrative and bureaucratic divisions among the national organs of law enforcement and prosecution impair the effectiveness of international cooperation in penal matters.[31]

Recommendations

1) Recognition of the maxim *aut dedere aut judicare* as a *civitas maxima* and the development of international standards including standards for effective and good faith prosecution and extradition.

2) Establishing by a multilateral treaty the criteria for criminal jurisdiction based not only on territoriality, nationality, passive personality, protected interest, and universality, but also other policy-oriented criteria that take into account national and international interests in achieving effectiveness and fairness, including criteria for conflict resolution and compulsory adjudication before the International Court of Justice, or before regional judicial organs.

---

29. See Bassiouni & Jean François Thony, The International Drug Control System, in I *International Criminal Law: Crimes* 905 (M. Cherif Bassiouni ed., 2nd rev. ed. 1999).

30. See Bassiouni, Legal Control of International Terrorism: A Policy-Oriented Assessment, 43 *Harvard International Law Journal* 83 (2002); M. Cherif Bassiouni, Perspectives on International Terrorism, in *Bassiouni Terrorism Conventions, supra* note 8, at 1.

31. The most common divisions in national systems are among law enforcement, prosecution, judiciary, and corrections. In addition, within each subsystem, there are still more separate bureaucratic and administrative units. All too frequently these subsystems are self-contained and have their own separate international activities. Moreover, each subsystem defends its respective turf and supports its own methods, goals, and purposes leading to the fragmentation of the system of international cooperation. A thorough discussion of the effects of bureaucratic subsystems on the administration of criminal justice is contained in report to the Seventh United Nations Congress on Crime Prevention and the Treatment of Offenders (Milan, Italy Aug. 26–Sept. 6, 1983), at 40–43, UN Doc. A/Conf. 121/NGO 1 (1986).

3) Developing a model international criminal code to serve as a model for codifying national legislation.

4) Adopting a multilateral convention on cooperation between law enforcement and intelligence agencies setting forth the means, methods, and limitations of such cooperation, including the protection of fundamental human rights.

5) Consistently including the integrated modalities of international cooperation in all substantive international criminal law conventions.

6) Developing a worldwide programme of technical legal assistance, and continuing legal education programmes for public officials, judges and prosecutors in international criminal law.

7) Developing networks of information and criminal justice data-sharing within states and between states.

CHAPTER 8

FORA FOR TRYING INTERNATIONAL TERRORISTS: THE ROLE OF THE INTERNATIONAL CRIMINAL COURT

8.1 INTRODUCTION

An important goal in the fight against terrorism is ensuring that terrorists are held accountable for their acts and are brought to justice. In achieving this goal there is almost inevitably a choice as to which jurisdictional forum is to be used to try suspected terrorists. In principle there may be flexibility in making this determination. It may even be possible for *ad hoc* tribunals to be created specifically to try suspected terrorists. Flexibility will, however, only be viable where the procedural safeguards guaranteeing a fair trial are in place. In view of this there are a number of advantages and disadvantages to the use of various fora which are explored in this chapter.

The newly created International Criminal Court (ICC), which came into being on 1 July 2002, may be an appropriate venue for the trial of some suspected terrorists. This chapter also explores the types of crimes which fall within the jurisdiction of the ICC, using as a case study the terrorist attacks of September 11, 2001.

8.2 THE CRIME OF TERRORISM IN THE INTERNATIONAL CRIMINAL COURT

The International Criminal Court is to have jurisdiction over the most serious crimes of international concern. As the crime of terrorism is not yet suitably defined, it is consistent with the principles of legal certainty and legality that it cannot constitute a crime under international customary law but only under treaty law. Initially there was support for including the crime of terrorism within the jurisdiction of the ICC, but attempts at drafting a suitable definition proved unsuccessful. The most significant obstacle in the way of reaching consensus was the decision whether or not to include 'freedom fighters' within this definition.

Resolution E of the Final Act of the United Nations Diplomatic Conference of Plenipotentiaries on the Establishment of an International Criminal Court,[1] does however note that the Assembly of States Parties may include the crime of terrorism at a later stage, once an accepted definition has been formulated.

In order to assess the importance of the ICC's role in combating terrorism, it may be useful to first consider the other fora which can prosecute acts of terrorism.

8.3 FORA FOR PROSECUTING ACTS OF TERRORISM

8.3.1 Domestic Courts

A country's courts will commonly have jurisdiction to prosecute perpetrators who have committed domestic acts of terror.[2] This jurisdiction might arise from the fact that the crime of terrorism has been written into the domestic legal system[3] or due to a domestic court exercising universal jurisdiction. The acts committed may also fall under common crimes, for example murder, which are recognised in the domestic legal system.

There are a number of advantages of trying a terrorist case within the domestic court: if the courts of the country in which the terrorist act occurred choose to prosecute, the proceedings are usually more accessible for the witnesses and families of victims. Obtaining evidence may also be easier. Further, prosecution within the state in which the acts of terrorism have occurred represents an important manifestation of the state's responsibility to protect its citizens and uphold justice. It may also allow the victims and communities affected by the terrorist attack to feel some 'ownership' of the criminal justice process.

There are, however, several disadvantages. Firstly, the way that individual domestic legal systems operate may differ, resulting in dramatically different outcomes, depending on the country in which the trial was held. This could not only cause legal uncertainty but could also create friction between different countries. A country whose nationals were victims of a terrorist act may feel that a second country is treating the perpetrators too leniently within their domestic legal system. Conversely, the severity of punishment or the procedural fairness of a trial may be deemed acceptable by the country doing the prosecuting but be entirely unacceptable to another country with an interest in the outcome of the trial. The second drawback relates to the impartiality of trying terrorists in the state in which the acts were perpetrated. Public sentiment and revulsion could

---

1. Annex I, Res. E.
2. Although states have varying jurisdictional principles upon which they base prosecution.
3. For example, the United Kingdom Terrorism Act of 2000.

be so high as to raise doubts within the international community as to the impartiality of the trial process. By the same token, if the prosecution takes place in a state in which the terrorist suspects are domiciled, the sentence may be perceived to be, or may actually be, more lenient. The third potential drawback relates to failures in the extradition process. Where the perpetrators of the terrorist act are abroad, the domestic court will seek to rely on extradition, which experience shows, commonly fails. Such failures are often attributable to political reasons with a state refusing to proffer its nationals for trial in a state with which it has poor diplomatic relations. Equally, concern about a lack of fair trial procedures and the application of the death penalty in the requesting state may lead to a refusal to extradite.

8.3.2   National Courts Constituted in Another State

In certain cases a national court can sit on foreign soil. An example of this is the special court which was established for the Lockerbie trial. This choice of forum may reduce the perception of partiality that may arise from a prosecution in the domestic courts within a country. However, the same problems associated with the diversity of approaches adopted by different domestic legal systems within specific countries, discussed above, apply here.

8.3.3   Special Military Tribunals

A distinction should be made between ordinary military tribunals, which, with their own rules of procedure, nonetheless make up part of the justice system, and special or *ad hoc* military tribunals, which are the focus of this section. To this latter category can be added regularly constituted military tribunals to which government officials refer non-military criminal cases. The ordinary military rules of procedure applied in such cases may, for example, exclude a right to appeal.

Special military tribunals are often created at times when the authorities perceive there to be threats to national security. At such times, it is crucial that any newly created judicial processes are given sufficient consideration and are evaluated against international standards of due process.

There are benefits to trying cases before a military court. Greater secrecy is usually possible with a special military tribunal. This may serve the purpose of protecting the national security of the prosecuting nation. It is however at the cost of legal transparency and therefore the use of such tribunals at times when there is no threat to national security or armed conflict taking place, may amount to an abuse of the fair trial guarantees. Even at times of war there are ways to protect national security interests, while still ensuring a fair trial. For example, the International

Criminal Tribunal for the Former Yugoslavia (ICTY), employed technology such as scrambling the voices of witnesses to ensure, *inter alia*, the protection of security interests. Moreover, by constituting special tribunals, the authorities may be in a better position to offer protection to judges, prosecutors, defence lawyers, participants in the trial and the general public from terrorist or other threats.

Weighed against these benefits are a number of disadvantages. The standard of procedural fairness in special military trials may be perceived to be, or in fact be, lower than in ordinary, domestic trials. If standards are lower, this may lead to incorrect convictions, not only violating the rights of those prosecuted but resulting in those who are in fact guilty not being brought to justice. Military tribunals may also be perceived as being less impartial than regularly constituted courts. A country using this kind of forum for prosecution therefore makes itself vulnerable to international criticism if its use is not justified. If a tribunal, which does not appear to be impartial and just is used to prosecute terrorists it may also fuel the animosity of those sympathetic to those on trial. This may result in further attacks against the citizens of the prosecuting country.

8.3.4   Coalition Treaty-Based Tribunals

Coalitions of different international players may choose to create a tribunal by treaty. The interested parties may be various countries, as was the case with the Nuremberg and Tokyo tribunals. Such tribunals may even constitute a country and the United Nations together, as was the case with the establishment of the Independent Special Court for Sierra Leone and the proposed mixed tribunal for Cambodia, which envisages international and Cambodian participation.

Coalition treaty-based tribunals have a number of benefits. First, it is possible that a coalition might be better able to reach consensus regarding an acceptable definition of terrorism. Second, by working together coalition members have the benefit of international financial, legal and policing services. Third, such a tribunal may be more reflective of different nations' legal systems and political ideals, thereby providing it with greater legitimacy. This, however, depends largely on who the members are. Fourth, the tribunal can be situated in a place other than the country in which the act of terrorism occurred. This may be beneficial for security reasons or simply for practical reasons regarding the procurement of evidence and witnesses. It may also project a more impartial image of the tribunal.

However, the coalition would be powerless to compel other nations to cooperate regarding the provision of evidence and suspects, and would have to rely on existing extradition and cooperation treaties. Further, where a mixed international/national court is established, the national component may dominate the international and thus introduce some of the acute problems of trial by national courts, considered above. Finally, the setting up of a tribunal of this nature may be both time consuming and costly.

8.3.5 The International Court of Justice

The International Court of Justice (ICJ) deals only with disputes between states and not with criminal acts of individuals. Given that terrorism is understood by the international community as applying to private individuals, it does not fall within the jurisdiction of the ICJ.

8.3.6 *Ad Hoc* International Tribunals

Security Council action under its Chapter VII powers has in the past led to the establishment of international tribunals for Rwanda and the former Yugoslavia. If such a tribunal were to be established for terrorism, it could exercise primary jurisdiction over individuals suspected of perpetrating the crime of 'terrorism'. The Security Council could compel UN member states to cooperate with the tribunal through use of its Chapter VII powers. The judges may be elected by the same procedure used in the Rwanda and Yugoslavia Tribunals. For those tribunals, a short-list of judges was compiled by the Security Council and the final selection was made from this list by the General Assembly. The input of the General Assembly allows for representation of the interests of the diverse legal systems of the world.

Ad hoc international tribunals have the advantage that judges appointed by the General Assembly are more likely to be impartial and representative of the general legal norms accepted by most nations and also to be perceived as such. Further, such tribunals may not have to rely on complicated extradition and cooperation treaties in order to obtain evidence and suspects, as such procedures will have been arranged in accordance with the Security Council's Chapter VII powers. Finally, a single set of procedural and substantive laws will apply for as long as the tribunal continues to function. This will remove both the uncertainty and possible unfair outcomes that may arise from individual prosecutions in a multitude of other fora.

Whilst there are advantages to *ad hoc* international tribunals, there are also a number of drawbacks.

First, the previous tribunals of this nature were, implicitly in the case of the former Yugoslavia, and explicitly in the case of Rwanda, set up to focus on specific periods of time. They will eventually complete their tasks and be dissolved. Terrorism has, however, been with us for many centuries and its motivations have been as varied as its targets have been widespread. It might therefore be preferable to prosecute this crime in a tribunal of a permanent nature such as the ICC, rather than establishing an *ad hoc* tribunal every time it becomes necessary. That would also be the more practical option, instead of keeping a tribunal functioning indefinitely to deal only with terrorism, when the need for such a tribunal may fluctuate.

Second, the start-up and running costs associated with tribunals of this nature are enormous and must be carried by the UN which is already functioning on a tight budget. Again the ICC would be a better option as it will be funded largely by the state parties. Costs can also be reduced as there will only be one 'start-up' and during times when there is a diminished need for a tribunal focused on terrorism, the court will still be dealing with the other crimes within its jurisdiction, so there will be no wasted running costs.

Third, if the tribunals are to rely on the support of the Security Council for their establishment and enforcement, there is always the possibility that they can be sabotaged by the political ideals of one or more of the Security Council members who have the right to veto decisions made by the other members. Alternatively, it might just take a long time for the Security Council to act and in the meantime valuable evidence, witnesses and even suspects may become unavailable.

Fourth, due to the inability of the international community to agree upon a legal definition of terrorism, there is a chance that such tribunals will lack the legitimacy they would require.

Fifth, Security Council members may be hesitant to create such tribunals as they could undermine the authority of the ICC.

Finally, tribunals of this nature, dealing with the widespread problem of terrorism, may be perceived as undermining state sovereignty.

It would appear from this discussion that the preferred forum for prosecuting acts of terrorism of an international nature would be an international tribunal. It is therefore important to determine how an *ad hoc* tribunal established by the Security Council and the ICC compare.

8.3.7 Prosecuting Acts of Terrorism in the International Criminal Court

As discussed above, the ICC does not currently have jurisdiction over the crime of terrorism *per se*, but it remains possible that this crime may be included within its jurisdiction in the future. It is also possible that terrorist acts may fall within the definition of one of the other crimes that are currently within the ICC's jurisdiction. A discussion of the advantages and disadvantages associated with the ICC prosecuting acts of terrorism therefore follows.

8.3.7.1 Advantages of ICC Jurisdiction

Putting suspected terrorists to trial before the ICC has a whole range of benefits. First, the procedure for the appointment of judges to the ICC ensures that they may be perceived to be impartial and representative of the general legal norms accepted by most nations.

Second, the Court does not necessarily have to rely on complicated extradition and cooperation treaties in order to obtain evidence and suspects as all those party to the ICC are compelled to cooperate with the Court.[4]

Third, states will often not extradite suspects to a certain country due to reservations regarding that country's legal system. This may, for example, occur if that country permits the death penalty to be imposed. The extraditing country may then prefer surrendering the suspect to the ICC for prosecution.

Fourth, a single set of procedural and substantive laws will apply to all parties to the proceedings of the ICC. This will remove both the uncertainty and possible unfair outcomes that may arise from individual prosecutions in a multitude of other fora. The detailed definitions and elements of crimes that have been incorporated into the ICC Statute are the result of agreement reached by extensive negotiation and debate, by the many nations involved in its formulation. This places the ICC at the cutting edge of global developments in international law. It removes legal uncertainty due to the precise description of the crimes within its jurisdiction. It also has greater legitimacy as it is reflective of the legal norms of more than one region of the world.

Fifth, due to the principle of 'complementarity', there is no reason to fear that the ICC might undermine state sovereignty. The ICC will only prosecute if a state with jurisdiction is unwilling or unable to do so.[5] This may however also be viewed as a disadvantage. The jurisdiction of the ICC will in all likelihood be excluded, most often, through the application of this principle. The first problem with this is that when a state with jurisdiction initiates an investigation, it may be difficult to determine whether it is doing so in good faith at the outset. The ICC will have to hold back until it is clear that such investigation is not being carried out in good faith. Valuable time can be lost in this way. On the other hand, even when a state with jurisdiction investigates and prosecutes in good faith, all the disadvantages associated with prosecutions in domestic tribunals, as discussed above, come into play.

---

4.   Article 86 of the ICC Statute states that, 'States Parties shall, in accordance with the provisions of this Statute, cooperate fully with the Court in its investigation and prosecution of crimes within the jurisdiction of the Court.'

5.   Article 17 of the ICC Statute states that a case is inadmissible where '(a) The case is being investigated or prosecuted by a State which has jurisdiction over it, unless the State is unwilling or unable genuinely to carry out the investigation or prosecution.'

Sixth, a case may be referred to the ICC by a state that is party to the ICC or an investigation may be initiated by the prosecutor of the ICC.[6] It then has jurisdiction to prosecute those crimes that fall within its jurisdiction, if either the state on whose territory the crime occurred, or the state of which the accused is a national, is a party to the ICC.[7] This means that perpetrators cannot escape the ICC's jurisdiction by fleeing to a state that is not a party to the ICC, so long as their own country, or the country where they committed the crime, is a member. Even if both these states are not parties to the ICC, either can agree to ICC jurisdiction for the prosecution of the perpetrator. In these cases the ICC will not have the power to compel a non-party state to surrender a suspect. This will however be true for any tribunal unless it can rely on a prior agreement with the surrendering state, or has been established by the Security Council under Chapter VII.

Seventh, the Security Council may refer a case to the ICC for prosecution.[8] The Security Council can also compel any UN member to cooperate with the ICC under its Chapter VII powers. However, it is not entirely clear from the Statute whether the Security Council, acting under Chapter VII, is permitted to refer a case to the ICC without having regard to the principle of 'complementarity'. But a reading of Article 103 of the UN Charter leads to the conclusion that the Security Council can override 'any other international agreement' when acting under Chapter VII.

Eighth, based on evidence presented by the Prosecutor, the Pre-Trial Chamber of the ICC can issue an international arrest warrant obliging all states parties to arrest the suspect.[9]

Ninth, the poorer nations of the world that are unable to finance the police and intelligence mechanisms required to prosecute terrorism will be able to refer the matter to the ICC, thereby not only ensuring greater justice for their own citizens but also preventing the existence of safe havens for terrorists.

Tenth, the greater international cooperation which is possible through the ICC should create greater international stability and expedience in the fight against terrorism. The very nature of terrorism creates the need for international cooperation if it is to be suppressed efficiently.

Finally, there is only a single start-up cost involved with the court, due to its permanent nature.

---

6. See Article 13(a) and (c) of the ICC Statute.
7. See Article 12(2)(a) and (b) of the ICC Statute.
8. See Article 13(b) of the ICC Statute.
9. See Article 57(3)(a) of the ICC Statute.

8.3.7.2 *Disadvantages of ICC Jurisdiction*

While trying suspected terrorists before the ICC clearly has many advantages, there are also a number of drawbacks.

First, the principle of 'complementarity' may result in delays and the problems associated with prosecution of acts of terror in domestic tribunals, as discussed above.

Second, the burden of financing the ICC will fall on the shoulders of the member states.[10]

Third, it is possible that the state parties will continue to disagree on the definition of terrorism. This may result in a very narrow definition being adopted, meaning that certain crimes that possibly should fall within the ambit of terrorism, will not fall under the ICC's jurisdiction. This may not be ideal but is still preferable to no jurisdiction at all. Any definition adopted by the ICC may then serve to develop this area of customary international law, creating greater legal certainty for all nations, not only those who are state parties. It should also alleviate objections of *nullum crimen sine lege.*

Fourth, the ICC only has jurisdiction over acts committed after 1 July 2002.[11] It will only be possible to include the crime of terrorism within the ICC's jurisdiction seven years after the Statute came into force, at the earliest.[12] If such an amendment is made to the Statute, it will only be binding on those existing states parties that accept it.[13] In the interim, other options for prosecution will have to be used, unless the acts can also fall under the definition of one of the crimes already within the ICC's jurisdiction. Whilst it would be ideal for the ICC to finally include the crime of 'terrorism' within its jurisdiction, the problems associated with defining such a crime may be with us for many years to come. It is therefore necessary to determine whether it is possible for terrorist acts to fall within the definition of one of the other crimes currently within the jurisdiction of the ICC.

8.4 COULD TERRORIST ACTS FALL UNDER THE DEFINITION OF ONE OF THE EXISTING ICC CRIMES?

For purposes of this exercise, the events of 11 September, 2001 will be used as examples of acts of terrorism. Clearly many other acts could also be considered so the same process of analysis can be applied to any terrorist act to determine whether it falls within the jurisdiction of the

---

10. See Article 115(a) of the ICC Statute.
11. See Article 11(1) of the ICC Statute.
12. See Article 121(1) of the ICC Statute.
13. See Article 121(5) of the ICC Statute.

ICC.[14] It is important to note that the ICC does not have jurisdiction over the actual events of 11 September 2001 as its Statute had not then entered into force. Also, even if the Statute had already come into force, the principle of 'complementarity' would mean that the acts committed would still be excluded from ICC jurisdiction, if they were being investigated or prosecuted in good faith by a country with jurisdiction to do so.

The acts committed in the attacks on the United States included murder, destruction of property, hijacking of aircraft, destruction of aircraft, incapacitating any individual on an aircraft, performing an act of violence against any individual on an aircraft or conspiracy to do so, forgery of passports or other immigration documents. Most of these acts would fall within the jurisdiction of domestic courts, either as common crimes, or as crimes defined in international terrorism treaties, which have been incorporated into the domestic criminal law of the country.

It is important to note that if a perpetrator has been legitimately convicted or acquitted for conduct in another court, the ICC will not be permitted to prosecute him or her for the same conduct. This means that if a domestic court prosecutes a perpetrator for murder, he or she cannot also be prosecuted for crimes against humanity for the same conduct, even if it is a different crime with different elements.[15] This differs from the prohibition of double jeopardy found in many legal systems.

The next question is whether these acts can be prosecuted in the ICC under one of the three major crimes within its jurisdiction. When determining this, the provision contained in article 22(2) of the Statute, should be borne in mind. It states that:

> 'The definition of a crime shall be strictly construed and shall not be extended by analogy. In case of ambiguity, the definition shall be interpreted in favour of the person being investigated, prosecuted or convicted.'

The three crimes which currently fall within the jurisdiction of the ICC, in terms of Article 5 are: crimes against humanity; war crimes; and genocide. These are now considered individually.

8.4.1 Crimes Against Humanity

On 17 October 2001, while speaking at the US Institute of Peace in Washington, the United Nations High Commissioner for Human Rights, Mary Robinson, expressed the opinion that the attacks of September 11 constitute a crime against humanity. A discussion of the definition and *essentialia* of this crime, in terms of the ICC Statute, should indicate

---

14. The ICC statute includes acts such as torture, rape and sexual violence.
15. See Article 20 of the ICC Statute.

whether those attacks fall within the scope of crimes against humanity, for purposes of ICC jurisdiction. The relevant articles in the ICC Statute, as well as the elements of crimes contained in Appendix 3 to the statute will be considered.

Article 7 contains a list of specific acts, including murder, torture and other inhumane acts intentionally causing great suffering. If these acts are 'committed as part of a widespread or systematic attack directed against any civilian population', they will constitute crimes against humanity, provided that they were committed with knowledge of the attack. There are a number of requirements that are absent from this definition. Firstly, no nexus is required between the act and an armed conflict. Secondly, no specific political, racial, national, ethnic, cultural, religious, gender, or other group need be targeted, with the exception of the act of persecution. The definition requires, however, that the acts be committed as part of a widespread or systematic attack, be directed against any civilian population and be committed with knowledge of the attack. These elements will now be considered individually.

Commission of the Act as Part of a Widespread or Systematic Attack

This threshold requirement also existed for the International Tribunals for Rwanda and the former Yugoslavia. The jurisprudence of these tribunals may therefore be of assistance in interpreting the meaning of this requirement. It should be noted that the requirement is disjunctive rather than cumulative.

'Widespread'

This term is open to two interpretations. Firstly, it could refer to the geographical spread of an attack. Secondly, it could refer to the number of victims of an attack. The ICTY has held that 'widespread' refers to the number of victims[16] and means acts committed on a large scale and directed at a multiplicity of victims.[17] This would imply that even a single act could be widespread. The ICTY specifically held that a crime may be widespread by way of the 'cumulative effect of a series of inhumane acts or the singular effect of an inhumane act of extraordinary magnitude.'[18] This tribunal has also implied that the term does not necessarily refer to geographical spread, by holding that crimes against humanity had been committed against the inhabitants of a single town.[19] If this line of reasoning is to be extended to the ICC definition, it would appear that a single act of terrorism, at a single location, would comply with the requirement of being widespread.

---

16. *Prosecutor v. Tadic* Case No. IT-94-1, Trial chamber, May 1997, para. 648.
17. *Prosecutor v. Blaskic* Case No. IT-95-14, 3 March 2000, para. 206.
18. *Id.*, para. 206.
19. *Prosecutor v. Jelesic* Case No. IT-95-10, 14 December 1999, para. 53.

'Systematic'

The ICTR held that this term requires a pattern in the execution of the act.[20] The International Law Commission has also interpreted it as requiring the existence of a plan or policy behind an attack.[21] The ICTY, in turn, required any of the following factors: the existence of a plan or political objective; very large scale or repeated and continuous inhumane acts; the degree of resources employed, military or other; the implication of high-level authorities in the establishment of the methodical plan.[22]

When applied to the acts of September 11, it would appear that these could comply with either the requirement of being widespread or systematic. If the term widespread is interpreted as implying a large number of victims, this requirement will clearly be met. Even if one prefers the requirement of a large geographical spread, the fact that the attacks were spread across the United States should satisfy this.

Similarly, the requirement that the attack be systematic is easily met. There is little doubt that these attacks were carried out with a political objective and that in order to have orchestrated an attack of this nature, there must have been methodical and detailed planning.

'Attack Directed Against Any Civilian Population'

Article 7(2)(a) states that:

> '"Attack directed against any civilian population" means a course of conduct involving the multiple commission of acts referred to in paragraph 1 against any civilian population, pursuant to or in furtherance of a State or organizational policy to commit such attack.'

The requirement that the attack be directed against civilians is consistent with previous definitions of crimes against humanity. If this distinction is strictly construed, it would seem possible that an attack on a military base would not qualify, even if some of the victims are civilian.[23] In addition, no distinction is drawn between an attack directed at non-civilians during times of armed conflict or during times of peace. The existence of this requirement can be explained if one bears in mind that earlier definitions of crimes against humanity under international law

---

20. *Prosecutor v. Jean Paul Akayesu*, Case No. ICTR 96-4-T, Judgement, 2 September 1998, para. 580.

21. Report of the ILC on the work of its 45th session 6 May, commentary to Article 18, 26 July 1996, 51 UNGAOR Supp. (No10), 9 UN Doc A/61/10 (1996).

22. *The Prosecutor v. Kordic and Cerkez*, Case No. IT-95-14/2, 26 February 2001, para. 179.

23. In *Prosecutor v. Jelesic*, *supra* note 19, para. 53, the ICTY took the approach that the targeted population need only be predominantly civilian.

required a nexus between the acts and an armed conflict. This nexus requirement has since fallen by the wayside and it therefore seems strange that the 'civilian' requirement has not gone the same way. If non-civilians are targeted but the level of armed conflict necessary for the application of war crime provisions is absent, it could result in the attack falling outside the jurisdiction of the ICC. This could mean that the attack on the World Trade Center does fall within this requirement but that the attack on the Pentagon does not. It can be argued that the airplane which was flown into the Pentagon was carrying civilians and that civilians could have been present in the Pentagon, thus not necessarily making it an act targeting non-civilians. On the other hand an attack on the Pentagon, the ultimate symbol of US military power, can be argued to be nothing other than an attack on non-civilians.

It is very unfortunate that such a splitting of hairs should be necessary. Ideally the ICC should acknowledge that the category of crimes against humanity developed as a result of a need to fill a gap in humanitarian law. It may therefore be wise to adopt a definition of 'civilian' which tracks the concept of a 'non-combatant' in the Geneva Conventions. This would mean that if these Conventions do not apply, due to an absence of an armed conflict, nobody would be considered to be a non-civilian either.[24]

At this point one can merely speculate as to what interpretation the ICC will give to the term 'civilian'. It can only be hoped that the interpretation will not give rise to the result that acts of terror committed against non-civilian targets during times of peace, will be excluded from ICC jurisdiction.

The inclusion of the word 'population' in Article 7(2)(a) would indicate that the attacks should not target individuals but rather be directed at people generally. Due to the indiscriminate nature in which terrorism claims victims, this requirement will normally be met.

'Course of conduct involving the multiple commission of acts'

This requirement excludes any one-off acts. Such acts are common crimes and should not be dealt with by the ICC. Acts of terrorism will normally satisfy this requirement. While terrorism is made up of individual acts, what distinguishes terrorism from common crimes is that all the individual acts of terrorism are committed with a single motive of achieving a common goal. It is not necessary for a particular perpetrator to have committed multiple acts, as long as other acts are committed with the same objective in mind.

---

24. Sadat, *The International Criminal Court and the Transformation of International Law— Justice for the New Millennium*, Transnational Publishers, (2002), p. 154.

'Pursuant to or in furtherance of a State or organisational policy'

This requirement of motive again distinguishes these acts from common crimes. The perpetrator's actions may not be motivated by purely personal reasons. The policy of either a state or organisation will be motivation for the actions. Terrorist acts are, by definition, committed pursuant to or in furtherance of an organisational policy.

'To commit such attack'

In the Elements of Crimes which is found in Appendix 3 of the Statute, this phrase is defined as requiring that the State or organisation actively promote or encourage such an attack against a civilian population. This would exclude acts committed by individuals who may share the motives of the particular organisation but who were not acting for such organisation.

'Committed with Knowledge of the Attack'

Article 30 states that:
'1. Unless otherwise provided, a person shall be criminally responsible and liable for punishment for a crime within the jurisdiction of the Court only if the material elements are committed with intent and knowledge.
2. For the purposes of this article, a person has intent where:
  (a) In relation to conduct, that person means to engage in the conduct;
  (b) In relation to a consequence, that person means to cause that consequence or is aware that it will occur in the ordinary course of events.
3. For the purposes of this article, "knowledge" means awareness that a circumstance exists or a consequence will occur in the ordinary course of events.'

The ICC will therefore not find a perpetrator guilty of a crime on the basis of negligence. Furthermore, as the material elements of a crime should be committed with intent and knowledge, the perpetrator will have to be aware not only of the attack, but also of the fact that it is directed at a civilian population and is pursuant to or in furtherance of a state or organisational policy. This mental state must be subjectively demonstrated and not merely inferred from circumstantial evidence.

From the discussion above it would seem that terrorist acts such as murder, torture and other inhumane acts could fall within the ICC Statute's definition of crimes against humanity. The problem that remains relates to the definition of 'civilian', as explained above. Offences such

as destruction of property and hijacking would not fall under the ICC Statute's definition of crimes against humanity.

8.4.2 War Crimes

Article 8 deals with the definition of war crimes for purposes of the jurisdiction of the ICC. Article 8(1) states that:

> 'The Court shall have jurisdiction in respect of war crimes in particular when committed as part of a plan or policy or as part of a large-scale commission of such crimes.'

Article 8(2) then goes on to divide war crimes, for purposes of the statute, into two main categories. The first applies to crimes committed during international armed conflicts, comprising grave breaches of the Geneva Conventions and other serious violations of the laws and customs applicable in international armed conflicts. The second category relates to crimes committed during non-international armed conflicts, comprising serious violations of Common Article 3 of the Geneva Conventions and other serious violations of the laws and customs applicable in non-international armed conflicts.

A list of acts that fall under both categories is included in the Statute. The use of the word 'namely' suggests that each list is exhaustive and not merely illustrative. To determine whether an act of terror falls within this Article, the following points will have to be considered: i)whether the act was committed as part of a plan or policy or as part of a large-scale commission of war crimes; ii) whether the act was committed as part of an armed conflict; iii) whether the perpetrator was aware of factual circumstances that established the existence of an armed conflict; and iv) for certain of the listed acts, whether the perpetrator was aware of factual circumstances that established the protected status of the victim.

'Act Committed, in Particular, as Part of a Plan or Policy or as Part of a Large-Scale Commission of War Crimes'

This phrase would suggest that isolated acts committed on the initiative of an individual, during an armed conflict, would not fall within the jurisdiction of the ICC unless the acts formed part of the plan or policy of the commanding authority. The phrase 'part of a large-scale commission of war crimes' implies that the act must be part of a continuous series of acts.

These two requirements are, however, softened by the use of the word 'particular'. This word has the effect that while these two requirements would normally exist, an exception can be made, in certain circumstances. Two considerations will be decisive in this regard. Firstly,

Article 1 of the Statute states that the ICC shall have the power to exercise its jurisdiction over the 'most serious crimes of international concern.' Secondly, by virtue of the *eiusdem generis* rule of interpretation, the exceptions must approximate those acts that are committed as part of a plan or policy and ones committed on a large-scale. This means that it would be possible for a single, isolated act, which is not committed as part of a plan or policy, still to fall within the jurisdiction of the ICC. This might be the case if an act is so shocking or gruesome that it would be inappropriate for the ICC not to consider the matter.

Although the attacks of September 11 are not considered to have taken place during the course of an armed conflict, terrorist attacks commonly do occur in such situations. Thus it is worth considering the likely position of the ICC had the events of September 11 been part of an armed conflict.

'Armed Conflict'

Article 8 requires that the act be committed during an armed conflict. This term is however not defined. In the preambular paragraph to the Elements of War Crimes in Appendix 3 to the Statute, it is stated that 'the Statute shall be interpreted within the established framework of the international law of armed conflict.' This is especially relevant when determining which category of armed conflict an act falls in for purposes of the Statute. In the *Tadic* decision the ICTY stated that:

> '. . . an armed conflict exists whenever there is a resort to armed force between States or protracted armed violence between governmental authorities and organized armed groups or between such groups within a State.'[25]

Acts committed during armed conflict not of an international character, for the purposes of the Statute, do not include 'situations of internal disturbances and tensions, such as riots, isolated and sporadic acts of violence or other acts of a similar nature.'[26] Furthermore, acts committed during armed conflict not of an international character, other than those included in the Statute in terms of Common Article 3 of the Geneva Conventions, also have to take place 'in the territory of a State when there is protracted armed conflict.'[27]

Had the terrorist acts committed on September 11 been classified as acts committed by an organised armed group on the territory of a state and directed at that State, the question is whether there was an armed conflict or whether it was an isolated and sporadic act of violence. If the

---

25. *Supra* note 16, Para. 70.
26. Article 8(2)(d) of the ICC Statute.
27. Article 8(2)(f) of the ICC Statute.

act is not disqualified as an act of armed conflict on this basis, then the following offences under Article 8(2)(c) become relevant: i) 'violence to life and person, in particular murder of all kinds, mutilation, cruel treatment and torture'; and ii) 'the taking of hostages'.

If the act passes the additional test of being protracted, the following offences under Article 8(2)(e) become relevant: i) 'intentionally directing attacks against the civilian population as such or against individual civilians not taking direct part in the hostilities'; ii) 'intentionally directing attacks against buildings, material, medical units and transport'; and iii) 'destroying or seizing the property of an adversary unless such destruction or seizure be imperatively demanded by the necessities of the conflict.'

If the attack could be considered part of an international armed conflict, by virtue of high level state collusion, then the following offences under Article 8(2)(b) could apply: i) 'intentionally directing an attack against civilians and civilian objects'; and ii) 'launching an attack in the knowledge that it will cause incidental loss of life or injury to civilians.'

The Appendix 3 elements require that the perpetrator was aware of factual circumstances that established the existence of an armed conflict. They do not need to have been aware of the fact that there was such an armed conflict for legal purposes, nor of the classification of such armed conflict as international or otherwise.

It is possible that terrorist acts might fall under the ICC Statute's definition of war crimes. The main obstacle to overcome will probably be in meeting the requirements of an armed conflict for purposes of the Statute.

8.4.3 Genocide

Article 6 of the ICC Statute states that:

'For the purpose of this Statute, "genocide" means any of the following acts committed with intent to destroy, in whole or in part, a national, ethnical, racial or religious group, as such:
(a) Killing members of the group;
(b) Causing serious bodily or mental harm to members of the group;
(c) Deliberately inflicting on the group conditions of life calculated to bring about its physical destruction in whole or in part;
(d) Imposing measures intended to prevent births within the group;
(e) Forcibly transferring children of the group to another group.'

The terrorist acts of September 11 do not qualify as acts of genocide. While the act of murder may be an element of both genocide and terrorism, the underlying motive for the two will generally be distinct. Terrorist acts are commonly committed with the intent of destabilising states or other groups by instilling terror, without an intent to wipe out a particular group. If there is such an intent then the act becomes one of genocide.

CONCLUSION

The events of September 11 have shown that the field of law dealing with terrorism needs to be developed to cater for such forms of criminality. If attacks of this nature can be carried out by international organisations with a network spanning the globe, international cooperation in curbing such attacks is even more vital. New fora for the prosecution of the perpetrator are also necessary.

It is clear that terrorism has well and truly moved into the international arena and that the most appropriate forum to deal with the problem is an international one. As far as the ICC is able to exercise its jurisdiction over acts of this nature, it should be allowed and encouraged to do so. The question of what impact the 'complementarity principle', absence of jurisdiction over the crime of terrorism *per se*, and the limitations inherent in fitting the acts into the three existing crimes under ICC jurisdiction will have, remains to be seen. The Task Force hopes that these issues will not handicap the ICC to such an extent that this preferred forum will not be able to prosecute acts of international terrorism effectively. It is further hoped that the introduction of bilateral agreements, which provide immunity from surrender to the ICC for nationals of the two states parties, will be a trend that does not perpetuate.[28] The Task Force believes that this thwarts the very object and purpose of the Rome Statute—to end impunity for the worst crimes.

Recommendations

1) Where a state has a choice as to which forum may legitimately try suspected terrorists, ensuring respect for the fundamental due process guarantees must be a major factor in reaching the decision.
2) When choosing a forum, consideration should also be given to the interests of the victims and their families.
3) In many instances international tribunals or, where it has jurisdiction, the ICC are the preferred fora to try suspected international terrorists.
4) Bilateral agreements which exempt the jurisdiction of the ICC must be rejected.

---

28. See 'Documents on impunity agreements', Coalition for the International Criminal Court, available http://www.iccnow.org/documents/otherissuesimpunitya-greem.html.

ABOUT THE INTERNATIONAL BAR ASSOCIATION

In its role as a dual membership organisation, comprising 16,000 individual lawyers and 180 Bar Associations and Law Societies, the International Bar Association (IBA) influences the development of international law reform and shapes the future of the legal profession. Its Member Organisations cover all continents and include the American Bar Association, the German Federal Bar, the Japan Federation of Bar Associations, the Mexican Bar Association and the Law Society of Zimbabwe.

Grouped into three Sections—Business Law, Legal Practice, and Energy & Natural Resources Law—more than 60 specialist Committees provide members with access to leading experts and up-to-date information as well as top-level professional development and network-building opportunities through high-quality publications and world-class Conferences. The IBA's Human Rights Institute works across the Association, helping to promote, protect and enforce human rights under a just rule of law, and to preserve the independence of the judiciary and the legal profession worldwide.

International Bar Association
271 Regent Street
London W1B 2AQ
United Kingdom
Tel: +44 (0)20 7629 1206
Fax: +44 (0)20 7409 0456
E-mail: member@int-bar.org
Website: www.ibanet.org

INTERNATIONAL BAR ASSOCIATION'S TASK FORCE ON INTERNATIONAL TERRORISM

'Terrorism . . . presents a global threat to democracy, the rule of law, human rights and stability' (Kofi Annan, UN Secretary-General)

MISSION STATEMENT

The International Bar Association (IBA), the world's largest association of lawyers, has established a Task Force on International Terrorism with a view to examining key legal issues surrounding this most complex topic.

The Task Force is composed of renowned international experts— **Ambassador Emilio Cárdenas** (Co-Chair) (former Permanent Representative to the United Nations for Argentina), **Judge Richard Goldstone** (Co-Chair) (Justice of the Constitutional Court of South Africa), **Dr Badria Al-Awadhi** (Professor of International Law at Kuwait University), **Professor Cherif Bassiouni** (President of the International Human Rights Law Institute at DePaul University, Chicago), **Sten Heckscher** (National Police Commissioner for Sweden), **Baroness Helena Kennedy QC** (Chair of the British Council and Chair of the Human Genetics Commission), **Fali Nariman** (President of the Bar Association of India), **Professor Michael Reisman** (Professor of International Law at Yale University).

Although international terrorism is not a new phenomenon, the unprecedented scale of the tragedy that unfolded on 11 September 2001 has acted as a sharp reminder that terrorism is a global scourge. Clearly it is vital for the international community to find cooperative ways to combat this threat and it may be necessary to reexamine time-honoured conventions and principles. Equally, there has never been a more important time to defend and uphold the rule of law in an effort to create stability and peace across all regions.

The objective of the Task Force is to critically examine legal issues that are crucial to the problem of international terrorism against the backdrop of existing national and international law. The Task Force will consider the challenges presented by methods of terrorism, including implications for the rule of law; current steps being taken to meet these challenges by national, regional and international organisations; the position of victims; ways to balance the concerns between effective security and civil liberties; and the role of the International Criminal Court.

Drawing upon the resources and experience of the IBA's global network of 182 Member Organisations and 60 specialist Committees, the Task Force will, where necessary, undertake legal research to aid in identifying the need for new norms of international law and interpreting existing ones, and provide expert opinion on aspects of international law.

A report will be published with the intention of contributing to international standards and practice in the field of terrorism. The aim is to reaffirm the rule of law while taking necessary measures to protect both individuals and societies in a manner consistent with the maintenance of international peace and stability.

APPENDIX III

United Nations

S/RES/1390 (2002)*

Security Council

Distr.: General
28 January 2002

Resolution 1390 (2002)

Adopted by the Security Council at its 4452nd *meeting, on*
16 January 2002
The Security Council,

Recalling its resolutions 1267 (1999) of 15 October 1999, 1333
(2000) of 19 December 2000 and 1363 (2001) of 3O July 2001,

Reaffirming its previous resolutions on Afghanistan, in particular resolutions 1378 (2001) of 14 November 2001 and 1383 (2001)
of 6 December 2001,

Reaffirming also its resolutions 1368 (2001) of 12 September
2001 and 1373 (2001) of 28 September 2001, and reiterating its support for international efforts to root out terrorism, in accordance
with the Charter of the United Nations,

Reaffirming its unequivocal condemnation of the terrorist attacks
which took place in New York, Washington and Pennsylvania on 11
September 2001, expressing its determination to prevent all such
acts, noting the continued activities of Usama bin Laden and the
Al-Qaida network in supporting international terrorism, and expressing its determination to root out this network,

Noting the indictments of Usama bin Laden and his associates
by the United States of America for, inter alia, the 7 August 1998
bombings of the United States embassies in Nairobi, Kenya and Dar
es Salaam, Tanzania,

Determining that the Taliban have failed to respond to the
demands in paragraph 13 of resolution 1214 (1998) of 8 December
1998, paragraph 2 of resolution 1267 (1999) and paragraphs 1, 2
and 3 of resolution 1333 (2000),

Condemning the Taliban for allowing Afghanistan to be used as
a base for terrorists training and activities, including the export of
terrorism by the Al-Qaida network and other terrorist groups as well

as for using foreign mercenaries in hostile actions in the territory of Afghanistan,

Condemning the Al-Qaida network and other associated terrorist groups, for the multiple criminal, terrorist acts, aimed at causing the deaths of numerous innocent civilians, and the destruction of property,

* Reissued for technical reasons.

02~21602* (E)

S/RES/1390 (2002)

Reaffirming further that acts of international terrorism constitute a threat to international peace and security,

Acting under Chapter VII of the Charter of the United Nations,

1. *Decides* to continue the measures imposed by paragraph 8 (c) of resolution 1333 (2000) and takes note of the continued application of the measures imposed by paragraph 4 (b) of resolution 1267 (1999), in accordance with paragraph 2 below, and decides to terminate the measures imposed in paragraph 4 (a) of resolution 1267 (1999);

2. *Decides* that all States shall take the following measures with respect to Usama bin Laden, members of the Al-Qaida organization and the Taliban and other individuals, groups, undertakings and entities associated with them, as referred to in the list created pursuant to resolutions 1267 (1999) and 1333 (2000) to be updated regularly by the Committee established pursuant to resolution 1267 (1999) hereinafter referred to as "the Committee";

(a) Freeze without delay the funds and other financial assets or economic resources of these individuals, groups, undertakings and entities, including funds derived from property owned or controlled, directly or indirectly, by them or by persons acting on their behalf or at their direction, and ensure that neither these nor any other funds, financial assets or economic resources are made available, directly or indirectly, for such persons' benefit, by their nationals or by any persons within their territory;

(b) Prevent the entry into or the transit through their territories of these individuals, provided that nothing in this paragraph shall oblige any State to deny entry into or require the departure from its territories of its own nationals and this paragraph shall not apply where entry or transit is necessary for the fulfilment of a judicial process or the Committee determines on a case by case basis only that entry or transit is justified;

(c) Prevent the direct or indirect supply, sale and transfer, to these individuals, groups, undertakings and entities from their territories or by their nationals outside their territories, or using their flag vessels or aircraft, of arms and related materiel of all types including weapons and ammunition, military vehicles and equipment, paramilitary equipment, and spare parts for the aforementioned and technical advice, assistance, or training related to military activities;

3. *Decides* that the measures referred to in paragraphs 1 and 2 above will be reviewed in 12 months and that at the end of this period the Council will either allow these measures to continue or

decide to improve them, in keeping with the principles and purposes of this resolution;

4. *Recalls* the obligation placed upon all Member States to implement in full resolution 1373 (2001), including with regard to any member of the Taliban and the Al-Qaida organization, and any individuals, groups, undertakings and entities associated with the Taliban and the Al-Qaida organization, who have participated in the financing, planning, facilitating and preparation or perpetration of terrorist acts or in supporting terrorist acts;

5. *Requests* the Committee to undertake the following tasks and to report on its work to the Council with its observations and recommendations;

(a) to update regularly the list referred to in paragraph 2 above, on the basis of relevant information provided by Member States and regional organizations;

(b) to seek from all States information regarding the action taken by them to implement effectively the measures referred to in paragraph 2 above, and thereafter to request from them whatever further information the Committee may consider necessary;

(c) to make periodic reports to the Council on information submitted to the Committee regarding the implementation of this resolution;

(d) to promulgate expeditiously such guidelines and criteria as may be necessary to facilitate the implementation of the measures referred to in paragraph 2 above;

(e) to make information it considers relevant, including the list referred to in paragraph 2 above, publicly available through appropriate media;

(0 to cooperate with other relevant Security Council Sanctions Committees and with the Committee established pursuant to paragraph 6 of its resolution 1373 (2001);

6. *Requests* all States to report to the Committee, no later than 90 days from the date of adoption of this resolution and thereafter according to a timetable to be proposed by the Committee, on the steps they have taken to implement the measures referred to in paragraph 2 above;

7. *Urges* all States, relevant United Nations bodies, and, as appropriate, other organizations and interested parties to cooperate fully with the Committee and with the Monitoring Group referred to in paragraph 9 below;

8. *Urges* all States to take immediate steps to enforce and strengthen through legislative enactments or administrative measures, where appropriate, the measures imposed under domestic laws or regulations against their nationals and other individuals or enti-

ties operating on their territory, to prevent and punish violations of the measures referred to in paragraph 2 of this resolution, and to inform the Committee of the adoption of such measures, and invites States to report the results of all related investigations or enforcement actions to the Committee unless to do so would compromise the investigation or enforcement actions;

9. *Requests* the Secretary-General to assign the Monitoring Group established pursuant to paragraph 4 (a) of resolution 1363 (2001), whose mandate expires on 19 January 2002, to monitor, for a period of 12 months, the implementation of the measures referred to in paragraph 2 of this resolution;

10. *Requests* the Monitoring Group to report to the Committee by 3 1 March 2002 and thereafter every 4 months;

11. *Decides* to remain actively seized of the matter.

APPENDIX IV

United Nations S/RE5/1373 (2001)

Security Council   Distr.:   General
                                                        28 September 2001

Resolution 1373 (2001)

Adopted by the Security Council at its *4385th* meeting, on

28 September 2001

The Security Council,

Reaffirming its resolutions 1269 (1999) of 19 October 1999 and 1368 (2001) of 12 September 2001,

Reaffirming also its unequivocal condemnation of the terrorist attacks which took place in New York, Washington, D.C. and Pennsylvania on 11 September 2001, and expressing its determination to prevent all such acts,

Reaffirming further that such acts, like any act of international terrorism, constitute a threat to international peace and security,

Reaffirming the inherent right of individual or collective self-defence as recognized by the Charter of the United Nations as reiterated in resolution 1368 (2001),

Reaffirming the need to combat by all means, in accordance with the Charter of the United Nations, threats to international peace and security caused by terrorist acts,

Deeply concerned by the increase, in various regions of the world, of acts of terrorism motivated by intolerance or extremism,

Calling on States to work together urgently to prevent and suppress terrorist acts, including through increased cooperation and full implementation of the relevant international conventions relating to terrorism,

Recognizing the need for States to complement international cooperation by taking additional measures to prevent and suppress, in their territories through all lawful means, the financing and preparation of any acts of terrorism,

Reaffirming the principle established by the General Assembly in its declaration of October 1970 (resolution 2625 (XXV)) and reiterated by the Security Council in its resolution 1 189 (1998) of 13 August 1998, namely that every State has the duty to refrain from organizing, instigating, assisting or participating in terrorist acts in another State or acquiescing in organized activities within its territory directed towards the commission of such acts,

Acting under Chapter VII of the Charter of the United Nations,

01-55743 (E)

S/RES/1373 (2001)

1.   *Decides* that all States shall:

(a) Prevent and suppress the financing of terrorist acts;

(b) Criminalize the wilful provision or collection, by any means, directly or indirectly, of funds by their nationals or in their territories with the intention that the funds should be used, or in the knowledge that they are to be used, in order to carry out terrorist acts;

(c) Freeze without delay funds and other financial assets or economic resources of persons who commit, or attempt to commit, terrorist acts or participate in or facilitate the commission of terrorist acts; of entities owned or controlled directly or indirectly by such persons; and of persons and entities acting on behalf of, or at the direction of such persons and entities, including funds derived or generated from property owned or controlled directly or indirectly by such persons and associated persons and entities;

(d) Prohibit their nationals or any persons and entities within their territories from making any funds, financial assets or economic resources or financial or other related services available, directly or indirectly, for the benefit of persons who commit or attempt to commit or facilitate or participate in the commission of terrorist acts, of entities owned or controlled, directly or indirectly, by such persons and of persons and entities acting on behalf of or at the direction of such persons;

2. *Decides also* that all States shall:

(a) Refrain from providing any form of support, active or passive, to entities or persons involved in terrorist acts, including by suppressing recruitment of members of terrorist groups and eliminating the supply of weapons to terrorists;

(b) Take the necessary steps to prevent the commission of terrorist acts, including by provision of early warning to other States by exchange of information;

(c) Deny safe haven to those who finance, plan, support, or commit terrorist acts, or provide safe havens;

(d) Prevent those who finance, plan, facilitate or commit terrorist acts from using their respective territories for those purposes against other States or their citizens;

(e) Ensure that any person who participates in the financing, planning, preparation or perpetration of terrorist acts or in supporting terrorist acts is brought to justice and ensure that, in addition to any other measures against them, such terrorist acts are established as serious criminal offences in domestic laws and regulations and that the punishment duly reflects the seriousness of such terrorist acts;

(f) Afford one another the greatest measure of assistance in connection with criminal investigations or criminal proceedings relating to the financing or support of terrorist acts, including assistance in obtaining evidence in their possession necessary for the proceedings;

(g) Prevent the movement of terrorists or terrorist groups by effective border controls and controls on issuance of identity papers and travel documents, and through measures for preventing counterfeiting, forgery or fraudulent use of identity papers and travel documents;

3. *Calls* upon all States to:

(a) Find ways of intensifying and accelerating the exchange of operational information, especially regarding actions or movements of terrorist persons or networks; forged or falsified travel documents; traffic in arms, explosives or sensitive materials; use of communications technologies by terrorist groups; and the threat posed by the possession of weapons of mass destruction by terrorist groups;

(b) Exchange information in accordance with international and domestic law and cooperate on administrative and judicial matters to prevent the commission of terrorist acts;

(c) Cooperate, particularly through bilateral and multilateral arrangements and agreements, to prevent and suppress terrorist attacks and take action against perpetrators of such acts;

(d) Become parties as soon as possible to the relevant international conventions and protocols relating to terrorism, including the International Convention for the Suppression of the Financing of Terrorism of 9 December 1999;

(e) Increase cooperation and fully implement the relevant international conventions and protocols relating to terrorism and Security Council resolutions 1269 (1999) and 1368 (2001);

(0 Take appropriate measures in conformity with the relevant provisions of national and international law, including international standards of human rights, before granting refugee status, for the purpose of ensuring that the asylum-seeker has not planned, facilitated or participated in the commission of terrorist acts;

(g) Ensure, in conformity with international law, that refugee status is not abused by the perpetrators, organizers or facilitators of terrorist acts, and that claims of political motivation are not recognized as grounds for refusing requests for the extradition of alleged terrorists;

4. *Notes* with concern the close connection between international terrorism and transnational organized crime, illicit drugs, money-laundering, illegal arms-trafficking, and illegal movement of nuclear, chemical, biological and other potentially deadly materi-

als, and in this regard *emphasizes* the need to enhance coordination of efforts on national, subregional, regional and international levels in order to strengthen a global response to this serious challenge and threat to international security;

5. *Declares* that acts, methods, and practices of terrorism are contrary to the purposes and principles of the United Nations and that knowingly financing, planning and inciting terrorist acts are also contrary to the purposes and principles of the United Nations;

6. *Decides* to establish, in accordance with rule 28 of its provisional rules of procedure, a Committee of the Security Council, consisting of all the members of the Council, to monitor implementation of this resolution, with the assistance of appropriate expertise, and *calls upon* all States to report to the Committee, no later than 90 days from the date of adoption of this resolution and thereafter according to a timetable to be proposed by the Committee, on the steps they have taken to implement this resolution;

7. *Directs* the Committee to delineate its tasks, submit a work programme within 30 days of the adoption of this resolution, and to consider the support it requires, in consultation with the Secretary-General;

8. *Expresses* its determination to take all necessary steps in order to ensure the full implementation of this resolution, in accordance with its responsibilities under the Charter;

9. *Decides* to remain seized of this matter.

APPENDIX V

INTERNATIONAL CRIMINAL ENFORCEMENT IN THE PROVISIONS OF ANTI-TERRORISM CONVENTIONS

Convention on the High Seas, U.N. Doc. A/Conf/13/L.52-55 & 56 & 58; 450 U.N.T.S. 11; 13 U.S.T. 2312 (29 Apr. 1958)
—Duty to prosecute, Article 13

Convention on Law of the Sea, U.N. Doc. A/Conf.62-121 & Corr.1-8; 1833 U.N.T.S. 3; 21 I.L.M. 1261 (10 Dec. 1982)
—Duty to prosecute, Article 99

Convention for the Suppression of Unlawful Acts Against the Safety of Maritime Navigation, IMO. Doc. Sua/Con/15; 27 I.L.M. 668 (10 Mar. 1988)
—Duty to prosecute, Article 7
—Duty to extradite, Articles 10, 11
—Duty to cooperate in prosecution, punishment (including judicial assistance in penal proceedings), Articles 12, 14

Protocol for the Suppression of Unlawful Acts Against the Safety of Fixed Platforms Located on the Continental Shelf, IMO. Doc. Sua/Con/16/Rev.1; 27 I.L.M. 685 (10 Mar. 1988)
—Establishment of a criminal jurisdictional basis, Article 3

Convention on Offences and Certain Other Acts Committed on Board Aircraft [Tokyo Hijacking Convention], U.N. Doc. A/C.6/418/Corr.1, Annex II; 704 U.N.T.S. 219; 20 U.S.T. 2941; 2 I.L.M. 1042 (14 Sept. 1963)
—Duty to prosecute, Articles 13 (implicit), 17 (implicit)
—Duty to extradite, Articles 13, 14, 16
—Establishment of a criminal jurisdictional basis, Articles 3, 4, 16, 17

Convention for the Suppression of Unlawful Seizure of Aircrafts [Hague Hijacking Convention], U.N. Doc. A/C.6/418/Corr. 1, Annex II; 860 U.N.T.S. 105; 22 U.S.T. 1641; 10 I.L.M. 133 (16 Dec. 1970)

—Duty to prosecute, Articles VI (implicit), VII (duty or right to prosecute if no extradition: Article VII)

—Duty to extradite, Article VIII

—Duty to cooperate in prosecution, punishment (including judicial assistance), Articles VI, X, XI

—Establishment of a criminal jurisdictional basis, Articles IV, VIII

Convention for the Suppression of Unlawful Acts Against the Safety of Civil Aviation [Montreal Hijacking Convention], U.N. Doc. A/C.6/418/Corr.2, Annex III; 974 U.N.T.S. 177; 24 U.S.T. 564; 10 I.L.M. 1151 (23 Sept. 1971)

—Duty to prosecute, Articles 3 (implicit), 6, 7 (duty or right to prosecute if no extradition: Article 7)

—Duty to extradite, Articles 6, 8

—Duty to cooperate in prosecution (including judicial assistance), Article 11

—Establishment of a criminal jurisdictional basis, Article 5

Protocol for the Suppression of Unlawful Acts of Violence at Airports Serving Civil Aviation [Montreal Protocol], ICAO Doc. 9518; 27 I.L.M. 627 (24 Feb. 1988)

—Establishment of a criminal jurisdictional basis, Article III

Convention on the Prevention and Punishment of Crimes Against Internationally Protected Persons, Including Diplomatic Agents [Diplomats Convention], U.N. Doc. A/Res/3166; 1035 U.N.T.S. 167; 28 U.S.T. 1975; 13 I.L.M. 41 (14 Dec. 1973)

—Duty to prosecute, Article 7 (duty or right to prosecute if no extradition: Article 7)

—Duty to extradite, Articles 7, 8 (duty to prosecute if offender not extradited: Article 7)

—Duty to cooperate in prosecution, punishment (including judicial assistance), Articles 4, 5, 11

—Establishment of a criminal jurisdictional basis, Article 3

Convention Against the Taking of Hostages [Hostage-Taking Convention], U.N. Doc. A/Res/34/146; 1316 U.N.T.S. 205; 18 I.L.M. 1456 (17 Dec. 1979)

—Duty to prosecute (duty to prosecute if no extradition), Article 8

—Duty to extradite, Article 10

—Duty to cooperate in prosecution, punishment (including judicial assistance), Articles 4, 11
—Establishment of a criminal jurisdictional basis, Article 5

Convention on the Safety of United Nations and Associated Personnel [U.N. Personnel Convention], U.N. Doc. A/Res/49/59 (17 Feb. 1995)
—Establishment of jurisdiction, Article 10
—Communication of information, Article 12
—Duties to prosecute, Article 14
—Duty to extradite, Article 15
—Mutual assistance in criminal matters, Article 16

Convention on the Marking of Plastic Explosives for the Purpose of Detection, U.N. Doc. S/22393/Corr. 1; 30 I.L.M. 721 (1 Mar. 1991)
—Duty to prosecute, Articles II and III

Convention for the Suppression of Terrorist Bombings, U.N. Doc. A/Res/52/164 (9 Jan. 1998)
—Duty to prosecute, Article 8
—Duty to extradite, Article 9
—Mutual assistance in criminal matters, Article 10

Convention on the Prohibition of the Development, Production and Stockpiling of Bacteriological (Biological) and Toxin Weapons and on their Destruction [BWC Convention], U.N. Doc. A/Res/2826; 1015 U.N.T.S. 163; 26 U.S.T. 583; 11 I.L.M. 309 (10 Apr. 1972)
—Duty to prosecute, Articles I, II, and IV
—Cooperation in investigation, Article VI

Convention on the Physical Protection of Nuclear Material, IAEA Doc. C/225; 1456 U.N.T.S.101; 18 I.L.M. 1419 (3 Mar. 1980)
—Duty to prosecute, Article 9
—Duty to extradite, Articles 9, 11
—Duty to cooperate in prosecution, punishment (including judicial assistance), Articles 5, 13
—Establishment of a criminal jurisdictional basis, Article 8

Convention on the Prohibition of the Development, Production, Stockpiling and Use of Chemical Weapons and on their Destruction [CWC Convention], U.N. Doc. A/Res/47/39; 1974 U.N.T.S. 3; 32 I.L.M. 800 (13 Jan. 1993)
—Duty to prosecute, Article VII (1)(a)
—Duty to cooperate in prosecution, punishment (including judicial assistance), Article VII (2), (3)
—Establishment of a criminal jurisdictional basis, Article VII (1)(a)

Convention for the Suppression of the Financing of Terrorism [Terrorism Financing], U.N. Doc. A/54/109 (9 Dec. 1999)
—Freezing and seizing assets, Article 8
—Duty to prosecute, Article 10
—Duty to extradite, Article 11
—Mutual legal assistance, Article 12

INDEX